WORDS LIKE
LOADED PISTOLS

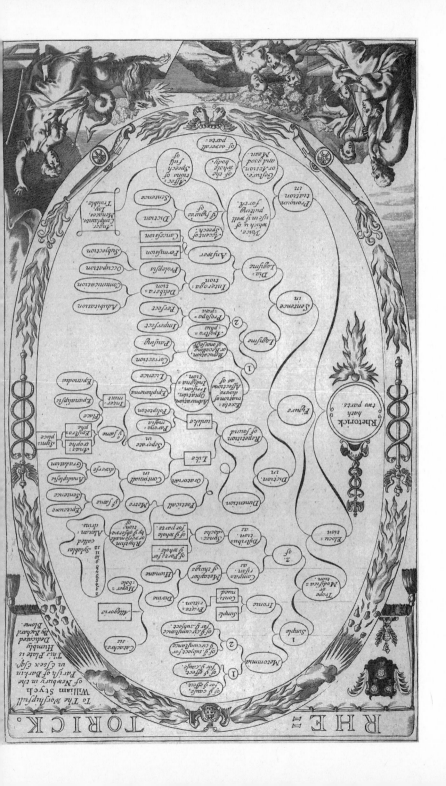

WORDS LIKE LOADED PISTOLS

RHETORIC FROM ARISTOTLE TO OBAMA

SAM LEITH

BASIC BOOKS

A Member of the Perseus Books Group
New York

Published by Basic Books,
A Member of the Perseus Books Group

Books published by Basic Books are available at special discounts for bulk purchases in the United States by corporations, institutions, and other organizations. For more information, please contact the Special Markets Department at the Perseus Books Group, 2300 Chestnut Street, Suite 200, Philadelphia, PA 19103, or call (800) 810-4145, ext. 5000, or e-mail special .markets@perseusbooks.com.

Designed by Trish Wilkinson
Set in 11 point Minion Pro

Library of Congress Cataloging-in-Publication Data

Leith, Sam.
    [You talkin' to me.]
    Words like loaded pistols : rhetoric from Aristotle to Obama / Sam Leith.
        p.   cm.
    Previously published as: You talkin' to me.
    Includes bibliographical references and index.
    ISBN 978-0-465-03105-4 (alk. paper) — ISBN 978-0-465-03107-8 (e-book)
1. Persuasion (Rhetoric) 2. English language—Rhetoric. 3. Rhetoric—History.
4. Rhetoric. I. Title.
P301.5.P47L45 2012
808.5—dc23   2012005866

10 9 8 7 6 5 4 3

For my mum

Also by Sam Leith

FICTION
The Coincidence Engine

NONFICTION
Dead Pets
Sod's Law

Contents

INTRODUCTION

LET ME START BY introducing you to a scene from *The Simpsons*.

> MARGE [*sings*]: *How many roads must a man walk down be-*
> *fore you can call him a man?*
> HOMER: Seven.
> LISA: No, dad, it's a rhetorical question.
> HOMER: Okay, eight.
> LISA: Dad, do you even know what "rhetorical" means?
> HOMER: Do *I* know what "rhetorical" means?

On this little scene, the whole premise of the book you hold in your hand hinges. Do *you* know what rhetorical means? Because you should. And if Homer Simpson, one of the greatest every-man figures of our time, can make a joke about rhetoric, you can be assured it is not a subject that needs to be intimidating.

So what is rhetoric? Rhetoric is, as simply defined as possible, the art of persuasion: the attempt by one human being to influence another in words. It is no more complicated than that. You

are probably accustomed to thinking of rhetoric in terms of formal oratory: the sort of public speeches you see politicians make on television, CEOs make at annual meetings, and priests make on Sunday mornings in church. True, that is, when rhetoric is at its most visible—that's when rhetoric puts on a dinner jacket and polishes its dancing shoes. But that is only one part of a huge area that the term covers.

Rhetoric is a field of knowledge: that is, something susceptible to analysis and understanding in the same way poetry is. Just as people studying poetry talk about anapests and caesuras and catalectic feet, people studying rhetoric have learned to recognize and name some of the ways in which rhetorical language behaves.

But rhetoric is also, and primarily, a practical skill—what one of its earliest and most important theorists, Aristotle, described as a *technè*, which is the root of the words "technical" and "technique." Rhetoric is directed at a practical goal; it's a means to an end.

Rhetoric is hustling, and our forefathers knew it. For fifteen centuries or so, the study of rhetoric was at the center of Western education. To be able to recognize rhetorical techniques, and to have them at your command, was a central accomplishment of any educated man (they were men, then, mostly—sorry).

It was right that it should be so. The business of state had at its heart, as it still has, two institutions: the courts and the machinery of government—and the practice of rhetoric was central to both. Yet it was and is present wherever there is language.

Inasmuch as the twentieth century—aka the Century That Rhetoric Forgot—paid much attention to rhetoric, the subject having been colonized largely by speech theorists, structural linguists, and literary critics, it was to point out just that: to note the intrinsic "rhetoricality" of all language.

Literary theorists and philosophers, you see, were initially intoxicated by the idea that language was ambiguous. Then they grew suspicious that it might be ambiguous for a reason: that metaphorical and figurative language could be serving the interests of Power. Then they wondered if, perhaps, the very nature of language itself was to be metaphorical and figurative and—important word here—"unstable."

Finally they concluded—to quote John Bender and David E. Wellbery, who offer a good example of the sort of high-sounding nonsense they talk—that

> rhetoricality . . . manifests the groundless, infinitely ramifying character of discourse in the modern world. For this reason, it allows for no explanatory metadiscourse that is not already itself rhetorical. Rhetoric is no longer the title of a doctrine and a practice, nor a form of cultural memory; it becomes instead something like the condition of our existence.[1]

In other words, language was Not To Be Trusted. But then, Aristotle could have told them that.

What I hope to do in this book is to give you the basics of rhetoric: to trace how people have taught, practiced, and thought about it from its ancient origins to its twenty-first-century apotheosis. I shall tell the stories of some of the great figures in its history—the heroes and villains of the persuasive arts. Men like Cicero, Erasmus, Adolf Hitler, and John F. Kennedy. I'll explain why George W. Bush wasn't so much of a doofus as all that, and why Winston Churchill wasn't always the great orator that posterity remembers.

I shall equip you with a working knowledge of the technical vocabulary. An alphabetical glossary at the back of the book

will give definitions and examples of the various terms, though I'll try to make clear, too, what each one means as it comes up in the text. More important, I hope to give some understanding of the principles that underlie those terms. I'll attempt to give a sense of how arguments prosper and founder: for the technical study of rhetoric is, at root, no more than a systematic way of doing that. Along the way I'll look at some of the great and not so great speeches of this and other ages, and take you through some of the more interesting byways of the Western mind.

By the end, in a word, you should get it. And even if you don't become a rhetoric nerd, you will be able to watch the keynote speeches at political conventions on TV and you won't just be able to say, "What a preposterous lying oily-faced scoundrel that politician is!" (Okay, you probably won't use that phrase if you live in America, but you get the idea.) You will add, with a sophisticated eyebrow hoist: "Do you think he could go ten seconds without using another *anaphora*? Anyone would think his copy of Lanham stopped at *A*."

I won't talk in detail, for the moment, about the tropes and figures that make up the rhetorician's box of tricks. Let's instead start with a broad view. Underlying the whole project of this book is, I hope, the awareness that practically any speech act can be understood, one way or another, as rhetorical—either in and of itself, or in the context of its utterance.

Let me give an example of the latter. If I say, "Tony has genital warts and halitosis." That is a statement of flat fact—or, at least, purports to be. But it can become more or less rhetorical depending on the context in which I utter it.

Context One: I am a doctor's receptionist, reading my employer the results of a patient's tests. Here, the phrase is as close

to neutral as you will find. There may be a bit of an edge in "halitosis," but I'm essentially conveying information without the urge to persuade. If it has the effect of persuading the doctor to take the afternoon off, that's incidental. If, mind you, I were a highly unprofessional receptionist—and while delivering the diagnosis, I clutched my throat and stuck out my tongue—we'd perhaps be straying into the region of *epideictic* rhetoric: the rhetoric of praise and insult.

Context Two: I am a prosecuting attorney in family court, attempting to unseat the defendant's claim that not only is he a virgin, but he was at a dental hygienists' appointment at the time when he is alleged to have fathered a child with Miss X. In this context, I'm trying to persuade my audience of something about the past. This falls into the realm of *judicial* or *forensic* rhetoric: the sort of rhetoric most commonly found in the courtroom.

Context Three: I am Miss Y's friend. We are in a nightclub. After a baker's dozen Bacardi Breezers she is starting to make sheep's eyes at Tony, the open-shirted smoothie throwing disco shapes at the other end of the bar. Fearing disaster, I offer a word to the wise. My aim is not to convey information, but to make going home with Tony seem like a less attractive prospect. (And, perhaps, going home with me like a more attractive one.) Again, I seek to persuade: and my concern is not with the past or with the present, but with the future. This is what's called *deliberative* rhetoric—and if it's useful in nightclubs, it is even more useful in politics.

So much for Tony. So much, too, for the division of rhetoric into *epideictic, forensic*, and *deliberative*—I'll return to that presently. For the moment, the point I mean to make is that rhetoric means a whole lot more than formal, stand-at-the-podium

oratory—it twines its tentacles into every corner of daily life and sprinkles its fairy dust into the most mundane of conversations. (Tentacles? Fairy dust? It is, as I suggested, a many-splendored thing.)

Rhetoric is language at play—language plus. It is what persuades and cajoles, inspires and bamboozles, thrills and misdirects. It causes criminals to be convicted, and then frees those criminals on appeal. It causes governments to rise and fall, best men to be ever after shunned by their friends' brides, and perfectly sensible adults to march with steady purpose toward machine guns.

And it is made of stuff like, well, the paragraph above. It is made of linked pairs—"inspires and bamboozles," "persuades and cajoles." It is made of groups of three. It is made of repeated phrases. It is made, as often as not, of half-truths and fine-sounding meaninglessness, of false oppositions and abstract nouns and shaky inferences.

But it is also made of ringing truths and vital declarations. It is a way in which our shared assumptions and understandings are applied to new situations, and the language of history is channeled, revitalized, and given fresh power in each successive age.

The technical language of rhetoric can seem forbidding. *Auxesis, homioteleuton, paralepsis, mesozeugma* . . . it looks to the casual reader like a glance across the labels of those miscellaneous firewaters you collected over half a decade's vacations on the Greek islands. But these technical terms, like those drinks, are actually tremendous fun once you get started with them. You won't soon forget a big night on the *epicheireme*. But they aren't anything in themselves. They are simply a way of describing a set of tricks and turns that already exist.

Your parents used rhetoric on you from the first moments of your life, and as soon as you were able to form words, you started using it right back at them. Your schoolmates, your workmates, and your chat partners in the dark back rooms of the Internet are using rhetoric. Your priests and your politicians, your television announcers and your commercial breaks are using rhetoric. You have been using rhetoric yourself, all your life.

After all, you know what a rhetorical question is, don't you?* We're all familiar with the way in which people ask questions to which they don't expect an answer: "Am I talking to myself here?"; "Could this new jacket look any more cool?"; "Why did I think having two children would be a good idea?"

That is, when you think about it, rather an abstruse way to use language. Why not just say: "Nobody's listening to me," "My new jacket looks very cool," or "My life has been ruined by these screaming brats"?

So embedded in everyday language is this strange flourish— this question aimed at nobody—that we scarcely notice it. In the very sentence I used to query the construction—that is, the one before last—I quite accidentally used it again.

And there it is: when we think we're speaking plainly, we're in fact filling our every sentence with rhetorical trickery. All of us are rhetoricians by instinct and training.

So it is small wonder that those terms—used unconsciously, understood instinctively—stud our language to this day. When you hear someone has delivered a "paean of praise," a "panegyric," or a "eulogy" to something, you're hearing terms from rhetoric.

---

*Don't answer that.

Even Derek Zoolander—in the glorious film that bears his name, a male model of surpassing stupidity—knows his stuff. Almost. "A eugoogalizer: one who speaks at funerals," he tells a reporter he suspects of looking down on him. "Or did you think I'd be too stupid to know what a eugoogoly was?"

When you hear words like "parenthesis," "apology," "colon," "comma," or "period"; when someone talks about a "commonplace" or "using a figure of speech," you're hearing terms from rhetoric. When you listen to the most bumbling tribute at a retirement party or the most inspiring halftime talk from a football coach, you are hearing rhetoric—and the basic ways in which it works have not changed a jot since Cicero saw off that treacherous fink Catiline. What has changed is that, where for hundreds of years rhetoric was at the center of Western education, it has now all but vanished as an area of study—divvied up like postwar Berlin between linguistics, psychology, and literary criticism. Even in universities, it is seen as a quaint and rather prissy minority interest.

So though rhetoric is all around us, we don't see it. Indeed, it's precisely because it's all around us that we don't see it. Explaining rhetoric to a human being is, or should be, like explaining water to a fish.

In the previous few paragraphs, I've used *auxesis, antithesis, chiasmus, digressio, apostrophe, erotesis, epistrophe, hendiadys,* and *argumentum ad populum*. There's even a bit of *polysyndeton* coming up. (Not to mention *occultatio; prolepsis,* I'll be getting to later.) And yet—at least I hope I'm safe in saying so— it reads more or less like . . . well, English.

It isn't an academic discipline, or the preserve of professional orators. It's right here, right now, in your argument with

the insurance company, your plea to the waitress for a table near the window, or your entreaties to your jam-faced kiddies to eat their damn veggies.

Like the fish in its water, we can and do swim in rhetoric unthinkingly. But there is so much you miss out on if you don't stop to think about it. Understanding rhetoric makes you better able to appreciate its wonders and pleasures, it equips you better to use it yourself, and it equips you to see through the next smooth-talking rascal who wants to sell you double-glazing.

But it's even more than that. To think about rhetoric is to think about something central to the foundation of our politics, to the DNA of our culture, and to the basic workings of the human mind.

We don't use language to pass on information flatly and to no purpose. We exchange information because it is either useful or delightful—because it does something for us: it gets us out of trouble or into bed.

We use language to cajole and seduce, to impress and inspire, to endear and justify. Language happens because human beings are desire machines, and what knits desire and language is rhetoric. To think about rhetoric—let's go back to my poor, not-wishing-to-be-bothered-with-all-this fish for a minute—is to get that bit closer to being able to see the fishbowl.

And think, for a second, about what rhetoric—in its basic sense of one person trying to persuade another person of a truth or of an ideal—has achieved. What has rhetoric ever done for us? Well, it has brought about all of Western civilization, for a start.

What is democracy, but the idea that the art of persuasion should be formally enshrined at the center of the political process? What is law, but a way of giving words formal strength in

the world, and what is the law court but a place where the art of persuasion gives shape to civil society? And what, in any society where one person or group exercises power over another—which is to say any society at all—is the instrument of that power but words?

Robert Mugabe and the late Kim Jong-il were not physically stronger than the people they governed—Mugabe's a doddery old thing, and even I wouldn't have had much trouble sticking the stack-heeled North Korean despot over my knee and giving him a good spanking—but they controlled the language. They positioned themselves—another central rhetorical idea—in a system of shared assumptions and shared fears.

When Shakespeare has his King Harry steal among the men before Agincourt, and thunder his exhortations at the gates of Harfleur, we are to understand that what made the difference here was the effect of his words. And that's not poetic license. Battles have been joined and averted, imperial powers seen off, and half the globe colonized by rhetoric. Gandhi never picked up a sword. Karl Marx never used a gun.

"WWJD?" asks the acronymic evangelical bumper sticker: "What Would Jesus Do?" We know what he did. He talked to people. That, and nothing else. He was crucified not because he bore arms against the Roman Imperium, but because they didn't like the way he was talking. The same goes for every religion of the book.

The thing is, the near-invisibility of rhetoric as an object of study in the modern age has had an unfortunate and unanticipated effect on the way we view it. It is, where we notice it working on us, profoundly mistrusted.

In realist painting, fiction, and filmmaking, it's commonly said that you strive for "the art that conceals art." You don't want

the viewer to be distracted by a pencil line you've failed to erase, or a too-intrusive author, or the display of a digital watch peeping through the fur at King Kong's wrist.

Your poem may be a Petrarchan sonnet put together like a steel trap—but you'll be admired more for it if it reads nearly like prose. This is, for the most part, the temper of the times.

So it is with oratory. We swallow the high style on certain occasions: at times of national grief or historic change, but for the most part we prefer plain speaking. This is a relatively recent development: for centuries people regarded oratory, be it in a sermon or in the law courts, as a form of entertainment in itself.

It's a commonplace in the theater that were most of us to see one of the greats of the eighteenth- or nineteenth-century stage deliver his Hamlet we would simply fall over laughing. It would seem implausibly stagy and histrionic. Even Laurence Olivier, to the eyes of today, looks like a colossal ham. Look at the film of his Othello. The camera zooms in, and—with his face covered in black shoe polish—Olivier booms and grimaces and rolls his eyes like a cartoon minstrel.

This description is not meant to disparage the actor. A modern audience's reaction is in part a shift from the age when acting meant being able to project both your voice and your gestures to the dimmest-eyed and deafest-eared spectator in the furthest corner of the auditorium—of an age before the intimacies of television and the wonders of amplified sound. But it is also a shift in style.

So it is, also, with rhetoric. Those rolling Churchillian periods seem to belong to another historical era. Routine political exchanges in the Houses of Parliament—and the setup in the UK, with questions going back and forth across the despatch box, already promotes a more conversational style—are

more commonly games of ping-pong than exchanges of mortar fire.

But the plain style to which we're accustomed is no less a rhetorical strategy than the high style that will strike us as hammy or false. What seems to you "rhetorical" today is, for the most part, rhetoric that isn't working. Rhetoric has come to be understood as a byword for all that is insubstantial, untrustworthy, windy, and needlessly ornate. If you type the phrase "mere rhetoric" into Google you get 492,000 hits. "Just rhetoric" gets you 560,000 hits. And the strongest negative, "empty rhetoric," earns more than 1.3 million hits—of which, as he entered the last year of his first term, well over a third were related to the search term "Obama."*

I started writing this book just after Obama's inauguration in 2009. As a one-time English literature student whose geekier hours had been spent not dropping acid in the college bar but poring through *A Handlist of Rhetorical Terms*, I took an interest in Obama's style of speaking. Here was oratory that proudly de-

---

*This paragraph is a fine example of the sort of argument you find in rhetoric. As we shall see, Aristotle said that the way rhetoric works, and the way logic works, are fundamentally different. Logical arguments proceed by syllogisms: ironclad chains of deduction that lead you infallibly from a premise to an inference without so much as a pee break. The equivalent in the field of rhetoric is something called an "enthymeme." Much more on this later, but it's what you might understand as "fuzzy logic": the affairs of the human world are not subject to the same black-and-white proofs as mathematical logic. In rhetoric, you may rest a "proof" on what seems likely or reasonable. And here's where there is room for maneuver. Google hits are a reasonable finger-to-the-wind measure of things. But they can be deceptive, too. I discovered this to my cost when in a *Guardian* article about the late Bill Hicks—complaining of the vocabulary of "naked religious devotion" in which devotees describe him—I observed that "if you Google 'Bill Hicks' and 'prophet' you get 47,000-odd hits." The online comment thread below—stuffed, I consoled myself, with tragic Hicks cultists—pointed out that if you Google "chicken" and "creosote" you get 503,000 hits, that if you Google "albumen" and "sumptuous" you get 9,750 results and that "disappointingly *Sam Leith testicles* returns only 3,870."

clared itself as oratory—and yet seemed neither old-fashioned nor quaint nor affected. And it certainly didn't seem irrelevant. In fact, it looked as if it was quite literally going to change the world.

When I wrote a longish newspaper article on the subject, I worried the number of recondite-seeming Greek terms might put readers off. As it turned out, nobody seemed to find the article indigestible—indeed, it seemed to touch off an appetite for this little-considered area of knowledge. The idea for the book in your hands is what came out of it.

So cast your mind back to that moment. It's a good place to start. The story of Barack Obama's campaign for the presidency is a great instance of both the power of rhetoric and the power of hostility to rhetoric.

It was, arguably, Obama's oratorical poise and fluency on his feet, more than anything else, that propelled him first past the far better funded and organized favorite, Hillary Clinton, to win the Democratic nomination. And as "Yes We Can" fever swept America, the Republicans—led by the less fluent John McCain* and the folksy but gaffe-prone Sarah Palin**—were put on the defensive.

What is interesting is that in very short order Obama found himself under attack not for his policies or for his voting history—but for his very ability to speak clearly and articulately and movingly. It seemed that, though we expected politicians to make speeches, we didn't like them to be too good at it. A distinctive and consistent line of attack emerged from his political enemies. Even Hillary Clinton sought to slight him as a man who just "gives speeches."

---

*A man who once called his wife a "cunt" in public.
**A woman who . . . oh, you know the drill. Insert your own examples.

The critic James Wood wrote a funny and penetrating short piece on the subject, in *The New Yorker* magazine in October 2008, entitled "The Republican War on Words." Wood quoted two prominent Republicans. Phyllis Schlafly, whom he ungallantly described as a "leathery extremist," was quoted speaking of her admiration for Sarah Palin on the grounds that "she's a woman who worked with her hands,"* whereas Obama was "just an elitist who worked with words." Another Republican, Rick Santorum, said that Obama was "just a person of words" and added that "words are everything to him."

Invoking both a historic current of American anti-intellectualism and a residual Puritan idea that "the letter killeth, but the spirit giveth life," Wood diagnosed "a deep suspicion of language itself."

The argument—and it went all the way up to Obama's presidential rival John McCain, who repeatedly accused his opponent of "parsing words"—was that words themselves were the enemy, and that Obama's care in their use marked him as intrinsically untrustworthy. By contrast, Sarah Palin defended John McCain from criticism by dismissing "an unfair attack, there again, on the verbage [*sic*] that he used."

Palin's implication was that Obama's well-chosen words served to conceal his essence (bad), and that McCain's ill-chosen words likewise served to conceal his essence (good). How, then, was the voter to divine the true essence of either man except through his words? Here, I suspect, we leave the province of politics and enter that of theology.

---

*You don't come in third in the Miss Alaska pageant just by sitting there looking pretty.

As we'll see, there is a very strong tradition indeed—a tradition that goes back to Plato—of hostility to rhetoric. It is seen as the tool of demagogues and liars. But the terms in which that mistrust is couched are invariably, well, verbal. Senator McCain and his supporters didn't start campaigning in sign language, or posting homemade Sculpey models of Republican superheroes into the mailboxes of voters.

He and his team continued to make speeches, send out leaflets, fund television and radio advertisements, canvass supporters by phone and email, and all the rest of it. They simply did it less successfully than Obama.

Being anti-rhetoric is, finally, just another rhetorical strategy. Rhetoric is what the other guy is doing—whereas you, you're just speaking the plain truth as you see it. Some of the great orators of history, men like Forrest Gump and Yogi Berra, have made that strategy their main selling point.

You might well seek to do the same thing. But you'll use that particular technique far more ably if you understand it as just that: one technique among many. And if you can understand what the other guy is doing, you'll be all the better equipped to go on the attack and expose his fancy-schmancy rhetoric for what it is.

Knowledge, it has been said, is power. And rhetoric is what gives words power. So knowledge of rhetoric equips you, as a citizen, both to exercise power and to resist it. As W. H. Auden wrote in "September 1, 1939," "All I have is a voice / To undo the folded lie." The folding of the lie and the undoing of it are both accomplished through rhetoric.

Still not convinced? Let me try to persuade you.

RHETORIC THEN AND NOW

LET'S START BY THINKING about where we are now—and then going back to the question of how we got there. We may no longer study or teach rhetoric in anything like the way our ancestors did, but many more of us rely much more heavily on it than ever before. Consider the conditions in which, at the dawn of the twenty-first century, we live. Our commerce, our politics, our cultural and social lives are all rhetorical to an extraordinary extent.

As the collar of the average Western worker made its journey from blue to white over the course of the last century, the value of the persuasive arts for career advancement has grown in proportion. Politicians like to tell us that we live in "a knowledge economy," but they might just as well call it a rhetoric economy. The rhetoric handbooks of our age are now to be found in the business sections of bookshops—books that promise to teach the would-be tycoon how to *manage up* and *manage down* with the appropriate *people skills*, how to shape a company's *ethos*, how to *get your message across.*

The great forward gallop of industrial capitalism has brought new tasks for the rhetorician's tool kit, too. The advertising industry throughout its development (and, in our age, the related industries of PR and marketing) has been stuffed with highly figural language and with appeals to ethos and pathos. What is a jingle but a sound bite applied to commerce?

Meanwhile, the Internet, probably the single most important human invention since the printing press, takes the whole process a step further. Persuasive communication is no longer the preserve of professionals—be they politicians, broadcasters, or advertisers. Anybody with a hooked-up computer can now communicate remotely and instantaneously—through the spoken word or through the written—with a potential audience of millions. Blogs and video-logs, and the online arguments in comment threads and chat rooms, have spawned new tropes and figures, and new uses for the old ones. We live, thanks to the reach of our technologies, in perhaps the most argumentative age of any in history.

And thanks at least in part to those technologies, we're seeing the tentative spread of democratic institutions in areas that have lived for years under dictatorships or near-dictatorships. Pro-democracy movements all over North Africa and the Middle East have made themselves felt in what has been called by some "the Arab Spring." People in Egypt, Yemen, Bahrain, and Libya, by pushing for democracy, are arguing, in effect, for the right to argue. A more democratic world—and one with the legal institutions that go hand in hand with democracy—is a more rhetorical one.

And that is, funnily enough, exactly where this story begins: two and a half thousand years ago. Not an Arab Spring: but a Syracusan one.

A prosperous city-state on the east side of the island of Sicily, Syracuse had been muddling along for years under a succession of tyrants. "Tyrant," in the classical context, just means absolute ruler—though five will get you ten they were tyrants in the modern sense also. But in 465 BC the last of these tyrants—one Thrasybulus—was overthrown in what appears to have been some sort of popular uprising.

Imagine, if you will, the sudden descent of democracy on an unprepared population. Just as in Iraq after Saddam Hussein's downfall, or as in Russia in the first days after the revolution, the evaporation of an established order left a power vacuum. There was looting and appropriation. Ad hoc pockets of power developed, and local thuggery thrived. Who would secure property rights? Who was in charge?

In Syracuse, tradition has it that a man called Corax—who, according to some sources, had honed his persuasive arts as a courtier to the previous tyrant Hieron—charged in and helped bring about some semblance of order.

> Coming into the assembly, where all the people had gathered together, he began first to appease the troublesome and turbulent element among them with obsequious and flattering words. After this, he began to soothe and silence the people and to speak as though telling a story, and after these things to summarize and call to mind concisely what had gone before and to bring before their eyes at a glance what had previously been said.
>
> These things he called "introduction," "narration," "argument," "digression," and "epilogue." By means of them he contrived to persuade the people just as he used to persuade a man.[1]

The various accounts that survive, though sketchy, broadly agree that Corax was the first person to set down precepts for the art of persuasion. He's credited with discerning the different parts of an oration—how to open your speech, advance your arguments in an orderly fashion, and close the deal—and with teaching his methods to others. He is also—and the importance of this is not to be brushed aside—seen as having grasped the essential notion that in rhetoric you are dealing with likelihood rather than certainty: there is room for argument, and it is precisely in that room for argument that the art of persuasion flourishes.

Corax's name is frequently mentioned alongside that of a sidekick—a colleague or pupil called Tisias. Indeed, in some accounts they seem to be more or less interchangeable, and one fifth-century account has Corax as pupil and Tisias as master. But let's follow the rough consensus and suppose Tisias was the pupil and Corax the master.

Tradition has it that they fell out over the terms of Tisias's instruction. Corax agreed to take Tisias on as a pupil, and the deal they struck was what may have been the first no-win, no-fee agreement in legal history. It went as follows: if Tisias won his first case, then he'd pay Corax the agreed fee for his services. If Tisias lost his first case, however, then Corax would waive his fee on the grounds that his instruction had been useless. Having received his course of instruction as promised, Tisias, in an apparent attempt to cheat his master, avoided going to court at all. Finally, Corax was forced to sue him for the outstanding money.

In court, Corax argued that if judgment were to be awarded in his favor, then obviously he should be paid his money as you'd

expect. He went further, though, arguing that if the case went against him, then Tisias would have won his first case—thus undeniably fulfilling the terms of their agreement . . . meaning that he'd have to stump up Corax's fee too. Either way, Corax ingeniously argued, he would have to be paid.

Tisias argued the exact opposite. A judgment for Corax, he said, would mean that he, Tisias, had lost his first case: so, by the terms of their agreement, he need not pay a fee. A judgment in his own favor, naturally, would indicate that the court deemed he had discovered the arts of rhetoric despite, rather than because of, Corax's instruction. Either way, Corax could go whistle for his fee.

This was a new one on the law courts of fifth-century Syracuse. So the judge pondered long and hard—and then threw both men out, with the words "*Kakou korakas kakon oon,*" which translate as, "Bad crow, bad egg." These survive in the Latin proverb *Mali corvi malum ovum*—an immemorial testament to the discovery that it is possible to be too much of a smart-ass.

Who was Corax? The answer is murky. Most of the sources for the story of the Corax versus Tisias dustup in court are Byzantine—that is, very much later—and though Plato knew of a Tisias and Aristotle mentions a Corax, there's not much on either of them in the ten centuries between their own lives and the fifth century AD.

A scholar named Thomas Cole, however, published an ingenious speculative essay in 1991.[2] Corax's name—giving extra piquancy to the judge's joke—means "crow" in Greek, and Cole starts out arguing from common sense. Corax is overwhelmingly likely, he says, to have been a nickname. Ancient Greek

parents were no more prone to call their sons "Crow" than modern ones—and would anyone called "Crow" have the brass neck to teach the art of public speaking for a living?

It was natural for contemporaries to associate the chatter of crows with a loud, inept, cacophonous racket (a Pindar poem premiered in 476 BC, when Corax was a boy or young man, compared bad poets to squawking crows), so the chances are that Corax's name came after he embarked on his chosen profession, rather than before.

"The epithet may have been totally derisive and contemptuous, or derisive and affectionate at the same time," writes Cole. "The question cannot be answered. But if one asks what Corax was called before he got his new name, the answer is almost inevitable: Tisias."

Here is Professor Cole's "aha!" moment: Tisias and Corax were one and the same. He accepts that many won't be persuaded of his conclusion, but he insists that, even if unprovable, it seems fitting: "What more appropriate fate for the putative founder of the entire rhetorical tradition, with the centuries-long study of figural speech it incorporates, than to be finally revealed as nothing more—or nothing less—than a figure of speech himself?"

What Corax began, Gorgias took out into the world. A native of Leontini, a Sicilian town just up the coast from Syracuse, Gorgias was born somewhere between 480 and 490 BC and lived to the ripe old age of 109.* We don't know much about his life or career, and there's speculation, but no evidence, that he learned directly from Corax.

---

*His pupil Isocrates lived to 98. Rhetoric is good for you.

But we do know that in 427 BC, early in the Peloponnesian War, he emigrated to Athens and took rhetoric with him, setting up shop as a teacher and presiding over a sort of big bang in the subject. Within a generation Athens would be stuffed with teachers and practitioners of rhetoric.

The "sophists"—colleagues, rivals, and imitators of Gorgias— were what you might think of as the spin doctors of the Attic golden age. They taught well-heeled Athenians how to construct speeches and sway audiences. There also grew up a whole class of speechwriters, or *logographoi*. Since litigants were required to represent themselves in court, those who could afford to do so would buy a speech from a professional. So Athens became the center of a burgeoning rhetoric industry, and with that came an increasing interest in systematizing the art.

Why did rhetoric catch on so rapidly in Athens? Well, for a start, here was a place just getting used to a radical and unprecedented experiment with democracy. It was only in the early fifth century BC that the popular assembly became the central repository of power in the Athenian state, and the oligarchies and tyrannies that had preceded it, pretty much by definition, weren't fertile ground for the growth of public speaking. But now the principle of persuasive speech was at the heart of government. Those aristocrats who regretted the waning of their influence saw a chance to claw some back, if they could master the skills required to dominate the assembly.

What was that assembly like? It little resembles the representative democracy we recognize today, so it's worth making a brief sketch of how it worked. At the time Gorgias arrived in Athens, there would have been maybe 300,000 people living in Attica. Male citizens of age, who were entitled and expected to vote in

the general assembly, made up no more than a quarter of the total adult population. Slaves didn't get votes. Women didn't get votes. *Metics*, or resident aliens like Gorgias himself, didn't get votes.

In order to vote, you had to be there in person, so those citizens who lived outside town were also, effectively, disenfranchised. In practice, therefore, power was concentrated in the hands of a small metropolitan elite.

There were three main bodies that comprised the Athenian government. The first was the general assembly, or *ekklesia*, which consisted of any male citizen who had completed his military training and reached adulthood.

This being a direct rather than a representative democracy, membership of the *demos*, or sovereign body, was by right rather than by election, and every decision was taken on a one-man, one-vote basis. If you didn't turn up, you didn't have a voice.

The decisions of the assembly were enacted by an executive body called the Boule, or council of five hundred, which contained the closest thing ancient Athens had to members of congress. Its members were selected by lot, with each of the ten Attic tribes sending fifty men to the council.

The Boule had little or no power, however. Basically, it was the job of the council to supply the assembly with any information it needed—and then to scurry back to the various tribes, spread the good word on any decisions made, and ensure that those decisions were enacted. Beneath them, a system of magistrates selected to serve by lot was used to carry decisions through.

The third part of the picture is the law courts. Here, ancient Athens resembles a modern democracy even less than in the previous particulars. For if its democracy looks less democratic than ours, its courts look far more so.

There already existed a sort of council of elders, called the Areopagus,* which consisted of senior ex-politicians and functioned as an aristocratic court of appeal. But by halfway through the fifth century BC—again, not long before Gorgias arrived—its judicial function had mostly been usurped by the Heliaea,** which was open to absolutely anyone. Any adult male citizen, that is, was eligible for the 6,000-strong jury pool. And, presumably for what nowadays we would call lulz, everyone turned up.

Forget twelve good men and true. The average size of a jury in the Heliaea was around 500, and the court wasn't even considered a quorum without a jury of 201 (rising to 401 in cases involving substantial sums). On at least one occasion, all 6,000 jurors heard a single case. These jurors, though they sat under oath, were subject to no regulation or review or supervision or appeal. And the state didn't exercise a monopoly on prosecutions, either: any citizen could bring a case against any other citizen—thus giving rise to a succession of nakedly political or grudge-motivated trials.

It was a bear pit: an endless procession of vexatious litigants and political opportunists settling personal scores in front of a shouting, hooting, uncontrollable rabble of, um, jurors. This was the closest thing one could get to institutionalized trial by lynch mob. Athenian juries were notoriously partisan and notoriously eager to convict—showing a chippy preference, too, for cutting the wealthy and prominent down to size.

No wonder the idea of learning how to talk round a large mass of people was something that Athenian aristocrats—traditionally

---

*So named, supposedly, because it met on a big rock above Athens. *Pagos* means "big rock."
**So named, supposedly, because it met in the sanctuary of the sun god, Apollo Heliaea.

the political class, and one bloodied but unbowed by the advent of democracy—got interested in. They were buying what Gorgias and the sophists were selling.

But no sooner had rhetoric established itself than anti-rhetoric did the same. The same claims that you see made today were established then: that rhetoric is nothing but a collection of low tricks designed to confuse and bamboozle an audience into thinking the weak argument is the stronger. In his comic play *The Clouds*, Aristophanes, writing in 420 BC, lampooned rhetoric as the art of weak reasoning, "which by false arguments triumphs over the strong." Personifications of "Just Discourse" and "Unjust Discourse" take the stage to slug it out. As the play's protagonist concedes, the pupils of Unjust Discourse are the occupants of all the positions of power and eminence in the city.

Plato had a less sarcastic but more forceful opposition. Plato didn't trust democracy. And because he saw how easily the mob could be swayed—he was traumatized by the judicial murder of his teacher and hero Socrates—he didn't trust rhetoric. He also regarded as suspect the instrumental nature, and murky methods, of rhetorical persuasion—which, by contrast with the strict logic of philosophical inquiry, they are.

In this Attic roughneck polity, you can think of Plato—with his radical idealism, intellectual rigidity, and hatred of the mob—as a sort of ancient precursor to Conservative MP Enoch Powell. His most sustained attack on rhetoric comes in his dialogue *Gorgias*, where he imagines Socrates giving the eponymous rhetorician the third degree.*

Gorgias, as it happens, is also the first text in which the term *rhetorike*, the Greek for "public speaking," makes an appearance.

Socrates first leads Gorgias up the garden path, enticing him to agree that "rhetoric is the artificer of persuasion, having this and no other business, and that this is her crown and end."

"Do you know any other effect of rhetoric over and above that of producing persuasion?" he asks.

Gorgias concedes, "No: the definition seems to me very fair, Socrates; for persuasion is the chief end of rhetoric."

Gorgias's brother Herodicus is a doctor, and the former attests that when trying to persuade a patient to submit to a course of treatment, his oratory is far more effective than his brother's medical expertise. Here, Socrates pounces. The oratory, in this case, is more effective on an ignorant audience than a well-informed one, is it not? And the orator need know nothing of medicine himself, hmm?

SOCRATES: Then, when the rhetorician is more persuasive than the physician, the ignorant is more persuasive with the ignorant than he who has knowledge? Is not that the inference?

GORGIAS: In the case supposed, yes.

SOCRATES: And the same holds of the relation of rhetoric to all the other arts; the rhetorician need not know the truth about things; he has only to discover some way of persuading the ignorant that he has more knowledge than those who know?[3]

That has continued to be the central complaint against rhetoric ever since: that it gives the plausible ignoramus or the self-interested dissembler—the knave or the fool—power over the good and the wise. It is, in consequence, a cousin of the arguments made against democracy itself.

The fact that "sophistry" has a bad name these days is down to Plato. The sophists—of whom Gorgias was one of the first examples—were essentially just private tutors who trained Athenian aristocrats in philosophy and rhetoric. And to the Athenian political class, they became indispensable.

Gorgias and the other sophists taught and worked haphazardly, but there would come a greater man. The Newton of rhetoric—the one person whose work in this department overshadows the whole history of the subject—was, of course, Aristotle.

Aristotle's *Rhetoric* was the first great systematic statement of how rhetoric works, and I draw on both its arguments and its structure throughout this book. Aristotle definitively identified the three branches of oratory—judicial, deliberative, and epideictic—and the three persuasive appeals—ethos (the speaker's self-presentation), pathos (the attempt to sway emotion), and logos (the intellectual argument)—that mingle in them. Those triads have proved enduring.

Aristotle was also the midwife of rhetoric's place in the liberal arts—making it an object of systematic study and finding a place for it in his system of thought. Rhetoric was, for Aristotle, dialectic's wayward cousin: having as its method not "this therefore that" but "probably this so likely that," and as its object not knowledge but persuasion. Rhetoric, he said, was a *technè*: a practical skill. It was teachable.

Aristotle was a pretty astonishing figure. Not only did he lay the foundations for all subsequent study of how poetry and drama work, but he more or less invented formal logic, knocked off the basis of the scientific method, produced significant advances in political theory, ethics, zoology, and for all I know invented skateboarding on a Wednesday afternoon when he had nothing better to do.

Born in 384 BC, he was the son of the personal physician to the king of Macedonia. Raised as an aristocrat, he was dispatched to the academy in Athens at the age of seventeen to study philosophy under Plato and spent two decades there. For most of that time, as far as we know, he was a straight-down-the-line Platonist.

That is why, on the face of it, it is rather odd that he ended up being the great scholar of rhetoric—and, for that matter, the great scholar of poetics too. As I've said, Plato mistrusted rhetoric—as he mistrusted poetry and drama. Rhetoric smears butter on the philosopher's spectacles, kicks sand in his face, and allows the demagogue to stroll off with the girl (or boy, as the case may have been).

Aristotle was a disciple of Plato, and to start with, this seems to have been his position too. But Aristotle was also a practical man. Plato had a mathematician's sensibility—his investigations into reality took place in the mind alone. Aristotle's investigations were a bit more hands-on: when he wanted to know what the inside of an octopus looked like, he grabbed a scalpel and opened one up.

Around the time of Plato's death—possibly in a huff because he wasn't asked to take over the running of the academy from the boss; possibly because Macedonians were, for political reasons, getting less and less popular in Athens—Aristotle shipped out of Athens.

It was not until 335 BC—when, among other things, Athens was once more safe for Macedonians—that he returned, aged fifty, and founded his own school there, the Lyceum. By the time he came to produce it, *Rhetoric* answered a directly practical problem. Aristotle needed to attract pupils—and while his rival Isocrates was teaching rhetoric, the Lyceum needed to be able to compete. Necessity, you might say, was the mother of invention.

The *Rhetoric* itself is, in many ways, a bit of a mess. It wasn't a book prepared for publication—but seems rather to have been a collection of notes for the lectures Aristotle gave his students, or notes taken by those students at the lectures. Stylistically, it is of Spartan—well, Attic—bareness. It doesn't have the structural elegance of the work of later handbooks, and it's written to instruct rather than to impress. But, obscure though it is in parts and repetitive though it is in others, it is filled with wise and interesting things.

The *Rhetoric*[4] gives us Aristotle as the austere, wan, sometimes amused observer of a fallen world: one where the young are foolish and the old mean-spirited, where most people will commit the crime if they think they can get away with it, and where slick and knavish operators can all too easily put one over on the general public. Nuggets of keen observation and odd tidbits about the ancient world glint in it, too. Reading it, for instance, you learn that, among the Spartans, long hair in a man is a mark of nobility: "as a sign of a free man, since it is not easy for a long-haired man to perform any manual task."* You hear of Polycrates, who delivered a panegyric to the mice that saved the Egyptians from an invading Assyrian army by gnawing through the enemy's bowstrings. And you hear how Gorgias, when a swallow shat on his head, rebuked it: "Shame on you, Philomela!"** (The remark, Aristotle says drily, "would have been excellent in a tragedy.")

All those enjoyments are incidental. The key thing is that it is halfway to being a handbook: here is not an academic exercise,

---

*I know: odd, isn't it?
**In Greek legend, Philomela was transformed into a swallow by the gods.

but a course of instruction in the basic principles behind the successful composition of speeches. It included a list of specimen arguments, explained how an audience could be swayed, and discussed everything from how to discredit a hostile witness to how best to modulate your voice when speaking. But while it is halfway to being a handbook, it is halfway to being something else too: it is an attempt to formulate a theory of rhetoric and give it a philosophical place in the world. Aristotle sought to rescue rhetoric from its place as a purely instrumental art: the highest rhetorical accomplishment, for Aristotle, was an expression of *arête*, or virtue. As he put it: "Character contains almost the strongest proof of all."

Rather than teach a series of tricks and tips for momentary success in speaking, as any catchpenny sophist might, Aristotle sought to form a coherent view of why those tips and tricks worked. If other rhetoric teachers were driving instructors, Aristotle was a mechanic: he didn't just want to know where the accelerator was—he wanted to understand what went on under the hood.

So when you grasp what Aristotle's about—that his theory of rhetoric is also essentially a theory of human nature—you cannot but find yourself in awe. Both the means and the ends of rhetoric, Aristotle finds, participate in the deepest human questions. He says the object of deliberative rhetoric, for instance, is "happiness"—and he therefore sets out to establish what constitutes the good. In relation to judicial rhetoric, he investigates what we mean by justice and fairness. And at every turn he is attentive to the notion that what is said needs to be fitted to the audience that hears it—and so everything from what is plausible in terms of motive, to the aesthetics of prose style, falls under his work's purview.

Aristotle shines, in other words, because he was the first person really to grasp that the study of rhetoric is the study of humanity itself.

So what came after? It belongs to a different, far bigger and more scholarly book to trace in detail the development of rhetoric teaching and theory between the ancient world and the present day. But it's worth including a thumbnail sketch, I think. If you can't wait to get to the nuts and bolts, by all means skip ahead. But I think to fully understand how things came to be as they are, it helps to get a sense of the history. Think of the classical tradition of rhetoric as a river: as it flows forward to the present day, it takes several twists and turns, and in some places it plunges underground. This is not figural: Aristotle's works spent a couple hundred years in a cellar in what's now western Turkey before someone dug them out in the first century BC. And thus it took over two hundred years after his death, in the fourth century BC, for his mantle to be assumed by Cicero.

Cicero, though he followed Aristotle, may not even have known his work firsthand. Cicero was the great eminence of the Roman age—a lawyer, a politician, and so not only Rome's greatest theorist of rhetoric but its greatest practitioner. He was followed by the Spanish-born Quintilian, who wrote the magnificently punchy and pragmatic *Institutes of Oratory*—looking wistfully back to the master—in the first century AD.

Confusingly, the other great Roman text to survive is *Ad Herennium*—which was roughly contemporary with Cicero, and was for centuries wrongly attributed to him. Thanks in part to that wrong attribution, *Ad Herennium* was the most popular handbook right through to the Renaissance. Shakespeare was most probably taught from it.

But before we reached Shakespeare, we had to get through the Dark Ages—when, no doubt, people communicated well enough in grunts, snarls, and the clanging of axes,* but nobody was paying too much attention to Aristotle's theories of metaphor. Fortunately, the Islamic world had its eye on the ball, and most of the classical texts we have now were preserved in Arabic translation. The early-medieval Renaissance saw them translated back out of Arabic and returned to the West.

Over the centuries that followed, there were two key influences on the way rhetoric developed: Christianity and the written word. Classical texts were wrestled into a Christian worldview as scholars like St. Augustine and Thomas Aquinas sought ways to claim the ancients as Christians *avant la lettre*. And, of course, in the shape of sermons, Christianity provided regular formal occasions for public speaking. We had a form of deliberative oratory whose aim was the winning or keeping of souls, rather than the good in public policy; and in theodicy—the justifying of the ways of God to man—and other aspects of Christian apologetics, you can see, if you like, the judicial and epideictic aspects of Christianized rhetoric.

The importance of written, rather than spoken, transmission is also pervasive. The main mutation was the growth of the *ars dictamini*s: a body of received wisdom about letter-writing that followed the classical canons of rhetoric and applied them in epistolary form. By Renaissance times, rhetoric had become so centrally embedded in the culture as a habit of mind that it shaped the way all knowledge was approached. Johannes Kepler's 1601 *Apologia Pro Tychone Contra Ursum*, for instance, is

---

*Some historical simplification has been necessary for reasons of space.

an immaculate judicial oration—on the subject of astronomy. Sir Philip Sidney's 1580s *An Apology for Poetry* is given the seven-part form of a classical oration.

In *Love's Labour's Lost*, Shakespeare has Berowne complain, "Taffeta phrases, silken terms precise, / Three-piled hyperboles, spruce affectation, / Figures pedantical; these summer flies / Have blown me full of maggot ostentation." That makes plain not only that formal rhetoric's "three-piled hyperboles" and "figures pedantical" were familiar to Shakespeare, but that he could have anticipated them being familiar enough to his audience to elicit a groan of recognition.

And so they would have been. In Shakespeare's day, rhetoric was one third of a basic education. The grammar school curriculum consisted of grammar, logic, and rhetoric—a three-part system of knowledge called "the trivium" that was regarded as the foundation of learning. It underpinned the more difficult "quadrivium"—arithmetic, geometry, music, and astronomy— that students went on to learn; all seven subjects taken *in toto* being the so-called liberal arts. This had been the outline of an education since medieval times.

The division of the liberal arts is not accidental; it articulates a coherent system of thought. The three arts of the trivium relate to the mind, and the four of the quadrivium to matter. Sister Miriam Joseph* categorizes the relation of the trivial arts as fol-

---

*Yes: a woman! And, yes: a nun! I know many of you will have despaired of coming across much of either in this volume, but there she is. Sister Miriam Joseph (1898–1982), born Agnes Lenore Rauh, was an American nun. Before she entered the novitiate, she trained as a journalist. Most of her adult life was spent teaching in the English faculty of a Catholic university. Inspired by a lecture from a visiting professor from the University of Chicago on "The Metaphysical Basis of the Liberal Arts," Sister Miriam attempted to reinstate

lows: logic is concerned with the thing-as-it-is-known; grammar is concerned with the thing-as-it-is-symbolized; rhetoric is concerned with the thing-as-it-is-communicated. She calls rhetoric "the master art of the trivium."

In the Renaissance, the art of rhetoric overlapped substantially with the arts of drama and poetry—not only because of their formal congruencies in terms of rhythm, sound effects, metaphor, and whatnot, but because those seeking to put language at the service of power were courtiers of an absolute monarch rather than citizens of an Athenian democracy. Poetry and drama were deeply involved in networks of patronage: praise-poems, sucky-up dedications, scurrilous broadsides, and vicious "flytings" of one's rivals.

A window into that world comes in the work of George Puttenham (c. 1530–1590), author of a 1589 book called *The Arte of English Poesie*, which is widely regarded as being "the central text of Elizabethan courtly poetics."[5]

In the preamble to the first book of the *Arte*, a history of poetry, Puttenham is clear "How the poets were the first Philosophers, the first Astronomers and Historiographers and Oratours and Musiciens of the world":

Vtterance also and language is giuen by nature to man for perswasion of others, and aide of them selues [. . . and poetry is] more eloquent and rethoricall then the ordinarie prose, which

---

the old-style trivium as a compulsory course for freshmen English students. She went on to write a PhD dissertation on the effect of formal rhetoric on Shakespeare's language, and remained an evangelist for the use of the trivium in education. She's the author of *The Trivium: The Liberal Arts of Logic, Grammar and Rhetoric—Understanding the Nature and Function of Language* (1937).

we use in our daily talke: because it is decked and set out with all manner of fresh colours and figures, which maketh that it sooner inuegleth the iudgement of man, and carieth his opinion this way and that, whither soeuer the heart by impression of the eare shal be most affectionatly bent and directed [. . .]So as the Poets were also from the beginning the best perswaders and their eloquence the first Rethoricke of the world.

So when Puttenham wrote about poetics, he was also writing about rhetoric. And what he's chiefly remembered for is a heroic attempt to domesticate the figures and tropes of classical oratory by giving them English names and English examples. The results never completely caught on—but they endure as a historical curiosity of some idiosyncrasy.

He lists 121 figures, and divides them according to a taxonomy that's highly serviceable today:* grouping them according to the type of thing they did. So he talked about "auricular figures" and "sensible figures"—that is, tweaks of language that help a sentence appeal better to the ear; and those that affect its argument—and subdivided those into figures that worked by "disorder," "surplusage," and "exchange."

Alliteration gets called "Like Letter," for instance. *Synecdoche*—using a part to recall the whole, like when you call a car "a set of wheels" or bark "all hands on deck!"—is renamed "Quicke Conceit." *Erotema* is "The Questioner." *Zeugma*—the figure where a

---

*Indeed, a version of it is one way you can search the absolutely invaluable online resource Silva Rhetoricae (http://rhetoric.byu.edu/) or "Forest of Rhetoric." You can look up Greek, Latin, and English names for the figures—and also browse by groups: figures "of Amplification," "of Balance," "of Overstatement," and what have you. I can't recommend this site, maintained by Dr. Gideon Burton of Brigham Young University, too highly.

single verb governs a number of subjects, as in "he put out the cat, his cigar, and the light"—gets called "Single Supply."

Hyperbole is the "Loud Lyer" or "The Overreacher." *Antiphrasis*, the sarcastic use of a word to mean its opposite—"take Einstein, over here"—is called "the Broad Floute"; and *mycterismus* (an insult which comes with an accompanying gesture: "I fart in your general direction") is Englished, magnificently, as "The Fleering Frumpe."

Sometimes Puttenham's terms are practical; sometimes, more fanciful. *Epizeuxis*—the repetition of a single word again and again without anything in between—"howl, howl, howl" or "break, break, break"—puts us appositely in mind of wall-to-wall carpets when Puttenham calls it "The Underlay" (or "the Cuckow spell").

From our vantage point, the project of giving English names to the classical figures of speech looks quixotic at best: something like George Bernard Shaw's attempt to rationalize English spelling, 1970s feminist campaigns for "herstory" and "womyn" to enter standard usage, the Académie Française's doomed crusade against Anglo-Saxon loanwords, or the hope that Esperanto might become the world language.

But at the time, it might even have looked sensible. After all, the Latin terms survive more or less in free variation with the Greek, and Puttenham's English equivalents are abundantly charming—albeit that charm is conditioned by a certain quaintness. We're the richer for his backing this horse, even if it was the wrong one.

The great joke about Puttenham, though, is that he survives not only for his work on rhetoric but as an instance of its effectiveness. It would be easy to assume—and for many years people did—that the author of *The Arte of English Poesie* was as

he represented himself: an experienced and urbane courtier, mannerly and well traveled, and able to give insight into the inner circles of the Elizabethan courtly life.

Puttenham, however, was in point of fact as chivalrous as Dominique Strauss-Kahn, as uxorious as Hugh Hefner, and as well connected to the inner workings of court as I am. He was a swindler, a welsher, a cad, and a rogue. His career saw him in and out of jail, constantly being sued, refusing to pay alimony, impregnating and abandoning a string of domestic servants, conspiring to duff up random clergymen, and at one point abducting a teenage girl and keeping her as a sex slave.* "Spouse abuse, sexual slavery, and multiple excommunications from the Church of England all figure in Puttenham's revised biography," as the above-mentioned Steven W. May sums it up.

Much of what he said of the Elizabethan court's style was, we now know, plain wrong; and May has a lot of fun pointing out how gauche his supposedly courtly poetry is: "Courtly finesse aside, mere common sense would have precluded any of her courtiers from describing the Queen, even by analogy, as 'Sore withered.'"

It's easy to laugh now. But this fraudulence carried all before it. For the best part of half a century, the author of the *Arte* was held to be a senior courtier and the work's contents the fruit of deep privileged knowledge. Its place in the canons of poetics and rhetoric, moreover, has largely survived the personal debunking of its author.

---

*That only came to an end when his wife happened to find her, and wrote to Puttenham crisply: "I haue in my custodie a damsell chosen by you as she confessethe for yor owne toothe."

It was said of Puttenham that he was "full of brables of sub-tyll practises and slanderous devyses . . . overconnynge in de-facinge of truthe, by wordes and speache eloquente and in invencon of myschieffe verie pertfytte." That's not meant in a nice way; but could there be a better epitaph for a rhetorician?

Outside the realm of courtly poetry, the handbook tradition continued to thrive. The rhetoric scholar Brian Vickers says that around two thousand rhetoric books were published between 1400 and 1700. The emphasis on rhetoric as part of an education didn't stress originality. School was very repetitive and boring: you were expected to memorize sententiae (wise sayings), and go through Ovid's *Metamorphoses* or similar revered texts identifying the rhetorical figures and marking them in the margins (Milton's own copy of *Orlando Furioso* is marked up in just such a way).

The eighteenth century saw something of a shift of emphasis to delivery, with "elocutionism" taking root as a formal disci-pline on its own. Teachers and written manuals proliferated, concerning themselves with the correct dress, stance, gesture, and vocal modulations of the orator, and—as *Pygmalion*, in 1912, indicates—the link between elocution and social class still had an iron grip on British society more than a century later.

One of the forgotten eminences of the eighteenth century was the Scottish teacher and minister Hugh Blair (1718–1800), whose *Lectures on Rhetoric and Belles Lettres* went into 130 edi-tions and was in print for more than a century. Admired by Jane Austen, Dr. Johnson, and David Hume, Blair edited the first Scottish edition of Shakespeare and a forty-four volume uni-form edition of the English poets. He was described three de-cades after his death as having had "so much taste and talent that his mind bordered on genius."

In his work on rhetoric, Blair applied a fresh tweak to tradition—emphasizing the importance of individual genius and the cultivation of taste over "servile imitation of any author whatever," and the written over the spoken word.

But he was with Quintilian in believing that there was a vital connection between virtue and rhetorical accomplishment. "Speech," as he wrote in his Introduction, "is the great instrument by which man becomes beneficial to man; and it is to the intercourse and transmission of thought, by means of speech, that we are chiefly indebted for the improvement of thought itself."

His warning about bad or phony rhetoric, I think, could do with being revived:

> The graces of composition have been employed to disguise or to supply the want of matter; and the temporary applause of the ignorant has been courted, instead of the lasting approbation of the discerning. But such imposture can never maintain its ground long. Knowledge and science must furnish the materials that form the body and substance of any valuable composition. Rhetoric serves to add the polish; and we know that none but firm and solid bodies can be polished well.

The other thing the eighteenth century saw, of course, was some radical shifts in the style of government. The French and the American revolutions both saw more or less tyrannical polities overtaken—at least on paper—by forms of representative democracy. The extent of their impacts, to adapt Zhou Enlai, it is still too soon to assess—but as the idea of democracy came into fashion in the West, there came with it a surge in the importance and effectiveness of rhetoric as a tool of political influ-

ence. We saw representative assemblies modeled, to a greater or lesser extent, on those of the ancient world. In some sense, things had come full circle.

In schools and universities, the nineteenth and twentieth centuries saw the study of rhetoric pushed aside. Its association with the classics, which in the twentieth century were themselves disappearing from curricula, did it no favors; and its territory was gradually colonized by more modern, more scientific-seeming disciplines such as linguistics, psychology, and literary criticism. But, as I argued at the beginning of this chapter, the practice of rhetoric continued to burgeon and spread—and it continued to behave in ways that were directly susceptible to the old tools of study and understanding. Those tools are set out in more detail in the chapters that follow.

The one thing that you won't find much of in the history of rhetoric, incidentally, is women. Of course, women from Elizabeth I to Emmeline Pankhurst have from time to time given blistering speeches. But it is true that rhetoric has generally been a boys' game. Men were not only the ones, in Western society, most likely to be in the jobs that gave occasion for speeches; they were, with very rare exceptions, also the ones educated to give them, and the ones whose speeches were most likely to be written down.

Indeed, the point at which schools stopped teaching traditional rhetoric was around the point at which they started teaching women. And the point at which women came to be not only enfranchised, but welcomed into the legislatures, courtrooms, and boardrooms of the modern world . . . was near enough the point at which our long history of understanding and consciously thinking about rhetoric sank beneath the waters of Lethe.

So it goes. But those great social earthquakes mean that, even if we regard the high watermark of male rhetoric as being be-hind us, we can say with certainty that we are now living at the dawn of the great age of rhetoric by women. With Margaret Thatcher as our Cicero, we have much to look forward to.

FIVE PARTS OF RHETORIC

FROM CICERO ONWARD, IT has been conventional to divide up the business of oratory into five basic parts—sometimes known as the "canons of rhetoric." I see no strong reason to do otherwise; the division may sound a bit odd at first, but it actually makes rather a lot of sense.

All you need to bear in mind is that rhetoric is a fuzzy art: these divisions overlap and interpenetrate. Different authorities have parceled their contents slightly differently—they don't appear like this in Aristotle, though you can argue that his *Rhetoric* implies or anticipates them—and I don't propose to follow any single one to the letter. Nor need you.

But here, for starters, is Quintilian: "The whole art of oratory, as the most and greatest writers have taught, consists of five parts: invention, arrangement, style, memory, and delivery."[1]

These five parts roughly correspond to the sequence in which you might imagine putting a speech—or, more broadly, any persuasive appeal—together. You think up what there is to say; you devise an order in which to say it; you light on the way in which you want to say it; you get all the aforementioned into your head; and then you take to your feet and let rip.

Let's look at them one by one.

THE FIRST PART OF RHETORIC

Invention

ARISTOTLE SAID THAT THE basic job of the rhetorician was to "discover the best available means of persuasion." That's what is meant, in this context, by "invention": not making things up, but exploring what there is to say on a subject. The word's root means to "come upon" something: to find what's available to be said.

Invention is doing your homework: thinking up in advance exactly what arguments can be made both for and against a given proposition, selecting the best on your own side, and finding counterarguments to those on the other.

There will almost always be more lines of argument available than it will be possible or prudent to use. The skill is to find the ones that will hold most sway with your intended audience. If you're running a rock venue, for instance, and you want to raise the ticket price on the door, the argument you'll use to justify the move to your customers—that it will allow you to invest in

better facilities, hire more famous bands, improve the gig-going experience, and so on—will not be the same as the argument you'll make to your shareholders.

Judging the audience is key, here. What are their positions in life? What are their interests and prejudices? What sex? What age? Aristotle, for instance, sets out in *Rhetoric* a whole series of characteristics that distinguish young people from old.

Young people, he says, are impatient, changeable, and appetitive—"and of the bodily appetites they are especially attentive to that connected with sex and have no control over it." They are ambitious, not yet mindful of money, and "sweet-natured through their not having yet observed much wickedness." They are optimistic, because unlike the worldly Aristotle, they haven't yet realized that "most things turn out for the worse."*

Idealism, he says, is a characteristic of the young because they prefer to do things for reasons that accord with their ideas of virtue rather than things that are in their interest; and they still like their friends, because they still take pleasure in companionship without the shadow of competing interests falling across it.**

The old, on the other hand, are shrewd, "sour-tempered," crabbed with disappointment, and have "many opinions but no knowledge": they never leap wholeheartedly into a thing, but always hedge around it with "maybe" and "perhaps." They are "morose," "live in memory rather than hope," are "slaves to profit," and are "prone to pity, though not for the same reasons as young

---

*He is a cynical old soul, our hero. He also states that "men, for the most part, do commit crimes when they can."

**Aristotle, it has to be said, never came across rioting students or permanently alienated emo kids, so his view of the young is a pretty rosy one.

men; for the latter are so from philanthropy, the former through weakness; for they think that all these things are near for themselves to suffer."

> The characters, then, of the younger and older generations are of this kind. So that since all men accept speeches directed at their own age and their kind, it is not hard to see by what employment of arguments men and speeches will appear to be of the appropriate kind.[1]

Aristotle identified three different lines of argument, or persuasive appeal, into which the process of invention divides. Thanks to my constitutional childishness, they have always sounded to me like the names by which the Three Musketeers really should have been known: Ethos, Logos, and Pathos.

These three fellows are the absolute bedrock of written and spoken persuasion. The first describes the way a speaker establishes—both overtly and more subtly—his bona fides as a speaker and his connection with the audience. The second is the way he seeks to influence them by reason (much the poor relation in all this, as witness the pervasive irrationality of human beings). And the third is the way in which he seeks to stir them to anger, pity, fear, or exultation.

One crude way I've chosen to encapsulate them in the past is as follows. Ethos: "Buy my old car because I'm Tom Magliozzi." Logos: "Buy my old car because yours is broken and mine is the only one on sale." Pathos: "Buy my old car or this cute little kitten, afflicted with a rare degenerative disease, will expire in agony, for my car is the last asset I have in the world, and I am selling it to pay for kitty's medical treatment."

Let's look at them musketeer by musketeer.

ETHOS—THE APPEAL FROM CHARACTER,
OR LOOK WHO'S TALKING

> Hi! I'm actor Troy McClure. You might remember me from such TV series as *Buck Henderson, Union Buster* and *Troy and Company's Summertime Smile Factory*. Today I'm here to tell you about Spiffy, the twenty-first-century stain remover. Let's meet the inventor, Dr. Nick Riviera . . .

The *Simpsons* character Troy McClure is a perfect instance of the way an appeal to ethos works, or tries to. He gets it right out there first: Here's who I am, and here's what I've done.

There is a killing poignancy in the fact that Troy's credentials are invariably a list of unwatched 1970s made-for-TV flops and infomercials for quack remedies, which is what makes us laugh. But it makes us laugh because we all instinctively recognize an ethos appeal falling flat on its face.

The ethos appeal is first among equals. How you present yourself—ordinarily the job of the opening few moments of your address—is the foundation on which all the rest is built. It establishes the connection between the speaker and the audience, and it steers how that speech will be received.

Your audience needs to know (or to believe, which in rhetoric adds up to the same thing) that you are trustworthy, that you have a *locus standi* to talk on the subject, and that you speak in good faith. You need your audience to believe that you are, in the well-known words, "A pretty straight kind of guy."

Perhaps most important of all, in ninety-nine cases out of a hundred, you will be seeking to persuade your audience that

you are one of them: that your interests and their interests are identical in this case or, to be more convincing, in all cases.

"Tremble, worms!" may work well as an opener for Ming the Merciless. But you could safely regard the commander of War Rocket Ajax as having no need to resort to ethos appeals.

Ethos will suffuse all that follows, logos and pathos alike. Your arguments will tend to prosper if they are founded on the common assumptions of your audience—or, in special cases, if the audience is minded to defer to your authority. Likewise, your hopes of stirring the audience to anger or pity depends on the extent to which they are prepared to identify with the anger or pity you yourself seem to feel.

It is the ethos appeal that gives us JFK's "Ich bin ein Berliner," Bill Clinton's "Ah feel your pain," and Margaret Thatcher's insistence that her management of the UK economy was simply the behavior of a thrifty housewife writ large. When this fails—think the patrician George H. W. Bush's claimed affinity for pork rinds, or any Democratic candidate at an NRA meeting—the result is often highly comical, if not cringe-inducing.

Kenneth Burke, author of the classic twentieth-century study *A Rhetoric of Motives* (1950) emphasized the importance of *decorum*—meeting the expectations of an audience—as an appeal to ethos: "You persuade a man only insofar as you can talk his language by speech, gesture, tonality, order, image, attitude, idea, identifying your ways with his."

Let's look at an instance: "Friends, Romans, countrymen. Lend me your ears!" The opening words of Antony's funeral oration in *Julius Caesar* are, covertly, an ethos appeal *par excellence*: a positioning of the speaker with relation to the crowd. He doesn't do much boasting about himself—but by interpellating

the crowd in particular terms, Antony is casting himself as one of their number.*

Those opening words look like an ascending *tricolon*—a set of three terms, increasing in force—though they are a special and subtle case of it. They feel like a crescendo, but they don't necessarily seem to add up to one in terms of meaning. Isn't "friends," you might think, a more powerful term of appeal than "countrymen"? Rather, they seem to be on the same level—and in a way, they are.

Antony is first appealing to his crowd on a human level, as friends: establishing a bond of common feeling which he hopes to extend to Caesar. Then, he reminds them that they are Romans— with all the civic and legal duties implied by citizenship. Finally, he produces a term that denotes a coming together of both of those two things—to be countrymen is to experience *romanitas* as fellowship—and a fraternity between speaker and audience.

What gives the three phrases their climactic force is actually a metrical effect. The first word's one syllable, the second's two (a stressed then an unstressed), the third's three (stressed, then

---

*Brutus's speech, which came before, is notably bossier. He reels out a whole string of imperatives: he demands silence, asserts his own honor, and appears to imply that the audience needs to pay attention and raise its game a bit. The showy use of climax doesn't help much, either—and there's something fishily circular in the idea that the audience should believe him for his honor, and respect his honor the better to, um, believe him. These are precisely the weaknesses Antony will use to skewer him—to the exact end that you should "awake their senses, that you may be the better judge," only not in the way Brutus was hoping.

> Romans, countrymen, and lovers! hear me for my
> cause, and be silent, that you may hear: believe me
> for mine honor, and have respect to mine honor, that
> you may believe: censure me in your wisdom, and
> awake your senses, that you may the better judge.

unstressed, then unstressed). A single stressed syllable, then a trochee, then a dactyl, for prosody nerds. Or, for air-guitarists, something like the opening to "Back in Black" by AC/DC: *DUM! DUH-dum! DUH-duh-dum!* Those three words do a lot of work.

Then, rather than command silence, he asks: "lend me your ears." The grammatical mood is imperative, but the rhetorical effect is one of intimacy and humility. He's asking for a loan—subtextually, a fraternal expression of trust.

In the next line—"I come to bury Caesar, not to praise him"—he plays the anti-rhetoric rhetoric card. He's not here to make a fancy speech, he tells us, but to get on with a job of work. A flat lie, but there we are. The contrast with Brutus is made, and reinforced when later he says:

> I am no orator, as Brutus is;
> But, as you know me all, a plain blunt man,
> That love my friend . . .

The cheek! The deliberate awkwardness of "plain blunt man," a molossus (three stressed syllables on the trot) interrupting the flow of the pentameter, serves to pile the message on further. Actually, as witness his unmusical opening—"Romans, countrymen and lovers"—it's Brutus who has the tin ear.

Antony goes on in his speech to make his shared bond with the audience a weapon against the conspirators:

> O masters, if I were disposed to stir
> Your hearts and minds to mutiny and rage,
> I should do Brutus wrong, and Cassius wrong,
> Who, you all know, are honorable men:

I will not do them wrong; I rather choose
To wrong the dead, to wrong myself and you,
Than I will wrong such honorable men.

In order to do the right thing by these "honorable men," which he promises fastidiously to do, he says that he would have to wrong not only himself but the dead Caesar and the whole crowd of Romans to whom he's speaking. Antony, in other words, puts the interests of the conspirators in one corner—and those of every living and dead Roman, himself included, in the other.

That is ethos on a stick. And that is what you are seeing in every modern politician shaping his or her "narrative": an attempt to position him- or herself as one of the people, rather than as one purporting to be above them.

George W. Bush, born in Connecticut to a life of unexampled privilege, cultivated in his dress and mannerisms the ethos of a Texan roughneck rather than the Yalie he is. Tony Blair's glottal stops and flattened vowels in office were an attempt to downplay his private school background, as is David Cameron's plausibility-stretching insistence that he's "middle class."

Ethos can be a slippery thing. One of the most famous speeches of modern times was the one made—apparently extempore—by a British army officer on the eve of the invasion of Iraq. In March 2003, Colonel Tim Collins addressed about eight hundred men of the 1st Battalion of the Royal Irish Regiment, as they waited in a camp in the Kuwaiti desert, ahead of their deployment to the Iraqi border.

The reporter who transcribed it, Sarah Oliver of the *Mail on Sunday*, reported afterward: He delivered the speech completely off the cuff. He said to me, "I'll have to say a few words

to the men to explain to them why they should take their an-
thrax drugs and malaria pills, or they just won't bother."

It just grew and grew into something magnificent—it made
you realize the true meaning of the term "rallying cry." It was
just after a sandstorm and all the men were standing around
him in a U-shape in the middle of a very dusty courtyard.

A lot of the Irish Rangers are very young and he wanted to
explain something of the history and culture of Iraq to them.
They knew that the public at home had doubts about the rightness of the war, and he wanted to reassure them and tell them
why they were there. He delivered the speech without a note
and went on at length. By the end, everyone felt they were
ready for whatever lay ahead.

If Ms. Oliver's account is to be believed—and we've no reason not to believe it—this was a pretty remarkable speech for
anyone to deliver off the cuff. He might have thought about it a
bit beforehand—and no shame in that. The most effective off-
the-cuff speeches are premeditated, and the best premeditated
speeches appear off the cuff.

"We go to liberate, not to conquer," Col. Collins began, and
continued in the high style, making allusion to "that ancient
land," describing Iraq as "the site of the Garden of Eden, of the
Great Flood, and the birthplace of Abraham,"* and urging his
men to "tread lightly there." They were to be "ferocious in battle
. . . magnanimous in victory," and to kindle the "light of liberation" in the eyes of the children. He talked of "nemesis" and "the

---

*Polysyndeton—"of the . . . of the . . . "—lends that resonant three-part phrase
an extra afflatus, and has—at least to my ear—a slightly and deliberately Biblical resonance.

mark of Cain," of enemy commanders with "stains on their souls," and "stoking the fires of hell."

"You will be shunned unless your conduct is of the highest— for your deeds will follow you down through history," he warned his men, adding zeugmatically: "We will bring shame on neither our uniform nor our nation." He ended with an almost Shake-spearean ellipsis: "Our business now is north."

The speech stirred the sinews and summoned up the blood quite brilliantly. It was reported around the world, and it was said at one point that President Bush had a copy of it installed on the wall of the Oval Office. Its rolling periods, its fine oro-tundities, its balanced pairs, and its vivid sense of how history pivoted on this moment, on these men . . . it was a tour de force. It made Col. Collins a star.

Some months later, I happened to be traveling in a car with a serving army officer of some seniority and Col. Collins's speech came up. To my astonishment, he hadn't thought much of it at all. In fact, he actually seemed quite angry about it.

To him, the speech had worked brilliantly—but on the wrong audience. It had impressed journalists, TV reporters, statesmen, and readers in comfortable homes who were thrilled by the high-sounding phrases and the nobility of the sentiments. He saw this as showboating—playing to the gallery.

On the eve of battle, he said—and he spoke with some authority—you want to hear your commander speaking to you in your own language. The soldiers Col. Collins was addressing would for the most part be lads in their teens and early twenties, most of them relatively unsophisticated, and many of them anxious that by the end of the following day, they would be in prospect of being killed.

"They don't want to hear," he said (and I paraphrase), "all that bollocks about Abraham and Isaac and the light of liberation."

I can't speak for Col. Collins's men, of course, and nor could he. But it was food for thought: effective rhetoric need not always be fancy rhetoric. Indeed, the opposite is often the case. An audience digesting war as spectacle may have a very different idea of the correct ethos for an eve-of-battle speech than the men at the sharp end.

In counterpoint, then, to Col. Collins's oratory, we could offer that of General George S. Patton—known as "Old Blood and Guts"—whose troops rolled the Germans up at such at an astonishing gallop in the closing weeks of the Second World War. He was no less memorable for speaking plain.

"Sure, we want to go home," he said. "We want this war over with. The quickest way to get it over with is to go get the bastards who started it. The quicker they are whipped, the quicker we can go home. The shortest way home is through Berlin and Tokyo. And when we get to Berlin, I am personally going to shoot that paper hanging son-of-a-bitch Hitler.* Just like I'd shoot a snake!"

From the school playground to the battlefield, from the mean streets of South Central Los Angeles to the annual meeting of the World Economic Forum, who you are is the first thing you need to establish if you intend to be heard.

So to return to Troy McClure and his terrible relevance to modern life, ethos is behind every celebrity endorsement you ever see on television. It's not just their visibility that attracts brands to an association with celebrities: it's their image.

---

*It was widely and belittlingly put about that Hitler had worked as a painter and decorator.

LOGOS–SOUNDING REASONABLE

If ethos is the ground on which your argument stands, logos is what drives it forward: it is the stuff of your argument, the way one point proceeds to another, as if to show that the conclusion to which you are aiming is not only the right one, but so necessary and reasonable as to be more or less the only one. If in the course of it, you can make your opponents sound venal or even deranged, so much the better.

Aristotle remarks, shrewdly, that the most effective form of argument is one that the audience is allowed to think it has worked out itself: one whose conclusion, in other words, the listener reaches just before, or just as, the speaker makes it. "The audience takes pleasure in themselves for anticipating the point."

Because *logos* shares a root with *logic*, it would be easy enough to assume that the two were roughly the same thing. They aren't. Indeed, they are but distant cousins: logos in rhetoric being another of those bendy shadows cast on the wall of Plato's well-known cave. Logos moves forward, but it leaps over gaps, sidles past obstacles, and—confronted with disaster— shouts, "Look! It's Halley's Comet!" and bolts for the exit.

Likewise, when we talk about a proof, in rhetoric, we're not talking about what, colloquially, you might understand by the term. In formal logic and in mathematics, proof is something absolute. You start with a set of axioms, and derive a series of conclusions by a watertight chain of deductions. A mathematical proposition is either demonstrably true, or it is not.

There's an old joke, told in Simon Singh's excellent book *Fermat's Last Theorem*, that gives a sense of the different degree of rigor of mathematical proof. An astronomer, a physicist, and a

mathematician set off for Scotland on the train. Not long after they cross the border, they look out of the window and see a black sheep standing in a field.

"Aha!" says the astronomer. "Scottish sheep are black."

"No," the physicist rebukes him. "Some sheep in Scotland are black."

The mathematician looks pained. "No: In Scotland there exists at least one field, containing at least one sheep, at least one side of which is black."

Along with being an unkind dig at astronomers, this tells us a bit about the methods of the natural sciences as against math. Logical deduction works fine for the world of ideas. Reasoning by induction—the process of generalizing from the available evidence—is the only real way of making progress in the world of things.

Anywhere outside pure math, we're in the territory of inductive reasoning. That is why the rigor of the scientific method depends not on the possibility of proof, but its opposite: the way science works is that you put up a hypothesis, and you let it stand until it's *disproved*. That is, essentially, a way of recognizing the provisional and imperfect nature of scientific reasoning.

Aristotle made a distinction between rhetoric and dialectics. In rhetoric, we're far closer to the astronomer than the mathematician. Rhetoric deals with probabilities rather than certainties: with analogy and generalization. If the philosopher deals with knowledge, the rhetorician is much more interested in *belief*. Zeno put it like this: "Rhetoric is an open palm; dialectic a closed fist."

For Aristotle, logos was the province of something he called an "enthymeme," which was the equivalent in rhetoric to the

syllogism in logic. Syllogisms and enthymemes can be understood as units of thought—that is, ways of articulating the relationships between ideas.

The syllogism is a way of combining two premises and drawing a fresh conclusion that follows logically from them. The classic instance you always hear quoted is the following: All men are mortal.* Socrates is a man.** Therefore, Socrates is mortal.***

The enthymeme is like that, only fuzzier. It is, if you like, a half-assed syllogism; typically one that, rather than having its premises right out in the open, has a hidden assumption somewhere.‡ "Elvis had to die sometime: all men are mortal" is an enthymeme rather than a syllogism, because it makes the assumption that Elvis was human, whereas anyone who has seen *Men in Black* knows otherwise.‡‡

Most enthymemes aren't on that level. They are generalizations, like the proposition that increasing corporation tax will damage the government's revenues because companies will migrate to territories with lower tax regimes. Like any economic proposition, there are all sorts of reasons why this might or might not turn out to be the case, but for the politician delivering a sound bite on the evening news, it is a case best stated with maximum generality: "High taxes hurt jobs."

---

*Premise one.
**Premise two.
***Ta-dah! Conclusion.
‡There is some debate over whether to characterize an enthymeme as an "abridged syllogism" (i.e., one in which there's a hidden premise) or as a "rhetorical syllogism" (i.e., one in which the propositions are probabilistic rather than categorical), but after a careful survey of the scholarly literature, the phrase "half-assed" seems to me to split the difference satisfactorily.
‡‡"Elvis isn't dead. He just went home."—Agent K

Another extraordinarily common, effective persuasive appeal in logos is analogy. Take the run-up to the invasion of Iraq. Among supporters of the war, one of the arguments that you heard most consistently was the idea that to allow Saddam Hussein to continue in power would be the equivalent of Neville Chamberlain's accommodation of Hitler.*

The analogy didn't hold in any way that bore close scrutiny. Nazi Germany was a direct threat to British interests—an armed-to-the-teeth European power with an aggressively acquisitive attitude to its neighbors' territory; Iraq was a nasty but second-rate Middle Eastern dictatorship without (as it turned out) so much as a spud gun to its name, no affiliation to al-Qaeda, and no obvious plans for a campaign of global conquest.

Nevertheless, the word "appeasement," carrying as it did a great burden of historical connotations, became a charged one in the debate over the war. The notorious "forty-five-minute claim"—where the British public was, perhaps accidentally, given the impression that Iraq had weapons that could rain chemical death on London in three quarters of an hour—only served to heighten the analogy.

But comparisons are odorous. Hence Julian Barnes, in *A History of the World in 10½ Chapters*: "And does history repeat itself, the first time as tragedy, the second time as farce? No, that's too grand, too considered a process. History just burps, and we taste again that raw-onion sandwich it swallowed centuries ago."

---

*This comparison has become so common in political rhetoric that it has taken on the status of a running joke. Godwin's Law—an Internet commonplace—states, "As an online discussion grows longer, the probability of a comparison involving Nazis or Hitler approaches 1."

Analogy, in political rhetoric, is the whiff of that burp. It can be powerfully oniony.

It can't be repeated too often: what you're talking about when you talk about logos is persuasion not proof absolute. That is why, when you look at judicial rhetoric in the UK and US, the standard stipulation is that "proof" means not certainty, but the ability to demonstrate a set of propositions "beyond reasonable doubt."

A good instance comes in the form of an apocryphal story. A man is in the dock, accused of murdering his wife. Although the body was never recovered, all the evidence points to the defendant: the trunk of his car was filled with twine, bloodstained hammers, torn items of his wife's clothing, and such like. He had abundant motive—as the cashing in of a huge insurance policy taken out on the eve of his wife's death demonstrates. And no sooner was his wife reported missing than he was holidaying in the Maldives with his pneumatically enhanced twenty-three-year-old mistress, and his Facebook page filled with photographs of him in Speedos and a snorkel, grinning his murderous head off.

Nevertheless, his lawyer at trial pulls off a remarkable *coup de théâtre.* "Ladies and gentlemen of the jury," he says. "The prosecution has presented you with a mountain of evidence that tends to show that my client is guilty of the crime with which he has been charged. But that evidence means nothing. For not only is my client not guilty of his wife's murder, but no murder has in fact taken place. My client's wife is, in fact, alive and well. And I can prove it. It is now five minutes to midday. At precisely midday, ladies and gentlemen of the jury, those doors over there will open"—he indicates the main doors into the courtroom with a flourishing sweep of the arm—"and my client's wife will walk through them into the court."

Gasps, naturally, go all round. For the next five minutes, the eyes of the presiding judge, the jury, and every functionary of the court are glued to the main doors. Eventually, the heavy hands of the courtroom clock tick round to midday, and a solemn bong is heard. The doors remain tight shut.

"Well?" says the judge. "Your promised miracle has not materialized."

"Indeed not," replies the defending attorney. "But every single one of you was watching those doors in the expectation that it would. In the absence of a body, that is surely an object demonstration that there remains a reasonable doubt over my client's responsibility for his wife's disappearance."

"Very good," says the judge. "However, I ask the jury to note that the only person in the courtroom not watching the doors was your client."

Nowhere in that story is anything demonstrated with the rigor that a philosopher would require. But first the lawyer, and then the judge, are able to use logos to sway the audience's conviction. The hidden premise of the lawyer's argument is that if the audience watches the door, they believe it possible that the woman is alive. The hidden premise of the judge's riposte is that if the defendant doesn't watch the door, he is shown to know that the woman isn't coming through it because, having killed her himself, he's quite certain she's dead.

Aristotle drew up a whole list of "topics"—like "invention" and "proof," the term has a special force in rhetoric. A topic is, essentially, the general form of an argument. Topics can relate to types of thing, to causality, to comparisons of scale, and so on and so forth.

Many of Aristotle's examples look pretty dry and obvious. If something is possible for a genus, then it's possible for a species:

that is, if something's true of insects, it's true of ants. If something can be stated of one thing, then the opposite can be stated of its opposite: if war is an evil, then it follows that peace is a good. If something has happened, then so must its antecedent have done: if a man has forgotten something, it follows that he knew it in the first place.

But what Aristotle is attempting is a basic taxonomy of forms of argument: and like so much in his book, those forms are so familiar to us that we have long ceased to notice them. When, for instance, he writes about the way mutual interrelations may be handled in argument, he cites the tax collector Diomedon, who asked of tax rights (Athens used to sell the right to collect taxes to local licensees): "If it is not shameful for you to sell them, then is it not so for us to buy?"

That same shape of argument is found (and confounded) in modern-day debates about the decriminalization of soft drugs: should it be legal to buy something and illegal to sell it? A similar relationship affects the double standard that has, for generations, applied to female virtue: men are admired for "sowing their wild oats"; whereas those women who provide somewhere for the oats to be sown are regarded as immoral.

A point that Aristotle makes that is particularly germane here is that arguments are made from accepted premises—"and many accepted premises are mutually contradictory." You can often argue both for and against a given proposition on the basis of the same evidence.

This is shown in caricature in the conflict between the Law of Induction and the Law of Averages. The former says that if the sun has risen in the east every morning since the dinosaurs walked the earth, you can bet dollars to donuts it'll do the same

tomorrow morning. The latter says that it's bound to be the west's turn by now.

But whenever you're reading a whodunit, or watching *Law and Order* reruns on a Sunday night, you find yourself sorting through candidates to be the criminal on the grounds that they are "too obvious."

For the conspiracy theorist, the very paucity of evidence to support their contention—that the moon landings were faked, a cabal of Jewish lizards is running the world, and Elvis was on the grassy knoll with the lead piping—is what passes as proof. The lack of evidence is evidence of a cover-up.

Aristotle offers as his own example the case of an assault. If a given suspect is a knock-kneed weakling, he says, he is less likely to be the culprit than a great big bruiser with HATE tattooed on his forehead.* On the other hand, the hulking thug can also be argued out of suspicion precisely because his physical demeanor would lead people to assume his guilt: who'd be stupid enough to commit a crime in the certain knowledge he'd be caught? "This is not probable, because it was likely to be thought probable."

Associated with these general topics are "commonplaces" (*topos* is Greek for a "place"). Any form of reasoning has to start from a set of premises, and in rhetoric those premises are very often commonplaces. A commonplace is a piece of shared wisdom: a tribal assumption. In the use of commonplaces, you can see where logos and ethos intersect.

In the modern West, we're confident that prevention is better than cure; that hard work deserves reward; that no means no; that you are innocent until proven guilty, and that all men are

---

*I'm translating the original Greek somewhat freely here.

created equal. But it would be a commonplace to a man of Aristotle's generation and time that the opinions of women and slaves were quite irrelevant.

Commonplaces are culturally specific, but they will tend to be so deep-rooted in their appeal that they pass for universal truths. They are, in digested form, the appeal to "common sense." You get nowhere appealing to commonplaces alien to your audience.*

As the handbook *Ad Herennium*—which, attributed to Cicero, had a central role in medieval and Renaissance rhetoric—warns, "That is faulty which is said against the convictions of the judge or of the audience."** Will Rogers put it more folksily: "When you go fishing you bait the hook, not with what you like, but with what the fish likes."

The Flanders and Swann song "The Reluctant Cannibal" tells the story of a young member of a cannibal tribe who refuses his dinner, insisting that "eating people is wrong." It draws its com-

---

*Sometimes, though, you can use a commonplace associated with an audience-within-an-audience to win round the wider group. Where provincialism is associated with honesty, the formula "Back where I come from, we like to say . . ." can play well to a national audience. Hence Sarah Palin's election aside: "I had the privilege of living most of my life in a small town. I was just your average hockey mom and signed up for the PTA. I love those hockey moms. You know they say the difference between a hockey mom and a pit bull? Lipstick."

**A painful-to-watch instance of this came when Piers Morgan was a guest on the British TV comedy show *Have I Got News for You?* At one point, asked a straightforward question, he replied: "Is the answer 'jam'?" There was bemused silence. "I thought I'd say that because last week Eddie Izzard said that and you roared with laughter," he explained. "But people like him," said his fellow contestant and frequent antagonist Ian Hislop, to loud applause. Seething through the rest of the show, Morgan eventually snapped. "Don't try the popularity line with me, Hislop," he said pettishly. "Why?" asked Hislop. Morgan then made a fatal *argumentum ad populum*, or appeal to the audience: "Does anyone like him?" he asked. "Does anyone here actually like him?" The audience—Hislop being a regular team captain—roared back as one: "Yes!"

edy from the fact that what, to Flanders and Swann's twentieth-century Western audience, is a commonplace, is heresy to the cannibals of the song. "Don't eat people?" the lad's incredulous father exclaims at one point. "You might just as well go around saying: 'Don't fight people,'" causing the rest of the tribe to fall about laughing at the intrinsic ridiculousness of the notion.

The wise persuader starts from one or two commonplaces he knows he has in common with his audience—and, where possible, arrives at one too.

PATHOS—MAKE 'EM LAUGH, MAKE 'EM CRY, MAKE 'EM AGREE

Pathos is the appeal to emotion—not just sadness or pity, which is what a film critic will tend to mean when describing this or that scene as "full of pathos," but excitement, fear, love, patriotism, or amusement.

As Quintilian argues, unless we "can entice [our hearers] with delights, drag them along with the strength of our pleading and sometimes disturb them with emotional appeals . . . we cannot make even just and true cause prevail."

Again, ethos, pathos, and logos—the Three Musketeers of the persuasive arts—can't be altogether separated. Emotion in a persuasive appeal is only effective inasmuch as it is *shared* emotion. One of the reasons laughter is so effective as a tool for persuasion—and any stand-up comic who has ever seen off a heckler with a zinging one-liner knows this—is that laughter is involuntary assent.

If you urge military intervention on behalf of "gallant little Belgium," or plead for clemency on the grounds that your client

is a broken man and has already suffered enough, you get nowhere if your audience couldn't give a toss about gallant little Belgium, or thinks that there's no limit to the suffering it would like your client to endure.

Pathos is the appeal you see uppermost in the heart-wrenching, expensively printed flyers that pop through your letterbox asking for donations to charity. Rather than use logos—detailed arguments and eye-glazing statistics about the ways in which the charity achieves the greatest good, distributes its funds, and so on—the ad shoots straight for the heart.

The cute chipmunk on the front cover gives way to a mass of fur and bloody entrails inside, making you think twice about investing in that fur coat. A reproachful, fly-haunted face locks eyes with you from the doormat, pleading for you to sign up. "By the time you throw this flyer in the recycling bin, thirty children will have died," one will say. "This is Sarah. She may not live to be two," will say another.

One highly effective campaign recently asked you whether you could poke your finger through the hole, approximately the diameter of a golf ball, cut in the front cover of the leaflet. You had to open the leaflet to do so—and on the inside you learn that one of the malnourished children the charity seeks to help could pass a whole arm though a hole that size.*

It's worth saying: an appeal to pathos is not in and of itself a "cheat." Feeling—and through it, fellow feeling—is the basis of pretty much everything that most of us regard as important in

---

*This is also a prime instance of *enargia*—the skill of painting a mental picture so it comes indelibly to the inner eye of the audience. You *see* that skinny arm.

being human. Without it, we wouldn't fall in love, nurture children, build communities, enact laws, remember our dead, or throw dinner parties. Feeling may not be logical, Mr. Spock, but to sway feeling is every bit the legitimate object of rhetoric.

During the eighteenth-century campaign in the UK to abolish the Atlantic slave trade, pathos was uppermost—though ethos featured there too—in one of the most enduring icons of the abolitionist movement. The potter Josiah Wedgwood, a friend of the campaigner Thomas Clarkson, cast a medallion showing a black slave in chains underneath the motto: "Am I Not a Man and a Brother?" The image still has the power to raise the hair on the back of the neck.

Long before President Nixon met his Waterloo over the Watergate burglary, he escaped from another tight spot with a magisterial speech, at the heart of which was a nakedly cheesy pathos appeal. While the "Checkers Speech" has become famous for that crowning moment, the whole speech is a rhetorical classic.

It was the autumn of 1952 and Tricky Dick, then a Senator from California, had just been selected as the Republican vice presidential candidate for that November's election. All seemed well, and he was rocketing around the country on his campaign train, the Dick Nixon Special, pressing the flesh of the voters and flashing his creepy smile.

Unfortunately, the press had a whiff of the private slush fund got up by his supporters to help pay his election expenses—and it was being put about by his political enemies that the "Nixon Scandal Fund" was corruptly funneling money from wealthy backers to Nixon in exchange for political favors. Though Nixon was angrily convinced that this was the work of "crooks and communists" out to smear him, the scandal got a grip on the

nation at large. Calls flooded in for his resignation from the Republican ticket, and impolite members of the public took to waving placards speculating on whether or not his wife Pat wore a mink coat.

Nixon, finally, defended himself in a masterful speech delivered live on television from the El Capitan Theatre in Los Angeles. He first set out the charges against him—that he had taken $18,000 from a group of his supporters—and he vaunted himself that, unlike other politicians, he would meet the charges head-on rather than "ignore or deny them without giving details."

"I believe we've had enough of that in the United States, particularly with the present administration in Washington, DC," he added, positioning himself as the courageous outsider and his tormentors as a crooked and shifty establishment, while at the same time, implicitly, identifying himself with the future tense of political change rather than a defensive *status quo*.

Straight out, he confirmed that he was the beneficiary of just such a fund, and embarked on a great run of *concessio*:*

> Now, was that wrong? And let me say that it was wrong. I'm saying, incidentally, that it was wrong, not just illegal, because it isn't a question of whether it was legal or illegal, that isn't enough. The question is, was it morally wrong? I say that it was morally wrong...

---

*This is the figure, called *paromologia* in the Greek, where you concede, or appear to concede, part of your opponent's point. It turns what is often necessity to advantage, because it makes you look honest and scrupulous, takes the wind out of your opponent's sails, and allows you to shift the emphasis of the argument in a way finally favorable to you. It's the equivalent of a tactical retreat, or of the judo fighter using an opponent's momentum against him.

And here's the turning point.

> . . . if any of that $18,000 went to Senator Nixon, for my per-
> sonal use. I say that it was morally wrong if it was secretly given
> and secretly handled. And I say that it was morally wrong if
> any of the contributors got special favors for the contributions
> that they made.

At this point, Nixon wheeled round and point by point, having defined the terms of the argument to his satisfaction, exonerated himself. Then, in folksy tones, he went on to use the business
of political expenses—he argued that the slush fund actually
saved the American taxpayer money—as the basis for a roaring
ethos appeal.

Making himself the spokesman for the ordinary American, he
wondered aloud how politicians met the costs of their political
expenses without putting those costs onto the taxpayer. "There
are several ways that it can be done, and that it is done legally
in the United States Senate and in the Congress," he answered
himself—that use of "legally" taking on a specially pungent force
given his earlier show of making morality more important than
mere legality.

The first way, he said, was to be a rich man—a privilege that
Dick Nixon, with his hardscrabble upbringing in East Whittier,
did not have. Then there was putting your wife on the payroll—
and though Pat Nixon, he said, did hours of work for the government unpaid, he had never put her on the government payroll
because "there are so many deserving stenographers and secretaries in Washington that needed the work that I just didn't feel
it was right."

He pointed out in a killer *paralipsis* that his opponent had had his wife on the payroll for a decade, but said, "I'm not critical of him for doing that. You will have to pass judgment on that particular point."

A third way of making ends meet, he said, would have been to continue to practice law—again, though, his personal probity forbade him, in the event his legal work and political work might have thrown up a conflict of interest.

Within a few paragraphs, Nixon had used the very venality of which he was accused as a stick with which to beat the wife-employing, law-moonlighting, silver-spoon-chewing Washington establishment over the head on behalf of the ordinary American man, of whom he was a representative.

To hammer that home—still under the guise of a straightforward piece of accountancy—he volunteered there and then, "and incidentally this is unprecedented in the history of American politics, I am going at this time to give to this television and radio audience a complete financial history: everything I've earned, everything I've spent, everything I own."

And with that he embarked on the whole story of his life: of honest toil and sacrifice, of the hard times of a newlywed, of military service in his country's defense, and of his climb up the political ladder, and then in an embarrassment of frankness, he enumerated his assets and outgoings.

> Well, that's about it. That's what we have. And that's what we owe. It isn't very much. But Pat and I have the satisfaction that every dime that we've got is honestly ours. I should say this, that Pat doesn't have a mink coat. But she does have a respectable Republican cloth coat, and I always tell her she'd look good in anything.

Then, the line for which the speech will always be remembered: the stone-cold stroke of brilliance.

One other thing I probably should tell you, because if I don't they'll probably be saying this about me, too. We did get something, a gift, after the election. A man down in Texas heard Pat on the radio mention the fact that our two youngsters would like to have a dog. And believe it or not, the day before we left on this campaign trip, we got a message from Union Station in Baltimore, saying they had a package for us. We went down to get it. You know what it was? It was a little cocker spaniel dog in a crate that he'd sent all the way from Texas, black and white, spotted. And our little girl Tricia, the six year old, named it "Checkers." And you know, the kids, like all kids, love the dog, and I just want to say this, right now, that regardless of what they say about it, we're gonna keep it.

No sooner had these words been uttered than America, as one, melted into a puddle of love for Nixon, his wife, his adorable little daughters, and itty-bitty waggy-tailed Checkers.

In the weeks that followed, no fewer than four million letters, telegrams, phone calls, postcards, and other expressions of support poured into the Republican Party's headquarters. They sent money. They sent collars and leashes. They sent dog food. Richard Nixon's candidacy was safe. And, we might add, look how well that turned out.

Champions of Rhetoric I

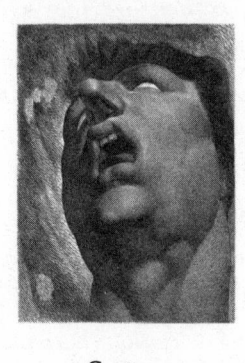

Satan
The Original Silver-Tongued Devil

NOBODY DOES IT QUITE *like the Prince of Lies. The ancients longed for logos in its purest form—the clear light of analytic philosophy—to be the only effective component of an argument. But Aristotle recognized and accommodated what Plato deplored: logos usually takes its place as number three in the trinity of persuasive appeals—the small voice of reason blown hither and thither by the emotional muddle of ethos and pathos.*

Logos, *in the first sentence of St. John's gospel, is the original Greek for the Word that "was with God and . . . was God." Rhetoric, as cannot be repeated too often, is the imperfect tool of an imperfect world. For Plato, the sublunary world was a distorted*

projection of the world of essences. For Christians, its imperfections go back to the Fall. Satan's interaction with Eve can be seen as the archetype of the birth of rhetoric.

It's no great surprise, therefore, that wherever Satan has appeared, audiences and critics have found it all too easy to take his side. Successful persuasion depends on an audience's being able to identify with the speaker—and we are much more often like the devil than we are like the Almighty.

The well-known remark of William Blake that our great laureate of the War in Heaven, John Milton, was "of the devil's party without knowing it" is testament to this. A succession of heretical readings of Paradise Lost, *television chocolate ads, and styling decisions for emporia of "adult toys" indicates, Milton wasn't the only one of whom Blake's remark could have been made.*

Everywhere in art and literature that we meet the devil or his minions, they are tempting and glozing and generally making themselves tricky. In Paradise Regained, *which describes the temptations of Christ in the wilderness, his words are described as "ambiguous and with double sense deluding."*

But it's in Paradise Lost *that he's to be found in properly blistering form—first as the defeated general rallying his troops in hell, and later as the tricksy serpent in the Garden of Eden. We first meet him in Book One, after he's been cast out of heaven. Picking himself up from the floor of hell, we can imagine him rubbing his head like a drunk coming to after a five-day bender. He's had a hell of a bump. He soon realizes that, lying next to him similarly battered, is his lieutenant, Beelzebub. Satan breaks the silence:*

> If thou beest he; But O how fall'n! how chang'd
> From him, who in the happy Realms of Light

Cloth'd with transcendent brightness didst out-shine
Myriads though bright . . .

(PARADISE LOST I: 84–87)

The project of the whole speech that follows is to make the best
of a bad lot. The situation as it stands is that Satan's rash challenge to God has been miserably defeated, earning every angel
foolish enough to take his side a one-way ticket to eternal perdi-
tion in a lake of fire. So Satan needs, one, to prevent his confederates throwing around anything so vulgar as blame, and, two, to
move the conversation away from the defeat in the immediate
past to the victory in some hypothetical future. In other words, he
wants to convince his audience that they're in this together, and
that losing the war with God was just a setback.*

*So he begins by being tenderly solicitous. He affects not even
to recognize Beelzebub, and then to be so overcome by emotion
that the grammar of his sentence breaks down into an* anacoluthon, *rupturing mid-sentence: "If thou beest he; But O how
fall'n! how chang'd . . ." Immediately, his ethos appeal is
launched. He flatters Beelzebub by suggesting that he outshone
all others in heaven (while actually, of course, that was Lucifer's
special eminence), and then strives to paint the two of them as
utterly united in defeat.*

Whom mutual league,
United thoughts and counsels, equal hope
And hazard in the Glorious Enterprize,

---

*There's a wonderful clip of the late Ian Richardson reading this bit on
YouTube, incidentally: http://bit.ly/hellspeech.

> Joynd with me once, now misery hath joynd
> In equal ruin.

Actually, of course, they did not have "equal hope and hazard" in rebellion: Lucifer stood to gain the throne of heaven, where the best Beelzebub could have hoped for was a promotion; and as for "hazard," Satan carefully avoids mentioning the possibility that forgiveness might be available to his confederates if they repent and learn their lesson. Likewise, "united thoughts and counsels" stretches the notion of collective responsibility to the breaking point. The blame-spreading continues: "till then who knew / The force of those dire Arms?" Satan wonders aloud, which is as much as to say: "How was I expected to know God was omnipotent? Anyone could have made that mistake. Anyone!"

As he goes on, Satan sets out to demonstrate that the defeat wasn't really a defeat at all. Our (eternal) lives are ruined—but He couldn't break our spirits, eh lads? Eh? Note the density of figures here, too: the rhetorical question to start with, then the repetition of "lost" (that's ploce, *to give it its technical name), then the* auxesis, *or buildup of those clauses linked with "and . . . and . . . and. . . ."*

> What though the field be lost?
> All is not lost; the unconquerable Will,
> And study of revenge, immortal hate,
> And courage never to submit or yield:
> And what is else not to be overcome?*

---

*"What is else not to be overcome" may sound confusing to modern ears. It unpacks as: "What does not being defeated ("not to be overcome") mean if not that [i.e., that your will, hate, courage, and determination are intact]?"

One thinks immediately of the Black Knight in Monty Python and the Holy Grail, *who after having both his arms lopped off declares, "It's just a flesh wound."*

But, in its context, this isn't delivered for comic or bathetic effect. This is the turning point of the speech—where Satan changes the tense from past to future, and sets into vowing never to surrender ("That glory never shall *his wrath or might extort from me") and promising that next time things will be different, thanks to the, um, valuable learning experience of this particular ass-kicking: "Since through experience of this great event / In Arms not worse, in foresight much advanc't, / We may with more successful hope resolve / To wage by force or guile* eternal Warr.*"*

Satan, in a classic rhetorical sleight of hand, doesn't directly ask the question his speech hopes to answer. In rallying his troops to "eternal warr," he never asks whether "eternal warr" is the right course of action: it is taken as a given, and he focuses instead on his optimism about the likelihood of success. The "you" and "I" of the speech situation have been gathered into the first person plural: "we" are making war on "our grand foe" who "sole reigning holds the tyranny of heaven." This is Satan the democratic insurgent—at least rhetorically—rather than Satan the prideful pretender. In this speech, Satan talks a big game about "force or guile"—but having tried force and lost, guile is his inevitable resort.*

Milton wasn't the only writer in history to give Satan the rhetorical chops he deserves. The 1967 film Bedazzled,** *written by and starring Peter Cook and Dudley Moore, is a case in point. It*

---

*There are literary-critical and theological questions over whether it occurs to Satan that there's the possibility of repentance, but we'll skate over those here.
**The Liz Hurley remake is to be avoided at all costs.

contains a memorable scene in which the Prince of Darkness appears to Dudley Moore's character, as he has appeared to so many of us, in the guise of a traffic cop. Notwithstanding that the devil, played by Cook, gives himself away at once by wearing red socks, the infallible mark of a cad, Dudley falls into conversation with him.

If at the heart of rhetoric is the ability to position oneself in regard to an audience, their exchange demonstrates Satan's mastery. He leads Dudley by the nose.

DEVIL: *It was pride that got me into this. I used to be an angel, you know. Up in heaven.*

DUD: *Oh yeah—you used to be God's favorite, didn't you?*

DEVIL: *That's right. 'I love Lucifer' it was in those days.*

DUD: *What was it like up in heaven?*

DEVIL: *Heh heh. Very nice, really. We used to sit round all day and adore 'im. Believe me, He was adorable. Just about the most adorable thing you ever did see.*

DUD: *What went wrong, then?*

DEVIL: *I'll show you. Here we are—give me a leg up, would you?*

Here, the Devil as it were primes the pump. He establishes that "pride" was at the root of his downfall, hints at the pathos of what he's lost, and appears unexpectedly generous to the God he might reasonably be expected to curse. Note, too, his use of the plain style—establishing an ethos connection with Dud. He calls heaven, litotically, "very nice"—as Dud might describe a suburban front lawn. What a reasonable chap! Dud gives him a leg up onto a red London mailbox, and the Devil sets about painting a mental picture—the technique known as enargia.

DEVIL: *I'm God. This is my throne, see? All around me are the cherubim, seraphim, continually crying "Holy, holy, holy," the angels, archangels, that sort of thing. Now you be me, Lucifer, the loveliest angel of them all.*

DUD: *What do I do?*

DEVIL: *Well, sort of dance around praising me, mainly.*

DUD: *What sort of things do I say?*

DEVIL: *Anything that comes into your head that's nice—how beautiful I am, how wise I am, how handsome . . . that sort of thing. Come on, start dancing.*

DUD: *You're wise! You're beautiful! You're handsome!*

DEVIL: *Thank you very much.*

DUD: *The universe! What a wonderful idea—take my hat off to you!*

DEVIL: *Thank you.*

DUD: *Trees—terrific! Water—another good one!*

DEVIL: *That was a good one . . .*

DUD: *Yes! Sex—top marks!*

DEVIL: *Now make it more personal . . . a bit more fulsome, please. Come on.*

DUD: *Immortal . . . invisible . . . you're handsome . . . you're glorious . . . you're the most beautiful person in the world!*

While all this goes on, Dud is capering around the mailbox like a champ—even attempting a headstand as his praise reaches its climax. Righting himself, he removes his hat and mops his brow.

DUD: *Here, I'm getting a bit bored with this. Can't we change places?*

DEVIL: *That's exactly how I felt.*

As the pair stroll away, that little bit of play-acting has done its work, and the devil continues, confidingly and with winning self-pity, "I only wanted to be like Him, and have a few angels adoring me. . . . But He didn't see it like that. 'Pride,' He called it. 'Sin of pride.'"

At the beginning of their exchange, if you'd asked Dudley whether the devil deserved his exile, he'd like as not have said that he did. He was, after all, guilty of the sin of "pride," wasn't he? In only a couple of minutes, though, not only has the Tempter put front and center in the conversation a definition of "pride" that sounds much more like "fairness," and cast God as an insufferable egomaniac, he has also put his interlocutor right in his own shoes. He has persuaded Dud not just to sympathize with, but actually to inhabit his position. The devil seems to put himself in your place, but in fact, fatally, he puts you into his.

It's the two of them against God (in this scene, both are dressed as traffic guards, a further subliminal attempt to emphasize the apparent identity of their interests), and "He didn't see it like that. "'Pride,' He called it." The repeated "He," has a sarcastic tone, and the hysteron proteron *in the second sentence foregrounds this notion on which the argument turns: Is pride really a bad thing? God may not see it like that—but the Devil and Dudley are now as one in seeing it like that. Who can blame the film's successive audiences for seeing it the same way?*

He does have a point. Doesn't he, silver-tongued devil that he is?

THE SECOND PART OF RHETORIC

Arrangement

IT IS A COMMONPLACE to say that a story needs a beginning, a middle, and an end. The same applies to any speech or extended piece of persuasive writing. After you've done your invention and discovered your proofs, you'll have a mass of material that wants putting into some sort of shape—a shape best designed to maximize the strong arguments, minimize the weak ones, and flow as if inexorably to its conclusion.

"It is not without reason," Quintilian tells us, "that arrangement is considered the second of the five parts of oratory, for though all the limbs of a statue be cast, it is not a statue until they are united, and if, in our own bodies or those of any other animals, we were to displace or alter the position of any part, they would be but monsters, though they had the same number of parts."

The historical authorities differ as to the number of sections a speech ought to be broken down into. Will "beginning, middle,

and end" do it—or is something more elaborate required? As Richard A. Lanham puts it in his indispensable *A Handlist of Rhetorical Terms*: "From the Greeks onward, the various parts of an oration have borne a body of theorizing so dense and extensive as almost to defy summary."

Quintilian didn't even try, saying more or less that arrangement, though vitally important, depended on circumstance, and that the orator was best using his "sagacity, his discernment, his invention, and his judgment, and must ask counsel from himself."[1]

That's wise advice. And, as you might imagine, certain kinds of speech need to be certain shapes. An extended rebuttal of your opponent's arguments isn't really necessary if you're delivering the father-of-the-bride speech at your beloved daughter's wedding. Nevertheless, it's worth having a sense of the basic off-the-rack structure of a speech before you dive into bespoke couture.

The simplest scheme is Aristotle's—who said that a speech is a thing of two halves. There's the *narration*, where you set out the points at issue, and the *proof*, where you make the arguments for your case. At most, and grudgingly, he admitted you could go up to four parts if you include an introduction and a conclusion.

The most influential rhetorical handbook between the ages of Cicero and Shakespeare, however, *Ad Herennium*, gives us six parts, which is the scheme I propose to adopt. Most more-and-less elaborate schemes are effectively variations. *Ad Herennium* sets the parts of a speech out as follows:

Exordium (also *prooimion*)

This is where you set out your stall. It's the point at which you establish your bona fides as a speaker, grab the audi-

ence's attention, and hope to keep it. The strongest up-front ethos appeal will tend to come here.

Narration (also *diegesis, prothesis,* or *narratio*)

Corresponding to Aristotle's notion of narration, this is where you levelly and reasonably set out the area of argument, and the facts of the case as generally understood.

Division (also *divisio, propositio,* or *partitio*)

Here's where you set out what you and your opponents agree about; and the areas on which you disagree.

Proof (also *pistis, confirmatio,* or *probatio*)

This is where you set out the arguments supporting your case. Here's where logos comes to the fore.

Refutation (also *confutatio* or *reprehensio*)

More logos. This is, as the name suggests, the part of an oration in which you smash your opponent's arguments into little tiny pieces.

Peroration (also *epilogos* or *conclusio*)

The grand finale. If you have flourishes, prepare to flourish them now, and if you have tears, prepare to shed them. In the peroration, you sum up what has gone before, reiterate your strongest points, and drive to your conclusion. It's usually the place for the pathos appeal to reach its height.

That, as it doesn't take much noticing, is more or less how we're taught to write essays at school. It's a pretty familiar pattern,

and the variations that are played on it—you can, for instance, add a decorative Digression in near the end; you can interleave some emotional appeals with the more evidential sections in the middle; or you can subdivide any of the constituent parts—don't alter its essential structure.

The job you are doing is to establish yourself with the audience, frame the terms of debate, find a way of appearing to take your opponent's arguments (actual or implied) into account, then load the dice in your own favor, and roll them with a triumphant flick of the wrist.

EXORDIUM

The purpose of the exordium is to put the audience into a receptive and attentive frame of mind. It's helpful to tell them—like the nightclub host who greets you, "Ladies and gentlemen: have we got a show for you tonight!"—that important, new, and unusual matters will be offered to their ears. And it's helpful to make clear why it's you who will be discussing them.

> We can by four methods make our hearers well-disposed: by discussing our own person, the person of our adversaries, that of our hearers, and the facts themselves.[2]

As a straightforward example, when the late Apple CEO Steve Jobs delivered a commencement address at Stanford University in 2005, he combined these methods effectively—flattering the audience, humbling himself, and pointing forward to what he was going to say.

"Thank you," he said. "I am honored to be with you today for your commencement from one of the finest universities in

the world. Truth be told, I never graduated from college, and this is the closest I've ever gotten to a college graduation. Today I want to tell you three stories from my life. That's it. No big deal. Just three stories."

This likeable but workaday opening does, when you go to nuts and bolts, more or less exactly the same work as the far more charged (and stylistically rococo) exordium to Earl Spencer's eulogy at the death of his sister Diana, Princess of Wales.

> I stand before you today, the representative of a family in grief, in a country in mourning, before a world in shock. We are all united, not only in our desire to pay our respects to Diana but rather in our need to do so. For such was her extraordinary appeal that the tens of millions of people taking part in this service all over the world, via television and radio, who never actually met her, feel that they, too, lost someone close to them in the early hours of Sunday morning. It is a more remarkable tribute to Diana than I can ever hope to offer her today.

There—and note the nice rising tricolon at the very outset— you can see a precise shaping of the speaker's relationship with the audience, and a fastidious, slightly bogus, self-abasement. Earl Spencer casts himself as a "representative" not only of his family but of his country and of the whole world, then suggests that he can't hope to match the mute tribute of the watching millions.

The opening section of his speech also goes on the attack, fulfilling *Ad Herennium*'s rather gleeful injunction to use this section to "make our adversaries unpopular."

> I don't think she ever understood why her genuinely good intentions were sneered at by the media, why there appeared to be

a permanent quest on their behalf to bring her down. It is baf-
fling. My own—and only—explanation is that genuine goodness is threatening to those at the opposite end of the moral
spectrum.

That was a zinger, to which was soon added the deadly
stiletto between the royal ribs of his promise (delivered to the
dead Diana, in a sustained *apostrophe*) that "we, your *blood*
family" would make sure her sons were raised right. "Blood
family" pointedly draws a line between us and them—with the
House of Windsor firmly on the other side.

This sort of rhetorical stance isn't the preserve of the English
aristocrat. Modern hip-hop is full of invective, with rappers forever bigging themselves up and promising to pop a cap in the ass
of a hater. Rap is often more or less all ethos and exordium—a
constant discussion of what the rapper is about to do,* his credentials for doing it, "shout-outs" to the crew with whom he in-
tends to do it, and "disses" to members of enemy crews who
propose trying to prevent him.

In "Till I Collapse," Eminem spits, "For shizzle my whizzle,
this is the plot, listen up: you bizzles forgot slizzle does not give
a fuck."** That is an exordium in capsule. He announces his credentials (in hip-hop and much rock music "not giving a fuck" is,

---

*Rap, usually; but sometimes shoot someone.
**You'll notice that, like Steve Jobs, Eminem asserts that he's telling the truth
("for shizzle . . . this is the plot")—a strategy that, from an intellectual view-
point, might seem redundant but, sheep that audiences are, seldom goes
wrong. Think of how many times you hear speakers say "to be frank," or
"honestly."

oddly enough, a positive ethos appeal*), he chastises the audience for having forgotten them, and he asks them to "listen up." The Beowulf poet does the same thing when he barks, "Hwæt!" which is Anglo-Saxon for "listen up."

NARRATION

Ad Herennium wants the narration to have three qualities: brevity, clarity, and plausibility. Note above all others the third of these. When setting out the facts of the case, the orator is no less able to shape the debate to his purposes than he is when openly mounting an argument—indeed he is probably more so because he speaks under cover of ostensible neutrality.

Narration is the who, what, when, and where of the case—the solemn reading from the policeman's notebook before the fur begins to fly. So let us say that, in the dock, there stands one Yogi Bear, accused of stealing a picnic basket from the table at a campsite in the Jellystone National Park.

In the narration, you would establish that Mr. Bear was a longtime resident of Jellystone, and that he had a history of picnic-basket-related offenses. You would say that the owner of the picnic basket, Mr. X, was recorded entering the park with a picnic basket at ten o'clock on the morning in question, and that at four o'clock that afternoon, Mr. X approached a park ranger claiming that his picnic basket had vanished while he was swimming. You would say that Mr. X claimed to have heard the words,

---

*Cf. the popularity of the late Kurt Cobain, who announced, "I hate myself and I want to die"—and meant it—but whose audience was not expected to share his feelings.

"Go, go, go, Boo-Boo!" and seen a rustling of trees, as he returned to his campsite from his swim. On these agreed facts, you could build your prosecution—or mount your defense.

The narration, briskly, fills the audience in. It need not do so in tones of absolute neutrality. When Neville Chamberlain addressed the House of Commons on September 1, 1939, his statement of the facts was brief, clear, and plausible, but suffused with moral and emotional judgment.

> No man can say that the Government could have done more to try to keep open the way for an honorable and equitable settlement of the dispute between Germany and Poland. Nor have we neglected any means of making it crystal clear to the German Government that if they insisted on using force again in the manner in which they had used it in the past we were resolved to oppose them by force.
>
> Now that all the relevant documents are being made public we shall stand at the bar of history knowing that the responsibility for this terrible catastrophe lies on the shoulders of one man, the German Chancellor, who has not hesitated to plunge the world into misery in order to serve his own senseless ambitions. . . .
>
> Only last night the Polish Ambassador did see the German Foreign Secretary, Herr von Ribbentrop. Once again he expressed to him what, indeed, the Polish Government had already said publicly, that they were willing to negotiate with Germany about their disputes on an equal basis.
>
> What was the reply of the German Government? The reply was that without another word the German troops crossed the Polish frontier this morning at dawn and are since reported to be bombing open towns.

That teed up what was to follow: the somewhat hangdog expression of national determination that was, a few days later, to lead to the formal declaration of war.

Barack Obama's sober scene-setting during his presidential campaign was textbook stuff. Here's part of the narration for a speech he gave in October 2008, where he went on to outline his "rescue plan" for America's middle class.

> We meet at a moment of great uncertainty for America. The economic crisis we face is the worst since the Great Depression. Markets across the globe have become increasingly unstable, and millions of Americans will open up their [pension] statements this week and see that so much of their hard-earned savings have disappeared. The credit crisis has left businesses large and small unable to get loans, which means they can't buy new equipment, or hire new workers, or even make payroll for the workers they have. You've got auto plants right here in Ohio that have been around for decades closing their doors and laying off workers who've never known another job in their entire life.

Though the solutions he'll go on to propose differ substantially, Obama's account of America's situation there is not all that different from what his Republican opponents would have acknowledged. Yet where a Republican narration—they then being the party in power—would likely focus on unity, leadership, and determination in tough times, Obama's emphasis is on crisis, instability, and uncertainty. It's an emphasis he was happier with, it's now possible to notice, when the other team was getting the blame.

The narration is one of the prime areas of a speech in which you are able to spin, and framing the terms of the debate is half the battle won. Don't talk about cutting welfare provision and giving tax breaks to the rich; talk about creating a Big Society where people are given control over their own destinies. Don't talk about repealing safety regulation; talk about cutting red tape. And so on.

The question of definition isn't restricted to using emotive or euphemistic language. It also carries over to logos: how you define the argument as a whole. We like to simplify things to a choice between A and B, so even if a given question is more complicated, we're vulnerable to someone presenting it in such a way.

In the months after 9/11, a whole series of questions arose as to whether to retaliate, how to retaliate, and who to retaliate against. But with public feeling running high, the dominant line, at least in the US, was: "You're either with us, or you're with the terrorists." Regardless of where you stand on the rectitude of the case that was built over those months for the invasion of Afghanistan and the eventual invasion of Iraq, you can probably agree that in rhetorical terms, what pushed it through was that binary opposition—rather than any argument seeking explicitly to connect Saddam Hussein's secular regime with the Wahhabi fundamentalists of al-Qaeda.

I said that defining your terms is half the battle won. To that may be added that if you're truly desperate, it can be the grounds you fight on long after the battle is lost. During the Monica Lewinsky affair, Bill Clinton, whose definition of the term "sexual relations" was already known to be eccentric, drifted into deep epistemological waters in a statement to the grand jury. Defending his testimony that "there's nothing going on between us"—delivered on a day when he hadn't happened to see Ms. Lewinsky—Clinton said it wasn't necessarily a lie: "It depends upon what the meaning of the word 'is' is. If the—if he—

if 'is' means is and never has been, that is not—that is one thing. If it means there is none, that was a completely true statement."

As this squirm-making instance illustrates all too well, the time to define your terms is in advance, not as part of a rear-guard action. Narration isn't the most exciting part of a speech—but it can be subtly influential on its outcome.

DIVISION

Division and narration are two ends of a pantomime horse. The former follows fairly briskly on from the latter; or should do, if onstage catastrophe is to be avoided. In division, you start by summarizing the salient points of agreement, then set out the points that are at issue.

So, to return momentarily to Jellystone, we might say that though it is a matter of record that Mr. Bear has a history of stealing picnic baskets, and doesn't deny that he was in the park at the time, at issue is whether he absconded with this particular picnic basket.

We have yet to establish whose was the voice that was heard saying, "Go, go, go, Boo-Boo!" It is possible that Mr. Bear was framed, and we intend to produce evidence to that effect. We may raise the possibility that Mr. X mislaid his picnic basket and chose to report it stolen in the hopes of making a claim on his insurance, and so on.

Ad Herennium gives two serviceable examples of division: "Orestes killed his mother; on that I agree with my opponents. But did he have the right to commit the deed, and was he justified in committing it? That is in dispute." Or: "They admit that Agamemnon was killed by Clytemnestra; yet despite this they say that I ought not to have avenged my father."

It adds shrewdly that in setting out the points at issue, it's best not to include too many: "We shall be using the Enumeration when we tell by number how many points we are going to discuss. The number ought not to exceed three; for otherwise, besides the danger that we may at some time include in the speech more or fewer points than we enumerated,* it instills in the hearer the suspicion of premeditation and artifice, and this robs the speech of conviction."

Richard Nixon's "Checkers" speech, mentioned above in the section about pathos, contains a nicely clean instance of division. As you'll remember, Nixon was at bay after a slush fund established to pay his election expenses was exposed in the press. In narration mode, Nixon concedes that the fund exists: "I, Senator Nixon, took $18,000 from a group of my supporters."

He then sets out, just as per the ancient rhetorical handbook, three points of disagreement.

> I say that it was morally wrong if any of that $18,000 went to Senator Nixon, for my personal use. I say that it was morally wrong if it was secretly given and secretly handled. And I say that it was morally wrong if any of the contributors got special favors for the contributions that they made.

Rebutting those propositions one by one is the task of the speech that follows.

---

*Cicero teased a lesser orator called Curio for having so faulty a memory that "at times when he had announced three points he would add a fourth or miss the third." Contemporary audiences need only call to mind Monty Python's Spanish Inquisition Sketch ("Our chief weapon is surprise! Surprise and fear . . . fear and surprise. . . . Our two weapons are fear and surprise . . . and ruthless efficiency. . . . Our three weapons are fear, and surprise, and ruthless efficiency . . . ") for details of how this can prove an embarrassment.

PROOF

This, and the section following, is where logos gets its day in the sun. You have established the facts, indicated the grounds of dispute, and now you set out to make your case in earnest.

You will use arguments of analogy and probability and induction, as discussed earlier. In the *Adventure of the Vanishing Pickernick Basket*, for instance, you would argue that it is in the nature of bears in general, and of Yogi Bear in particular, to steal picnic baskets and shit in the woods.

You would also seek out corroborating evidence. Yogi's known accomplices, such as Boo-Boo, might be asked to come up with an alibi. Jellystone's CCTV footage would be called into evidence, the Park Rangers cross examined, and so on.

These are what—in connection with forensic rhetoric in particular, though they have their analogues in the deliberative sphere—Aristotle calls "nontechnical proofs." What he means is that these proofs, or pieces of evidence, are not part of the *technè* of rhetoric. Technical proofs are the arguments that the orator contrives. Nontechnical proofs are there already: available to be used rather than needing to be invented.

Aristotle names five of them: laws, witnesses, contracts, tortures, and oaths. Not all of these apply equally commonly in all parts of the modern world, obviously. We're not, supposedly, big on torture in the civilized West—though whether we can say that with a straight face is an argument for another day.

"Laws" sounds like a rather obvious thing to take into consideration—but it's not always straightforward. In both judicial and forensic rhetoric, it can be necessary to establish not only whether x did y or x should do y, but whether or not that falls within the law.

Before the 2003 invasion of Iraq, for instance, a great deal turned on the question of whether a "second" UN resolution was required to authorize the use of force against Iraq, or whether Resolution 1441—which threatened force in the case of non-compliance with the UN's conditions—was itself sufficient authority for an invasion.

Aristotle advises—and it is advice supporters of the Iraq war would very likely approve—that "if the written law is contrary to our position, we must use the general law and the principles of greater equity and justice, and claim that this is the meaning of the 'to the best judgment' principle."[3]

This is the argument, he says, that Antigone makes in burying her brother Polynices: it may be against the arbitrary and temporary law of the tyrant Creon, but not against the unwritten law of justice.

With contracts, as with laws: "A contract is a private and particular law, and contracts do not make the law binding, but the laws do make legal contracts so." So there's always room to wriggle. Arguments can make contracts sound, "if they are one's own, binding and authoritative, if of one's adversary, the reverse." You can appeal, as above, to the written or universal law in support or against a given contract.

What Aristotle has to say about oaths is fairly peripheral for the modern courtroom, where everyone is expected to speak under oath. In Attic courts, you had the option to challenge your adversary to swear an oath to the truth of what he said on whatever he held holy—where you were, effectively, gambling on quite how god-fearing your opponent was.

The oath still has considerable informal rhetorical power, though. From the satisfaction-guaranteed end of the advertising market, to the statesman showily making "solemn prom-

ises" (as if to imply that everything else he says may be regarded as frivolous and insincere), the oath is still very much present in the culture.

An eccentric nobleman of my acquaintance, some years ago, quietly bought a castle without telling his wife. She cottoned on to this—as the story has it, when she found a receipt: "To one castle" in the waste paper basket; the story, I suspect, has grown fondly in the telling—and confronted him.

"Did you buy a castle, H——?" she asked.

"No, love. No. I didn't buy a castle."

"Really?"

"No, honestly I didn't."

"Do you *swear*?"

"I swear. I didn't buy a castle. I didn't."

"Swear on B——'s life," she said—referring not to one of his children but to the pit bull terrier (sadly now deceased) that was the apple of his eye.

He winced. He gulped. He stammered. He couldn't do it.

"I did. I did buy a castle. Sorry."

When he moves onto "witnesses," Aristotle includes in the term what we would probably regard as a slightly different category of things. Under the umbrella term, he includes both "modern witnesses"—those who give evidence in a courtroom or notables who have given judgment in similar cases—and those he calls "ancient witnesses," which is to say authorities from the past, in which category he even includes proverbs. A commonplace, he implies, can seem to stand as a witness too.*

---

*Anamnesis, incidentally, is the fancy term for recalling past events or sayings in a speech—whether ambling publicly down memory lane like Ronnie Corbett on his barstool and Justice Shallow in *Henry IV, Part 2*, or wondering: "Was it not Robert Lowell who said, 'Memory is genius'?"

This opens onto a vital point. Appealing to authority—whether by quoting a commonplace or the words of a named source—always strengthens an argument. Rhetoric is about connecting with an audience; that means finding shared assumptions. And those shared assumptions are usually pretty conservative: we don't reinvent the world from scratch every time we float a theory.

As a species, we follow living leaders and—oddly, but it seems universally—we one way or another honor our dead. The idea of authority is all over our moral and intellectual lives like orange on Doritos—whether we're applying Karl Marx's ideas to the behavior of modern capitalism, or the teachings of the Koran to our own day-to-day lives.

So however questionable they may seem on intellectual principle, those great oxymorons—"common sense" and "received wisdom"—are profoundly important in persuasion. Well-known quotations embody both of these things: they come with the imprimatur both of ancient derivation, and of the many people who, by passing it on, in some way are understood to have endorsed it.

So though it shouldn't make a difference, in strictly logical terms, whether I say, "There are three forms of persuasive appeal—ethos, pathos and logos," or "Aristotle tells us there are three forms of persuasive appeal—ethos, pathos and logos," the latter is undoubtedly going to be of more account to you. You've heard of Aristotle. Who the hell am I?

Most great leaps forward in human understanding have been developments from, or arguments with, the understandings of the past. The so-called renaissances in the twelfth and sixteenth centuries were based on a rediscovery of classical antiquity, and to this day the simple fact of quotation marks around a statement has the effect of making it more plausible.

This reliance on popular wisdom and authority has down-sides. Galileo demonstrated that the earth went round the sun, but the authority of the accepted wisdom was too great to dislodge. The evidence for a germ theory of disease was available for hundreds and hundreds of years before medical orthodoxy was capable of looking at it freshly enough to accept it. And, to take a more modern example, a pair of researchers demonstrated in the early 1980s that gastric ulcers were caused by a bacterium and not, as had previously been thought, stress; but it still took two decades for their findings to be accepted.

For a long time, originality itself was mistrusted. Thomas More claimed to have based *Utopia* on the report of a knowledgeable traveler, and Chaucer's work is full of references to "myn auctoritee" or "myn auctour." What was in "olde bokes" was to be revered, and even when Chaucer was just making it up, he liked to pretend—though perhaps half in jest—that he was basing his work on a previous text.

When Barack Obama wishes to win his electorate to radical change, he doesn't declare that he proposes to rip up all that has gone before and start from scratch; rather, he makes a doubly determined attempt to root his project in the received values of the American people. He clothes his ideas in the language of the Bible and tops it with the stovepipe hat of Abraham Lincoln. And when Lincoln himself piped up at Gettysburg, he began with the words: "Four score and seven years ago our fathers brought forth . . . "

When a politician on the British Right speaks now, he will genuflect to Mrs. Thatcher; on the Left, Aneurin Bevan and Keir Hardie. Republicans in America inevitably bring up Ronald Reagan. Going a bit further back, Enoch Powell's "rivers of blood" speech, as it became known, was based on a classical allusion:

"Like the Roman, I seem to see the River Tiber foaming with much blood." The Peasants' Revolt in the 1380s had as one of its slogans an appeal to Biblical authority: "When Adam delved and Eve span, who was then the Gentleman?" Dante went nowhere without his Virgil.

That is as true of advertising as it is of politics or literature. A company will boast of having been "purveyors of fine jewelry to the gentry since 1861." When you pick up a new book in the bookshop, you'll very likely see quotations—kindly remarks about the book on the jacket from names you know and trust. The absent witnesses—proverb and commonplace, custom and authority—are not to be underestimated.

Where it comes to the more specific question of living witnesses, Aristotle is as ever pragmatic. If you're coming up short on that front, he says, you can argue that witnesses muddy the waters and the audience should judge only the probabilities of the case: "because it is not possible to make probabilities deceive with silver and probabilities are not caught in perjury."

If, on the other hand, you've witnesses on your side and your adversary doesn't, you can argue the opposite: that "probabilities are not answerable to the court, and that there would be no need of witnesses, if it was sufficient to consider the matter from the speeches."

Then there's good old torture—standard practice for slaves giving evidence in the Athenian courts.* It's worth mentioning as a historical curiosity. Aristotle tells us, oddly, that to his contemporaries the evidence of tortured slaves was "thought to carry

---

*Though a slave would never be tortured without the consent of his master. Who do you think these people are: barbarians?

conviction, since a certain compulsion is present." He goes on, though—in considering how you'd seek to minimize the impact of torture evidence against you—to make a startlingly modern point:

> If they are against us and with the adversary, one might refute them by telling the truth about the whole genus of tortures. For no less under compulsion do men tell lies rather than the truth, either enduring rather than telling the truth or easily making false accusations so that the torture may stop sooner.

We can only hope, when it comes to our missing picnic basket, that the more enlightened side of Aristotle's counsel would have prevailed before Boo-Boo got waterboarded.

REFUTATION

Proof and refutation are another of these linked pairs. In most adversarial situations, to prove your own case is to disprove your opponent's—though rhetoric being as slippery as it is, the task is seldom precisely symmetrical. If you can't dazzle them with brilliance, as the old bumper sticker has it, baffle them with bullshit. The skilled orator is out not necessarily to knock down his opponent's case *tout court*—but to misrepresent his opponent's case in such a way as to make it easier to attack.

You can indignantly answer a charge nobody made, or fiercely deny something adjacent to the truth. "I did not have sexual relations with that woman," Bill Clinton told the American people at the height of the Monica Lewinsky scandal—choosing not to gloss his remark with the information that he didn't regard oral sex as "sexual relations."

You can burlesque your opponent's position in a way that makes it unattractive to the audience. President Obama's proposed healthcare reforms in 2010, for instance, were characterized by ideological opponents as "socialist" or "communist,"* and he was accused of proposing to set up "death panels" to decide whether invalids lived or died.

If your own case is weak, you may even want to reverse the order in which proof and refutation come: reduce your opponent to smoldering rubble in the hopes that nobody then notices how feeble the case you mount afterward is. The nature of the Western tradition in rhetoric (as in dialectic) is adversarial: it is better at dealing with either/or propositions than and/also possibilities or neither/nors.

In other words, the world is full of cases where both proposition A and proposition B are correct; or where both are wrong. But very often the two—presented as opposing sides in a set-to—will look as if they are mutually exclusive. It was possible, for example, that O. J. Simpson was both framed by the police and guilty of murder.

But that confusion can be turned to rhetorical advantage. If you characterize something as the opposite of your own proposition, and then attack it—"Down with tuition fees! Up with opportunity!"; "Down with cheese! Up with mice!"—a slow-witted audience will think that by damaging the apparent opposition, you've proved your case.

---

*A leaked memo to reporters from a managing editor at the right-wing TV station Fox News played on popular mistrust of government: "1) Please use the term 'government-run health insurance' or, when brevity is a concern, 'government option' whenever possible; 2) When it is necessary to use the term 'public option' (which is, after all, firmly ensconced in the nation's lexicon) use the qualifier 'so-called' as in 'the so-called public option.'"

Nontechnical proofs can be refuted too. The discrediting of witnesses can be a highly effective tactic, and Quintilian observes that it can be done against whole categories of witnesses, as well as against individuals.

> In regular speeches, we commonly offer observations, first of all, for and against witnesses in general. This is a common topic for argument, one side maintaining that there is no evidence stronger than that which rests on human knowledge, and the other, to detract from the credit of such knowledge, enumerating every cause by which testimony is rendered false. The next step is when pleaders make special attacks, though on bodies of men, for we know that the testimonies of whole nations have been invalidated by orators, as well as whole classes of evidence, as in the case of hear-say witnesses, for pleaders maintain that they are not in reality witnesses, but mere reporters of the words of unsworn individuals.[4]

An ugly instance of undermining witness credibility can be found in those rape trials where the sexual history, clothing, and moral character of the victim are dragged in to muddy the water. A more comical one can be found during the Profumo scandal, in the pert rejoinder of Mandy Rice-Davies when told that Lord Astor had denied sleeping with her: "Well, he would, wouldn't he?" *Erotema* and *chiasmus*! Not just a pretty face, that lass.

Helpful though it can be to go on the attack, it is a mistake to regard retreat on any front as a sign of weakness. Giving more ground than your opponent expects can throw them off balance. Recognize which battles you have no choice but to lose; then lose them on your own terms.

Say your husband catches you in a lie. You spent the afternoon eating Walnut Whips off your lover's toned six-pack in a fancy room at the Savoy, but you told your husband you spent all day at home. Then he finds a parking ticket in your coat, proving you spent two hours in the middle of the day parked somewhere in the center of town. He confronts you. You deny it. He produces the parking ticket. You burst into tears of indignation. Yes, you say, I *was* in the center of town. Since you must know, I went in to arrange *your* surprise birthday party. And this is how you repay me?

Now who feels bad?

The usual term for the figure is *concessio*; or, if you insist on the fancy Greek one, *paromologia*. It has always struck me that were newspapers better able to see the virtue of this figure, they'd be readier to print apologies. The *Guardian*'s introduction of a "Corrections and Clarifications" column seems to me not only an admirable move, but a shrewd one. Other newspapers have resisted doing the same because they think it looks weak to admit to routinely making mistakes, but actually, it just makes the newspaper look honest.

I used to write gossip columns for a living, and apologies always struck me as enormously useful. We'd resist them a little—but when we had plainly got something wrong, it seemed to me that the fulsome apology was the way to go. Not only did it usually fill space and send the complainant away happy, it made us look honest. By apologizing for the one mistake in ten that someone bothered to complain about, we made the cavalcade of defamatory innuendoes, half-truths, and outright fabrications that filled the column day in, day out, look, by implication, like cast-iron facts.

An instance of *concessio* from an unlikely source illustrates just how widely and well this principle applies: as I hope should be clear, the traditions of formal rhetoric didn't create the way an argument works—they simply described it.

In 1905, the anthropologist Matilda Stevenson was investigating the Native American Zuni tribe in New Mexico. While Stevenson was with them, a boy was accused of witchcraft after a twelve-year-old girl he had touched died from a seizure.

The boy denied having anything to do with witchcraft, as well he might, but his fellow tribesmen refused to believe him. Something must have been responsible for the death of the girl. The boy changed his position. He said that he had inherited magical powers that allowed him to assume the shapes of animals. Asked to demonstrate, he said sadly that his powers had departed him following the incident with the girl. He was freed—on the grounds that he was no longer a sorcerer.

As Aristotle tells us, *pithanon tini pithanon*: "What is convincing is what one can be convinced by."

PERORATION

The peroration is where the orator can really have fun. This is the opportunity to end on a twenty-one-gun salute, to move the audience to tears of pity or howls of rage, to wheel out your grandest figures and highest-sounding words. It can be like watching Bruce Springsteen and the E Street Band close a show with "Born To Run" and belt the final chorus out four times in a row.

Figures of auxesis and repetition—often pulling together words or themes from earlier in the speech—commonly proliferate in

the peroration, and many orators will crank it up a little in the direction of the grand style.

But it can also be the place for a dying fall—where you bring the ship of your speech into the calm waters of harbor. Sometimes you want to leave an audience thoughtful, rather than excitable. The point is that the peroration shapes the impression—intellectually, yes, but above all in terms of emotion or tone—with which the audience comes away from your speech.

For *Sturm und Drang*, there's not much to beat the peroration of Frederick Douglass's 1852 Fourth of July address. Douglass (1818–1895) was born into slavery in Maryland, but escaped to the North and became one of the most celebrated campaigners for abolition.

He settled in Rochester, New York, and in 1852 he was invited to address an Independence Day party thrown by well-intentioned local poobahs. The irony was not lost on Douglass. He opened his speech with a pointed *erotema*—a sort of anti-ethos appeal in which he wondered what his qualification to speak was:

> What have I or those I represent to do with your national independence? Are the great principles of political freedom and of natural justice, embodied in that Declaration of Independence, extended to us?

Then he really cranked it up, concluding as follows:

> At a time like this, scorching irony, not convincing argument, is needed. Oh! Had I the ability, and could I reach the nation's ear, I would today pour out a fiery stream of biting ridicule, blasting

reproach, withering sarcasm, and stern rebuke. For it is not light that is needed, but fire; it is not the gentle shower, but thunder. We need the storm, the whirlwind, and the earthquake. The feeling of the nation must be quickened; the conscience of the nation must be roused; the propriety of the nation must be startled; the hypocrisy of the nation must be exposed; and its crimes against God and man must be denounced.

What to the American slave is your Fourth of July? I answer, a day that reveals to him more than all other days of the year, the gross injustice and cruelty to which he is the constant victim. To him your celebration is a sham; your boasted liberty an unholy license; your national greatness, swelling vanity; your sounds of rejoicing are empty and heartless; your shouts of liberty and equality, hollow mock; your prayers and hymns, your sermons and thanksgivings, with all your religious parade and solemnity, are to him mere bombast, fraud, deception, impiety, and hypocrisy—a thin veil to cover up crimes which would disgrace a nation of savages. There is not a nation of the earth guilty of practices more shocking and bloody than are the people of these United States at this very hour.

Go search where you will, roam through all the monarchies and despotisms of the Old World, travel through South America, search out every abuse and when you have found the last, lay your facts by the side of the everyday practices of this nation, and you will say with me that, for revolting barbarity and shameless hypocrisy, America reigns without a rival.

That's what I call a peroration—though heaven knows where Douglass's hosts would have been looking as he delivered it.

CHAMPIONS OF RHETORIC II

Marcus Tullius Cicero
The Attack Dog of the Roman Forum

THOSE OF US STILL *waiting for the Justin Bieber craze to vanish from the earth may be forgiven for casting an anxious eye at the example of a previous cult of personality. The Roman orator Marcus Tullius Cicero died in 43* BC*. Nearly sixteen centuries later, so many people were still infatuated with him—Christian Italians had even taken to calling God "Jupiter" and Christ "Apollo"—that the great humanist Erasmus felt it necessary to write a play mocking them. His 1528* Ciceronianus[1] *includes a character who has purged his library of all books not by Cicero, included Cicero in his calendar of the Apostles, installed paintings of Cicero in his*

chapel, library, and every doorway in his house, and who wears a miniature of Cicero engraved on a gem.

Erasmus's burlesque attack is a mark of Cicero's enduring influence. And as Erasmus believed, to treat Cicero as an abstract and ossified model of style appropriate for every age was to miss the point of him: had he been living in the fifteenth century AD *it would have been in the idiom of the fifteenth century that he'd have spoken.*

Cicero was both theorist and practitioner of rhetoric—lawyer, politician, and teacher. It is to Cicero that we owe the classic instance of the five canons of rhetoric—the spine of this book—and it was Cicero who gave us the notion that rhetoric seeks to move, educate, and delight (movere, docere, *and* delectare). *Cicero's key works on rhetoric are* De Inventione, *a handbook written when he was a young man, and* De Oratore—*an extended dialogue "on the ideal orator" in which he sets out a very humanistic view of how oratory should be more than a set of persuasive tools.*

Like an ancestor volume of Machiavelli's The Prince, De Oratore *is a treatise on statecraft that casts light on the idea of the state. For Cicero, oratory was both the crowning expression of a whole set of civic virtues, and their grounds of existence: "Eloquence is the comrade of peace, the ally of leisure, and, in some sense, the foster child of a well-ordered state."*

Cicero was a model of the practical rhetorician. When he talked about judicial rhetoric, Cicero wasn't talking about an abstract exercise in style—he was talking about the underpinnings of civilization as he understood it: "the desirableness of maintaining the laws, and the danger with which all public and private affairs are threatened."

Despite Erasmus's best efforts, Cicero's model held more or less continuous sway up to the nineteenth century. His works were key

texts from the end of the Dark Ages through the Renaissance and French Revolution to the drafting of the American Constitution. He was influential even through works he didn't write: in the same way that orphaned quotations get attributed to Oscar Wilde, one of the most influential rhetoric handbooks, Ad Herennium, was also assumed to be by his hand.

But though Cicero now stands as the very icon of romanitas, the historical man—born in 106 BC—was a classic instance of a semi-outsider made good. His family was well-to-do, and may have run a fuller's business (soaking wool in urine for cloth-making), but they came from provincial Arpinum, so were half-in and half-out of the snobby Roman club.

Cicero was literate in both Latin and Greek—a mark of cultivation and an entry to Roman high society. His ambitious father sent him as a teenager to Rome, where he studied under two very eminent Roman rhetors, but also under a Greek one, Archias—leading him to pick up the nickname "the Little Greek Boy." It's significant that the man who went on to shape the canons of Roman rhetoric did so having thoroughly digested the Attic tradition.

Like more of the great orators than one cares to mention, Cicero was not a naturally dominating presence. The young Cicero was a shrimp and dweeb, confessing that he wrote poetry in the hours his contemporaries dedicated to "parties and gambling and ball games." Before he spoke, he was terribly nervous—but how he described those nerves gives an insight into how thoroughgoing was his theory of oratory:

> Personally, I am always very nervous when I begin to speak. Every time I make a speech I feel I am submitting to judgment, not only about my ability but my character and honor. I am afraid of seeming either to promise more than I can perform,

*which suggests complete irresponsibility, or to perform less than
I can, which suggests bad faith and indifference.*

Already in there you can see the consciousness of how damaging he regards the appearance of bad faith, and how penetratingly the orator is exposed to his audience.

The young Cicero overcame some of that shyness by taking lessons from the theater, going on to model his style on Clodius Aesopus. The original Russell Crowe–style method actor, it was said of him that he got so carried away playing Agamemnon that he ran through and killed a stagehand.

After a brief interlude as a slum landlord ("two of my shops have collapsed and the others are showing cracks—even the mice have moved out," he complained), Cicero turned in earnest to making a name* for himself in the courts.

His break came in 80 BC, when he took on a hot potato of a case that had been turned down by bigger names. He was to defend Sextus Roscius, on trial for killing his father. The Roman abhorrence for parricide—and thus the taint of involvement in the case—was indicated by the punishment as Cicero set it out in his defense:

*According to the custom of our ancestors it was established that
the parricide should be beaten with blood-red rods, sewn in a*

---

*Cicero, incidentally, is Latin for "chickpea"—possibly, his biographer suggests, indicating that he had an ancestor with a particularly striking wart or interestingly shaped nose. Toward the beginning of his career as an orator, Cicero was advised to change his name. He declined, saying that he intended to make the name of Cicero as famous as those of Scaurus and Catulus, political giants of previous generations. Their names mean "fat ankles" and "puppy" respectively.

leather sack together with a dog, a cock, a viper and an ape, and the sack thrown into the depths of the sea or a river.

Cicero's defense was ballsy to the point of recklessness. He not only exonerated Roscius, but went on the attack against his two accusers, rounding on a known favorite of the then-dictator Sulla. But he triumphed—managing, too, to emerge with his neck intact— and was launched as a public man.

A year later, however, he set off for the Eastern Mediterranean on something like a cross between a gap year and oratory boot camp—showing, again, how he regarded oratory as a physical more than simply intellectual craft, and one that benefited from a long and various apprenticeship:

> I always spoke without pause or variation, using all the strength of my voice and the effort of my whole body. . . . I thought that by a more restrained and moderate use of the voice and a diligent way of speaking I could both avoid the danger and acquire more variety in my style. . . . The reason for my going to Asia was to change my method of speaking.

He retrained there under Apollonius Molon—"not only a pleader in real cases* and an admirable writer, but excellent as a judge and critic of faults and a very wise teacher and adviser. . . . I came home after two years not only more experienced, but almost another man; the excessive strain of my voice had gone, my style had so to speak simmered down, my lungs were stronger and I was not so thin."

---

*See how Cicero values real-world experience: this is rhetoric as *technè*, as a practical skill.

So here's Cicero the practical man—making himself into the orator he needs to be. Experience shaped him further. When he returned from his first political posting, as quaestor in Sicily, for instance, he imagined his fame would have spread far and wide. His friends had barely noticed he'd gone.

"I've been in my province."

"Ah yes—Africa."

"No! Sicily!"

Cicero eventually gave up and, in a huff, pretended to have been a tourist. He ever after recognized the importance in politics of being the man on the spot: "I took care to be seen in person every day." And—a trick that works for politicians to this day—he taught himself to remember people's names.

That doesn't mean Cicero was all touchy-feely, though. Invective—as he demonstrated by dissing the dictator in his first big case—was a Ciceronian specialty. Cicero's gift for invective was as important then as it is to speakers today. Etymologically, "invective" is a cavalry charge, and when Cicero hit a gallop, woe betide whoever was in the way. In one speech, for instance, he accused an enemy in short order of being a "monster," "funeral pyre of the commonwealth," "butcher," "scoundrel," "most foul and inhuman monster," and "gelded pig." He further attacked his mark's forehead, eyebrows, cheeks (hairy), and teeth (stained).*

The key thing about invective or ad hominem *attack is that it is a sort of reverse ethos appeal: the purpose is to isolate your opponent from the community. Cicero very well understood this—having himself been attacked for social climbing, his failed marriage, and as "an immigrant citizen of Rome." (Winston*

---

*"In Pisonem."

Churchill's dismissal of Gandhi as "a seditious Middle-Temple lawyer now posing as a fakir" is out of the same drawer.)

It is interesting, in that light, to note that the outsider's invective is typically more stern and solemn: an insider, more comfortable reading the audience's social codes, can risk a joke. That points to something wider: while the fusillade of insults moves its object out of the embrace of the community, it seeks to move its speaker closer to the center. There's nothing to affirm a tribal identity, or consolidate power around a leader, like having an Other to denounce. On the small scale, it gives you the Yankees–Red Sox rivalry; on the large one, it gives you more questionable twentieth-century regimes than I care to mention.

Cicero's finest hour—or one of them: he had a whole career full of finest hours—was his denunciation of Catiline, a thwarted populist politician and sometime rival who, bad loser that he was, got up a conspiracy to seize power by force when he lost the election to consulship.

There was about the antagonism between Cicero and Catiline something of the settling of old scores. Catiline ran with an aristocratic bad crowd, and Cicero had on a previous occasion used enargia to withering effect in describing the comportment at a party of Gallius, one of his close friends:

There are shouts and screams, screeching females, there is deafening music. I thought I could make out some people entering and others leaving, some of them staggering from the effects of the wine, some of them still yawning from yesterday's boozing. Among them was Gallius, perfumed and wreathed with flowers; the floor was filthy, soiled with wine and covered with withered garlands and fish-bones.

Cicero had made sure he was well informed before he moved. Ahead of his denunciation of Catiline, he was being fed information by the disgruntled mistress of one of Catiline's coconspirators. Cicero called a special meeting of the Senate, to which—adding to the theater—Catiline had the brass neck to show up.

Cicero made full use of Catiline's presence in the room, opening his oration with the run of epiplexis that is one of his most quoted passages:

> When, O Catiline, do you mean to cease abusing our patience? How long is that madness of yours still to mock us? When is there to be an end of that unbridled audacity of yours, swaggering about as it does now? Do not the nightly guards placed on the Palatine Hill—do not the watches posted throughout the city—does not the alarm of the people, and the union of all good men—does not the precaution taken of assembling the Senate in this most defensible place—do not the looks and countenances of this venerable body here present—have any effect upon you? Do you not feel that your plans are detected? Do you not see that your conspiracy is already arrested and rendered powerless by the knowledge which everyone here possesses of it?

Here, already, he moves to isolate Catiline from "everyone"— "the people," "all good men," "this venerable body"—and to present his arrogance as so contrary to common sense as to be bewildering and unnatural. He also plays the old trick of presenting as a fait accompli what is, in fact, the nub of the argument, and to give the force of inevitability to something contingent.

During the course of the speech, the audience is said to have visibly moved away to leave Catiline isolated—something Cicero

didn't stint to point out. He also played a clever dialogic trick. Because of Catiline's presence in the room, as Cicero discussed his banishment, an embarrassed silence prevailed—but he turned what could have seemed a setback into a rhetorical victory by asking immediately afterward how his audience would have responded had he called for the exile of two popular senators he named: "before this time the Senate would deservedly have laid violent hands on me, Consul though I be, in this very temple."

After that full-pelt exordium, Cicero moved on to upbraid not Catiline himself, but the senior senators, for their failure to have put him to death long since: "We, we alone—I say it openly—we, the consuls, are wanting in our duty."

He uses a familiar Aristotelian topic of comparison: if Tiberius Gracchus (good chap, nice family, not too far out of line) was rightly put to death by one man, Publius Scipio, can it be right that before the full majesty of the Senate, Catiline—"openly desirous to destroy the whole world with fire and slaughter"—be tolerated? Then the occultatio: *"I pass over older instances, such as how . . ."*

If the first oration against Catiline can be said to have a dominant figure, though, it is the rhetorical question. By the time Cicero reaches his peroration, he has asked something in the order of fifty questions to Catiline—each designed to make his failure to go into voluntary banishment look bizarre and unnatural.

As Cicero explains showily, he himself hesitates to directly order the banishment—because then, he says, not only would he appear cruel and tyrannical but Catiline's coconspirators would still fester in the heart of the city. "But I know that if he arrives at the camp of Manilus to which he is going, there will be no one so stupid as not to see that there has been a conspiracy, no one so hardened as not to confess it." Catiline, in other words, is wedged

firmly between a rock and a hard place. After the detailed evidence Cicero has brought against him, he can hardly stay, but if he goes, he is condemned by his own actions.

Cicero ends with a final address to Catiline, and then with a contrastive apostrophe to Jupiter—effectively putting Catiline's decision to depart under the compulsion of a God. Both these long sentences roll and gather powerfully, even allowing for the distortions of translation. A run of doubled-up terms—the tautological "impious and nefarious," "misfortune and injury," and the hendiadys *"wickedness and atrocity" help inflate his final denunciation of the traitor:*

> *With these omens, O Catiline, be gone to your impious and nefarious war, to the great safety of the republic, to your own misfortune and injury, and to the destruction of those who have joined themselves to you in every wickedness and atrocity. Then do you, O Jupiter, who were consecrated by Romulus with the same auspices as this city, whom we rightly call the stay of this city and empire, repel this man and his companions from your altars and from the other temples—from the houses and walls of the city—from the lives and fortunes of all the citizens; and overwhelm all the enemies of good men, the foes of the republic, the robbers of Italy, men bound together by a treaty and infamous alliance of crimes, dead and alive, with eternal punishments.*

Catiline's attempt to reply was shouted down, and he fled the scene—just as Cicero intended.

Nobody as rebarbative as Cicero, in a state as turbulent as Rome during the first century BC, could expect not to run into trouble sooner or later. Cicero's final comeuppance came after the

assassination of Julius Caesar. As relations with Mark Antony broke down, Cicero moved to open condemnation, delivering no fewer than fourteen Philippics* denouncing Antony. Unfortunately, Antony survived and Cicero was marked for death. One account of it has it that his severed head was brought to where Antony was having supper. Antony's wife Fulvia then took out her hairpins (Antony's biographer Adrian Goldsworthy says that "like every aristocratic Roman woman she affected a fashionably elaborate hairstyle") and stabbed them through the dead man's tongue.

Cicero, then, offers an object lesson for orators in the importance of watching your mouth. But, after all that, what a mouth!

---

*These were so named because he modeled them on Demosthenes's attacks on Philip of Macedon.

THE THIRD PART OF RHETORIC

Style

DECORUM

Most discussions of style over the years have followed Cicero in identifying, at least roughly, three kinds—the high or grand style, the low or plain style, and the middle style.*

Matthew Arnold, discussing the business of translating Homer, wrote: "Alas! The grand style is the last matter in the world for verbal definition to deal with adequately. One may say of it as is said of faith: 'One must feel it in order to know what it is.'" I think he's overfastidious. Roughly: the more "rhetorical" it sounds—the more stuffed with extended metaphors, elaborate verbal patterning, and five-dollar words—the higher the style.

---

*These are sometimes called Asiatic, Attic, and Rhodian: hence "Atticism" and "Asianism" in this book's glossary.

Thus, it's in the high style that Shakespeare's chorus sets the scene in *Henry V*:

> O for a Muse of fire, that would ascend
> The brightest heaven of invention,
> A kingdom for a stage, princes to act
> And monarchs to behold the swelling scene!
> Then should the warlike Harry, like himself,
> Assume the port of Mars; and at his heels,
> Leash'd in like hounds, should famine, sword and fire
> Crouch for employment. But pardon, and gentles all,
> The flat unraised spirits that have dared
> On this unworthy scaffold to bring forth
> So great an object: can this cockpit hold
> The vasty fields of France? or may we cram
> Within this wooden O the very casques
> That did affright the air at Agincourt?

I'd judge Oliver Cromwell's speech dissolving the Second Protectorate in 1658 to be a fair example of the middle style. It conforms to Alexander Pope's definition of simplicity as "the mean between ostentation and rusticity." Here is a certain grandeur of address, but with a flinty, plain-spoken grip:

> God is my witness, I speak it; it is evident to all the world, and all people living, that a new business hath been seeking in the army against the actual settlement made by your own consent. I do not speak to these Gentlemen [gestures with his right hand] or Lords, or whatsoever you will call them; I speak not this to them, but to you. You advised me to run into this place, to be in capacity by your advice, yet, instead of owning a thing

taken for granted, some must have I know not what; and you have not only disjointed yourselves, but the whole nation, which is in likelihood of running into more confusion in these fifteen or sixteen days that you have sat, than it hath been from the rising of the last session to this day.

The plain style—valued for clarity, brevity, and the effect of sincerity—is the one of which, in the twentieth century, George Orwell was both the great champion and the great exemplar:

Modern English, especially written English, is full of bad habits which spread by imitation and which can be avoided if one is willing to take the necessary trouble. If one gets rid of these habits one can think more clearly, and to think clearly is a necessary first step towards political regeneration: so that the fight against bad English is not frivolous and is not the exclusive concern of professional writers. I will come back to this presently, and I hope that by that time the meaning of what I have said here will have become clearer.

Even making allowances for the different periods from which these pieces of writing are taken and the different purposes they serve (dramatic exposition, political debate, and critical essay), I think the fundamental difference in their lines of attack should be pretty clear.

A good orator will hope to have a command of all three—and will be capable where appropriate of mixing them up a bit in a single speech. A narration might ask for the clarity and emotional temper of the plain style, for example, whereas the peroration—where you typically seek to stir your audience—gives the opportunity for a higher style.

In deciding which style to use in a given circumstance, it is *decorum* that shapes your choice. Decorum can be seen as the ethos appeal working at the level of the language itself. Indeed, bracketing decorum under the heading of style is, to some extent, to put the cart before the horse.

As a rhetorical concept, decorum encompasses not only the more obvious features of style, but *kairos*, or the timeliness of a speech, the tone and physical comportment of the speaker, the commonplaces and topics of argument chosen, and so on. It is a giant umbrella concept meaning no more nor less than the fitting of a speech to the temper and expectations of its audience. So not all of decorum comes under the heading of style. But everything there is to say about style has to do with decorum. "Indecorous" may sound like the reproach of a maiden aunt, but we all exercise an intuitive sense of stylistic decorum from the moment we begin to speak: it's at the center of our social being.

Linguists talk about the phenomenon of "accommodation"— which is the way in which we seek to adapt our own language to fit into a speech community. That's how we pick up accents— sometimes to the extent that our interlocutors think they're being mocked—and how we lose them. It's how idioms travel around the world. You may not think of it as the conscious exercise of decorum, but when you write a letter applying for a job, you instinctively know that text-speak and winking-face emoticons are probably not the way to go. Meeting your in-laws for the first time, likewise, you'll tend to rein in the blue jokes. When you're giving evidence in court, you're unlikely to address the judge with "yaknowwhamean?"; and conversely the language you use in court would cause your peer group back on the street to fall about laughing.

The Internet—given that its tribes don't have any geography to mark out their separate identities—sees decorum operating in a dramatically exaggerated way. "Memes"—the in-jokes that circulate online—are part of a whole raft of community-defining trends that behave like passwords: by the time they have leaked out to the wider community, the core community will have adopted new ones. Subcultures spawn languages, and there is decorum to how those languages are used. "1337 haxxors" used to say "w00t! pwned!"* But they stopped as soon as their grannies caught on.

So decorum is, literally, speaking your audience's language. Pomposity is a failure of decorum, as is vulgarity or boastfulness. Shakespeare frequently uses violations of decorum for comic effect, as witness Bottom's muddled attempts at eloquence, Pistol's braggadocio, and Polonius's foolish high-sounding waffle. But in *Henry IV, Part 2*, the poignancy of Falstaff's final appeal to the newly crowned King Henry—"my royal Hal! . . . my sweet boy!"—is that it fails because it is indecorous: he is addressing a dear old drinking buddy, but the person who hears him is a king. Falstaff will never be decorous: and he is cast off.

As I've remarked earlier, the most effective rhetoric is often the least obviously rhetorical. Decorum, therefore, is a tricky quality to instance: when it is there, you don't see it. It is most visible when least present.

---

*Do I really need to explain? Sigh. "l337" is a cute way of spelling "leet," which is an abbreviation of "elite." It means "really good." "Haxxors" are "hackers," i.e., computer programmers. "W00t!" is an all-purpose expression of excitement, i.e., "Hooray!" "Pwned" is a cute way of spelling "owned" (probably a frequent mistype that has been whimsically adopted as orthodox), which is slang for "defeated conclusively."

The best man's speech can provide a caricatured instance of decorum misfiring. A speech suitable for the stag night may not go down so well at the wedding, and decorum is a mobile thing—any good speaker reads his or her audience as he goes along. So if the joke about the groom losing control of his bowels hasn't drawn the laugh you hoped it would, don't plow on assuming that since the joke about the groom sleeping with a prostitute is *even funnier*, the father of the bride won't be able to help bursting his dog collar laughing when you get to it.

P. G. Wodehouse's *Right Ho, Jeeves* offers what is among the funniest instances of a failure of decorum in all of literature. Bertie Wooster's shy friend Gussie Fink-Nottle has been invited to give the prizes at a school speech day in the provincial town of Market Snodsbury. To overcome his shyness, he has imbibed just a bit too heavily. As a result, our narrator observes him "with a smile so fixed and pebble-beached that I should have thought that anybody could have guessed that there sat one in whom the old familiar juice was plashing up against the back of the front teeth."

Gussie is to speak in front of an audience described as follows: "a mixed drove of boys, parents, and what not, the former running a good deal to shiny faces and Eton collars, the latter stressing the black-satin note rather when female, and looking as if their coats were too tight, if male." That is to say, a status-conscious, prim and proper audience of sternly respectable burghers.

To this stiff-necked audience, Gussie blithely but incompetently delivers a ribald joke about two Irishmen, announces, "We are all sorry that the Reverend What-ever-he-was-called should be dying of adenoids," and talks about "shoving along with it" when prompted to get on with it and deliver the prizes.

To the first honoree, he announces, "Well, here's your book. Looks rather bilge to me from a glance at the title page, but, such as it is, here you are." To the second, he says, "Well, here it is, cocky. You off?" And so on.

Quintilian's discussion of decorum picks up some hints from Cicero (whom he commends for brevity and comprehensiveness, seeming "not to have omitted anything when he says that one kind of style cannot suit every cause, or every auditor, or every character, or every occasion") but expands the discussion.

Having acquired the ability of writing and thinking, as well as of speaking extempore when necessity requires, our next study must be to speak with aptitude, an excellence which Cicero shows to be the fourth in elocution and which is indeed, in my opinion, the most important of all. For as the dress of oratory is various and manifold, and different forms of it are suited to different subjects, it will, unless it be thoroughly adapted to things and persons, not only not add luster to our eloquence, but will even destroy the force of it. . . . Of what service will our eloquence be if we adopt a grand style in trivial causes, a poor and constrained style in such as are of high moment, a florid style on grave subjects, a calm style when forcible argument is necessary, a menacing style in deprecation, a submissive style in spirited discussions, and a fierce and violent mode of speaking on topics intended to please?*

---

*There follows an illiberal analogy about transvestites: "The same kind of result would be produced as when men are disfigured with necklaces, pearls, and long robes, which are the ornaments of women, while a triumphal habit (than which nothing can be imagined to add greater majesty to men) is to women but an unbecoming encumbrance." Whatever floats your boat. His larger point holds.

Quintilian goes on to argue, interestingly, that sometimes what might be decorous in practical terms could be unbecoming *sub specie aeternitate*. The instance he gives is that Socrates could have got on the right side of the judge by presenting a humble defense in the plain style, but that Socrates determined to comport himself as one deserving of the highest honors: "He committed himself to the judgment of posterity, and purchased, by the sacrifice of a short portion of extreme old age, a life that will last forever." Most of us will be untroubled by that sort of dilemma: decorum is fitting the language to the task.

JOKES

Humor can be very persuasive. Even Aristotle counseled playing to the gallery to keep an audience lively, advising "what Prodicus called 'slipping in a bit of the fifty-drachma show-lecture for the audience whenever they began to nod,'" and quoting with approval Gorgias's advice "that one must destroy the seriousness of the other with laughter, and their laughter with seriousness."

As I argued fleetingly in my discussion of pathos, the joke can do more than just perk up a drowsing audience. It can be a powerful rhetorical tool. It participates in the pathos appeal inasmuch as it stirs an audience's emotions to laughter—but more importantly, it participates in the ethos appeal, inasmuch as laughter is based on a set of common assumptions. As Edwin Rabbie argues in "Wit and Humour in Roman Rhetoric,"[1] "Jokes usually presuppose (even rest on) a significant amount of shared knowledge."

There's anecdotal evidence of archives of *bons mots* and jokes being collected as early as the fourth century BC, and a Greek joke book called *Philogelos*, "The Laughter-Lover," survives from the fourth or fifth century AD—just as *facetiae* were

collected in the Renaissance and lists of off-the-rack jokes supposedly suitable for best man's speeches proliferate on the Internet. Three books of Cicero's jokes, now lost, were published
after his death by his freedman Tiro.

None of the ancients seemed quite able to agree that any of
the others were funny, however. Cicero and Quintilian, for instance, both regarded the Greek orators in general—and Demosthenes in particular—as unfunny. Quintilian commends Cicero
on "an extraordinary vein of delicate wit," but bitchily adds that
his readiness with a gag damaged the quality-quantity ratio: "I
could wish, too, that his freedman Tiro, or whoever it was that
published the three books of his jests, had been more sparing as
to their number and had used greater judgment in selecting than
industry in gathering."

That Greek jokes fell flat on Latin ears should not surprise us;
Shakespeare's jokes don't cause most modern audiences to fall
about either. The speed with which humor dates is an index of
how closely it is wired into a set of shared assumptions—and
consequently how bound up with an orator's ethos appeal. When
a stand-up puts down a heckler, he has to do so by being funnier:
compelling laughter, very directly, gets the audience on his side.

Cicero adds a perspicacious emphasis on decorum. "We say
these things for a reason," he warns, "not to look funny, but
to achieve something." That something is to win the audience
round. A badly judged joke sends your connection with the audience down in flames.

SOUND EFFECTS

How a piece of rhetoric sounds—and this applies just as much
whether it is heard out loud or scanned by the inner ear while

being read on the page—is vital to its effectiveness. Here, again, we see where rhetoric and poetics share territory. Why does sound matter? It matters in rhetoric for the same reason that it matters in poetry.

W. H. Auden's celebrated definition has it that poetry is "memorable speech," and Auden is right. Poetry comes out of oral tradition, and it has long been suggested that most of the effects of sound and rhythm that characterize formal verse—from the alliterative and stress-based forms of Anglo-Saxon poetry, to end-rhymed classical prosody—originated as devices to make long poems stick in the mind.

Repetition (because rhyme, alliteration, and the tick-tock of a pentameter are all, at root, no more than forms of repetition) makes things memorable, as we know from learning our times tables. Fixed epithets like Homeric formulae—wine-dark seas and rosy-fingered dawns and all the rest of it—are thought to have acted as filler, giving a poet the time to remember or improvise the next few lines while he spiels them out. And repetition in larger narrative structures—as witness the shape of everything from fairytales and myths to *The Gruffalo*—is what makes them seem coherent, memorable, self-achieved, and, in effect, meaningful.

To say that sound matters in rhetoric for the same *reason* that it matters in poetics is not to say that it matters in exactly the same *way*. It was as obvious to Aristotle as it is to you or me that though a speech might—to its advantage—be poetic, it is not delivered in poetry:

> The form of the diction should be neither fully metrical nor completely without rhythm; the former is unconvincing (as it is thought to be artificial), and at the same time it is distracting;

for it makes one expect the recurrence of a similar rhythmic
pattern. . . . On the other hand, the rhythmless is unlimited,
and the speech should be circumscribed but not by meter; for
what is unbounded is unpleasant and unrecognizable. . . . So
the speech must have rhythm, but not meter; otherwise it will
be a poem. But it should not have a precise rhythm.[2]

You can't formulate rules for sound in rhetoric as you can for
regular metrical verse (though some of the vocabulary of the latter can be useful). But you can hear when a sentence is sinuous
and forward-moving, and you can hear when one (intentionally
or otherwise) is cacophonous. The thumping, obdurate stresses
of "blood, sweat, toil and tears" were no accident of rhythm. And
if it was an accident of rhythm that the opening line of the US
Declaration of Independence—"We hold these truths to be self-
evident"—is a perfectly cadenced iambic pentameter . . . well, it
was a happy accident. Good rhetoric uses the bricks and mortar
of poetry, but it doesn't lay its walls as regularly.

When you talk about Churchill's "great rolling periods"—
meaning his long, mellifluous sentences—you are primarily talking about sound effects: the gather and surge of a sentence
toward its climax. Pauses or parentheses may change the flow of
meaning—but they also, often more importantly, change the flow
of sound.

T. S. Eliot once said something to the effect that meaning, in
poetry, is the bone that the burglar throws to the watchdog: the
meaning of a poem is there to distract the conscious mind while
the poem does its real work round the back. The same isn't entirely true of rhetoric—the meaning of a speech is important—
but it is partially true: the sound of a speech works on the mind

and emotions of the audience beneath the conscious level at which the meaning is considered.

That is why the lengths of cola matter—isocolon being a balancing of clauses of the same length: "The louder he talked of his honor, the faster we counted our spoons"—and why a "rising tricolon," strictly defined, is one in which the clauses increase not necessarily in importance but in length: "I came, I saw, I conquered."*

Aristotle notes that ordinary speech is broadly iambic, which is to say that it falls into a *di-dum di-dum di-dum* pattern (this is true of English as well as of Greek). He says that trochaic speech (*dum-di, dum-di, dum-di*) is "too rumbustious" to work in oratory. He suggests that the *paean*—which, helpfully, he describes as a rhythmic unit that "speakers have used from the time of Thrasymachus, but without being able to say which it was"—is the best suited to rhetoric. If what he means is that rhetoric needs to sound right, and good rhetoric always does sound right, and that "sounding right" is impossible to set a definition for . . . well, I concur.

CONTROLLING THE TENSE

Controlling the tense of an argument is a very good way of controlling its direction because it is, essentially, a way of controlling which branch of oratory you find yourself in. A wily speaker will have the capacity to jump back and forth between the judicial and the deliberative branches like an oratorical orangutan.

---

*In Latin, *veni, vidi, vici* is isocolonic. In English, it's a rising tricolon.

If you're uncomfortably on the spot about something in the past, move to the future tense. "Yes. Mistakes have been made, and we're in the process of being bailed out by an IMF loan that our children's children will still be beggared by. But what matters now is that we stop slinging recriminations about, pull together, and set about building a brighter future."

On the other hand, if you're arguing against someone about what to do in the future, find something in the past with which to discredit him. "It's all very well for you to say we need to increase corporation tax to pay off our debt to the IMF. But do you really expect us to take your advice on economics, O'Malley, given that the whole governmental Ponzi scheme that got us here in the first place was your damn-fool idea?"

If you're scared of both the past and the future, having a dismal record in the former and no ideas for the latter, you can always just wallow in the present tense of demonstrative rhetoric. Find something to praise or deplore, and do it in such a way that you draw the tribe together: "Yes. We have our troubles. But the people of Ireland are steadfast in adversity. When I think of this country of ours, this great nation gleaming like an emerald in the Irish sea, I know that there is no place better fixed—no people better fixed—to ride out the storms of a crisis and come safely into the harbor of prosperity. God bless all of us."

In the televised debates between party leaders ahead of the 2010 elections in the UK, incumbent Prime Minister Gordon Brown made the mistake of choosing the wrong tense, and was punished for it.

He was doggedly determined to fight the election on his record—and a broken record was just what he sounded like. The problem was not, or not just, that his record as prime minister

had been compromised by the financial crisis and a series of damaging revelations about his private behavior—it was that it made him sound like a man with nothing to offer for the future.

While his Conservative and Liberal-Democrat opponents talked about the future with the easy optimism of opposition politicians, Mr. Brown relentlessly yoked what he proposed to do in the future to gruff boasts about what he had done in the past.

Asked about immigration, he responded: "When I became prime minister, I did a number of things . . . " Asked about policing, he said, "We've built up the police force from a period when it was understaffed to a period where they now have more police than ever before." Asked about prisons, he said, "At Reading Prison, we've been working . . . " On education: "Since 1997, 1,600 underperforming secondary schools in 1997 went down to 250." On the armed forces: "The important thing is that we're doing the right thing by our troops. And that's why we've increased the spending on equipment dramatically over these last few years."

While there may be a highly respectable intellectual case for stressing a continuity of policy, the rhetorical case for it was very weak: Brown effectively misread the mood of an audience that wanted to feel in control of its destiny. The idea that the future would be ineluctably shaped by the past was exactly what a country that had plunged into recession didn't want to hear.

THE FIGURES

"All the rhetorician's rules," wrote Samuel Butler, "teach but the naming of his tools." The naming of those tools—the figures and tropes—is what gives rhetoric its sometimes opaque-seeming technical vocabulary. But as I'll hope to show, figures and tropes

are essentially very straightforward things that happen to have Greek and Latin names.

The survival of the Greek and Latin names (all rather higgledy-piggledy and overlapping) is a historical accident. As Richard Lanham explains, "The confusion began because Rome was bilingual. The Greek rhetorical terminology put on a Latin doubleture, and then in the Renaissance both sets of terms absorbed the numinosity of classical culture itself."[3] They have come to us, essentially, through persistent linguistic ancestor-worship, and we're stuck with them. No bad thing.

A figure (as in "figure of speech") and a trope, or turn (as in "turn of phrase"), are ways of describing twists of language. They are sometimes called *flores rhetoricae*—"the flowers of rhetoric." The different ways language becomes metaphorical, the different ways it performs, are given names. Think of them in the same way you might think of dance moves. There's more to a dance than a list of moves. But the moves are a good place to start.

Lists of figures—which made up much of the substance of rhetorical handbooks down through the ages—are an attempt to categorize or give a system to the impossibly wide range of things that language can do. As you can imagine, therefore, after hundreds and hundreds of years of handbooks, we inherit not a clinical Excel spreadsheet of neat categories, but a giant soupy mess of overlapping ideas, picky distinctions, dead ends, and redundant terms. That, too, is no bad thing. This is the stuff of language, the stuff of the human mind. Glory in it.

There is a sort-of attempt to make a distinction between figures and tropes—the former operating at the level of a phrase or sentence, and the latter being shifts in meaning for single words. So calling your car, synecdochically, your "wheels" would be a trope, but exclaiming, "Bring me my bow of burning gold! Bring me my

arrows of desire!" would put you into the territory of a larger figure, or "scheme." But in the end, these distinctions are pretty hard
to sustain. When you call soldiers "boots on the ground," for instance, is that not essentially the same thing as calling a car
"wheels"? Those distinctions can safely be left to the theorists.

There's also a distinction sometimes made between figures of
speech and figures of thought. *Reductio ad absurdum*, by this token, would be classed as a figure of thought, whereas *isocolon*—a
sequence of phrases the same length—or *alliteration* would be figures of speech. But that, too, is hard to sustain. Where would you
put *hyperbole*, for instance? Or *chiasmus*? Everything overlaps.

It is a literary-critical commonplace to say that style and
substance can't be disentangled. Every stylistic element of oratory serves a purpose. Figures of antithesis or parallelism may
serve to frame or advance an argument; *apoplanesis** to avoid
one. *Apostrophe*** or *aporia**** or *comprobatio‡* or *argumentum
ad populum‡‡* serve to put the speaker in a given relation with

---

*Evading an issue by digression. You may have noticed it happening on the
news. "Minister, did you or did you not tell a flat lie to the House of Commons?"
"Very interesting you should ask that question. The key issue here, I think we
can all agree, is my campaign to save schools and hospitals."

**Breaking off to address someone or something other than the audience. "Ye
Gods!" is a simple example; it's also seen when someone speaking at a funeral
turns to address the departed. Earl Spencer, at the funeral of Diana, Princess
of Wales, began by addressing the audience but then continued: "Today is our
chance to say thank you for the way you brightened our lives, even though
God granted you but half a life."

***This describes the real or pretended sense of doubt or deliberation, of a
speaker wrestling with himself on the spot. Hamlet is, as you'd expect, heaving
with the stuff. "To be, or not to be . . . " may be the most celebrated aporia in
literary history.

‡Sucking up to the audience, basically. You seldom go wrong with it.

‡‡An appeal to the crowd.

the audience. *Aposiopesis*—a sudden breaking off as if at a loss for words—can be intended to stir pathos. And even where something appears merely decorative—a run of alliteration or a mellifluously turned sentence—it serves to commend the speech more easily to memory, and to give pleasure to the audience. Delight is an end, as well as a means.

So if I'm using the discussion of style to talk about the figures, I do so because it's worth addressing them as a corpus, and here seems as good a place as any—not because they belong in a box marked "style." They pervade everything. The figures are the stuff that rhetoric is made out of, and they give shape to the speech at the level of the paragraph, the sentence, and the word in the same way that the parts of "arrangement" give shape to its larger movement.

You can find a list of the figures, along with explanations and examples, in the glossary at the back of this book (as well as some reminders of other rhetorical terms). That glossary isn't complete—there are hundreds of the flowers of rhetoric in the overstuffed greenhouse of oratory—but it should provide a solid starting point. I've also suggested some thematic groupings, according to nothing more scholarly than my own taste.

CHAMPIONS OF RHETORIC III

Abraham Lincoln
"A Few Appropriate Remarks"

THE SIXTEENTH PRESIDENT OF *the United States of America did not, as you might imagine, speak in a rich chocolaty baritone. He had a high, squeaky voice and a strong Kentucky accent. Nor— coming from a humble background—could he automatically be expected to have a confident grasp of classical rhetoric. That would have mattered. We may think of the American Revolution as a bold and unprecedented new beginning, the casting off of a European yoke, but it would be hard to overstate quite how deeply immersed in the traditions of classical rhetoric the framers of the US Constitution and their inheritors were. Every town in Massachusetts had a grammar school, and from the age of eight,*

pupils there would be taught the classics from eight in the morning until dark fell. Candidates for higher education would be expected to have tracts of Cicero, Virgil, Isocrates, and Homer by heart.

Samuel Adams's master's thesis was "delivered in flawless Latin,"[1] Alexander Hamilton copied Demosthenes into his commonplace book, and Thomas Jefferson modeled his oratory on the prose of Livy, Sallust, and Tacitus. John Adams spent the summer before he became president reading Cicero's essays. Pamphlets and articles were written under classical pseudonyms—Samuel Adams alone was, inter alia, "Clericus Americanus," "Candidus," and "Sincerus." Displaying classical knowledge was a way of demonstrating education and sophistication—it was, if you like, an ethos appeal in itself.

Rome was more than just a literary touchstone: England, in the narrative of the Revolutionary War, was cast as the bloated and corrupt Roman Empire of late antiquity, whereas the founders saw themselves as harking back to the virtues of the Republic. They sought visible symbols of this. Thomas Jefferson built the University of Virginia on strict classical lines, and when the Capitol was to be built in Washington, he insisted that its architecture should see "the adoption of some one of the models of antiquity which have had the approbation of thousands of years."

When George Washington was called "the Father of the Country," that was an echo of what Cato said of Cicero; and Cincinnatus—a plowman who led Rome as dictator but then relinquished his power to return to the fields—was frequently invoked as a spiritual cousin to Washington.

So this was the soil out of which, a generation later, Lincoln's rhetoric was to grow. But as the largely self-educated son of a Kentucky farmer, he wasn't able to tap into the knowingly arcane by-

ways of classical history with which his predecessors were able to signal their patrician credentials. Lincoln was a clever, gangly, pugnacious, provincial lawyer.

His special distinction as a speaker was not to deliver the full-bore, self-consciously Greco-Roman ornamentation of his predecessors. It was to tame those techniques—to yoke classical figures to a crisply vernacular style, and to offset his intermittent stylistic flourishes with a folksy swoop down to a register where he all but claps the individual audience member on the shoulder.

In the "House Divided" speech, with which Lincoln accepted the Illinois Republican Party's nomination to run for the Senate, Lincoln talks the audience through the history of the argument so far—could the union make sense with some states countenancing slavery and others free?—in an absolutely plain and straightforward way, wryly dramatizing it as you might dramatize an argument between friends. "Then opened the roar of loose declaration in favor of 'Squatter Sovereignty.' . . . 'But,' said opposition members, 'let us be more specific.' . . . The election came, Mr. Buchanan was elected, and the endorsement, such as it was, was secured. . . . At length, a squabble springs up . . ."

Seeking to avert civil war, in his First Inaugural Address, Lincoln spoke in the same way—reasonable-sounding and without pomp: "I add too, that all the protection which, consistently with the Constitution and the laws, can be given, will be cheerfully given to all the States when lawfully demanded, for whatever cause—as cheerfully to one section as to another." Note the studied impression of a mind at work: the sense of "and another thing," the naturalness of the qualifying parentheses, and the amiable excellence of "cheerfully"—yet all in a sentence whose clauses build and interlock artfully in both sound and sense, moving from "laws" to "lawfully," "all" to "all," "given" to "given," "cheerfully" to "cheerfully."

The peroration to that same speech is not blood and thunder, but an antithesis so intimate in tone—charged with such feeling—its effect is still startling: "I am loath to close. We are not enemies, but friends. We must not be enemies."

The widely agreed pinnacle of Lincoln's rhetorical achievement was the speech now known as the "Gettysburg Address"—delivered on November 19, 1863, at the dedication of the graveyard for the Union dead after the battle of Gettysburg in the Civil War.

As any student of American history ought to know, though, Lincoln did not deliver the official Gettysburg address. The honor of that fell to Edward Everett, a distinguished classicist then regarded as one of the greatest orators America had ever seen—now, all but forgotten.

Lincoln was sixth on the bill—making "Dedicatory Remarks" after music from Birgfield's Band and the Marine Band, a prayer, a hymn, and the main speaker. Lincoln, in other words, was the supporting act. He was asked along, relatively late in the day and more or less informally, to make "a few appropriate remarks" after Edward Everett's oration.

It's a pretty good testament to the transformative power of rhetoric that Gettysburg remains so hallowed in the annals of American history. A turning point though it may have been in the war, it wasn't exactly a flawless demonstration of military prowess. The battle itself started by accident: four Confederate infantry brigades had set out on a foraging expedition after rumors had reached them that a warehouse full of shoes was to be found somewhere in the area. When they bumbled into the 1st Cavalry division of the Union Army, it all kicked off.

After a long and bloody encounter in which something like 50,000 casualties were incurred, the Union troops routed the Confederates—but then squandered the best opportunity they'd

yet had to smash General Lee's army decisively. With thousands of corpses festering in the summer sun, the cleanup operation was horrific, and the local lawyer who oversaw it, David Wills, "meant to dedicate the ground that would hold them even before the corpses were moved. He felt the need for artful words to sweeten the poisoned air of Gettysburg."[2]

It was not to Lincoln he turned. Nor, indeed, originally to Edward Everett—who came on board only after three eminent poets (Longfellow, Whittier, and Bryant) had turned the gig down. But Everett was well qualified: universally revered, and a dab hand at battlefields, he'd already played Concord, Lexington, and Bunker Hill.

Speech-making is a practical as well as a spiritual affair. Everett spent months preparing—researching the battle in journalistic detail, which amid the fog of war was no mean task, then polishing and memorizing his speech. There were more mundane practical preparations to make too: at sixty-nine, Everett suffered from prostate problems and had to ensure there was a special pee-tent right by the stage where he could relieve himself immediately before and immediately after his speech.

The great man, suitably eased, spoke for over two hours—a rolling classical speech that evoked Pericles's funeral oration during the Peloponnesian War, and likened the dead of Gettysburg to the fallen soldiers at Marathon while running back over the events of the battle itself in minute detail.

Lincoln—whose hat was still circled by a black mourning band in honor of his dead son—spoke for a couple of minutes, and delivered 250-odd words. But those "few appropriate remarks"— delivered to an audience of between 10,000 and 20,000 people— remain probably the single most influential piece of rhetoric in American history.

Four score and seven years ago our fathers brought forth on this continent a new nation, conceived in liberty, and dedicated to the proposition that all men are created equal.

Now we are engaged in a great civil war, testing whether that nation, or any nation, so conceived and so dedicated, can long endure. We are met on a great battle-field of that war. We have come to dedicate a portion of that field, as a final resting place for those who here gave their lives that that nation might live. It is altogether fitting and proper that we should do this.

But, in a larger sense, we cannot dedicate . . . we cannot consecrate . . . we cannot hallow this ground. The brave men, living and dead, who struggled here, have consecrated it, far above our poor power to add or detract. The world will little note, nor long remember what we say here, but it can never forget what they did here.

It is for us the living, rather, to be dedicated here to the unfinished work which they who fought here have thus far so nobly advanced. It is rather for us to be here dedicated to the great task remaining before us—that from these honored dead we take increased devotion to that cause for which they gave the last full measure of devotion—that we here highly resolve that these dead shall not have died in vain—that this nation, under God, shall have a new birth of freedom—and that government of the people, by the people, for the people, shall not perish from the earth.

I've mentioned that Lincoln was a late addition to the bill. That said, the president himself didn't treat the occasion as offhandedly as posterity has sometimes had it. Lincoln had a strong sense of the importance of the Gettysburg dedication as war propaganda—not to mention having one eye on upcoming elec-

tions in Pennsylvania whose outcome might have an indirect effect on his own reelection campaign.

He was determined enough to be there that, even with his wife near-hysterical with grief over the recent death of their son, he made a point of leaving Washington a day early to make sure he got there. He was wise to do so. Had he taken the train his staff originally booked him for, he'd have missed the ceremony altogether.

Likewise, though myth has it variously that the speech was scribbled on a bit of cardboard, composed in Lincoln's head while Everett droned on, or literally written on the back of an envelope, the chances are that Lincoln paid rather more attention to it than that.

Lincoln was, by habit, a slow and careful polisher of his speeches. It stretches plausibility to the breaking point that he would have decided to deliver one as important as this off the cuff. He was also an accomplished actor, who loved to declaim Shakespeare aloud. He thought about delivery as well as about composition. The care with which he was thinking about it in advance is evidenced by the fact that, a few days before, he asked the man who landscaped the cemetery to bring him the plans, so he could familiarize himself with the layout of where he'd be speaking.

The speech, like the myth of its offhandedness, is one thing that appears another. It is an absolute masterpiece of the plain style. It is fiercely well patterned in almost every phrase—"government of the people, by the people, for the people," its most resonant coinage, manages to be tricolonic, zeugmatic, and epistrophic all at the same time—yet sounds clear as day.

The particulars of the battle and the politics behind it are barely alluded to—there's no mention of the Union or of Gettysburg; no

honoring of the particular dead; there are no proper nouns, and no descriptive adjectives. And look at the modest, talky straightforwardness of phrases like, "It is altogether fitting and proper that we should do this."

Yet underneath it is a web of muscle. Sentence is bound to sentence with repeated words—"conceive," "dedicate," "consecrate"—and with the antitheses of "we" and "they," "living" and "dead." Its shape is guided by the image of birth, death, and rebirth: the birth of a nation, the death of its soldiers, and the "new birth" of liberty that comes out of it.

The speech's very abstraction gives it its strength: it has the gnomic, exemplary force of parts of the Bible (not to mention the conscious Biblical echo with which it opens). Also, as scholars have pointed out, it follows exactly—whether consciously or not—the shape of a classic Attic funeral oration: it begins by praising the dead and aligning them with noble ancestors; it asks those present to temper their mourning with knowledge of the great deeds that the dead have done; and it enjoins the living to carry on the work that has yet to be done.

So though it looks like a polar opposite of the speech that went before it—Everett verbose and ornate where Lincoln was clipped; Everett concrete where Lincoln was abstract—it is a modification rather than a rebuke. Everett was showily classical, but Lincoln's classicism purrs powerfully under the hood.

The historian Garry Wills's view that Everett's speech was "obsolete within a half-hour of the time when it was spoken" seems to me a little over the top. Lincoln set a new standard for political oratory, but he didn't abolish what went before—and the high style is still visible in Lincoln's successors. More nuanced and more revealing is Wills's other remark—that "Everett's clas-

sicism was as much the forerunner of Lincoln's talk as its foil or contrast."

Lincoln's speech was a political as well as a literary tour de force, and what was really clever about it—not to mention cheeky—was that he used it, in effect, to game the Constitution. He used the emotional force of the occasion, channeled through his rhetoric, to quietly shift the political ground and redefine the casus belli in a way that suited him.

> Four score and seven years ago our fathers brought forth on this continent a new nation, conceived in liberty, and dedicated to the proposition that all men are created equal. Now we are engaged in a great civil war, testing whether that nation, or any nation, so conceived and so dedicated, can long endure.

Good luck—in the face of words so forceful—to the pedant who squawked: "Hey! Swizz! No we aren't! That's not the proposition to which the nation's dedicated—and that's not what we're testing!" By the time Lincoln finished his speech, like it or not, that was the proposition and that was what was being tested.

The point here was that the Declaration of Independence contained the phrase "all men are created equal," whereas the American Constitution itself, albeit in weasel words, expressly allowed slavery. The Civil War was being fought in the hopes of keeping the Union together and upholding the Constitution—not for the abolition of what Southerners liked to call "the peculiar institution." But by appealing to the spirit of the Constitution rather than its letter—or, rather more bluntly, by simply acting as if the Constitution had been framed in the spirit of the Declaration of Independence—Lincoln shifted the ground.

Without mentioning slavery at all, Lincoln had subtly, retrospectively made its abolition the cause for which the Civil War was being fought. Garry Wills describes the speech as "a giant (if benign) swindle" and says, "Everyone in that vast throng of thousands was having his or her intellectual pocket picked."***

Here was logos—sinuous old rhetorical logos—cleverly spinning the pathos of an occasion to establish a commanding set of facts on the ground. That speech turned an equivocal, a provisional victory on the field of battle—thanks to the alchemic power of Lincoln's words—into a turning point in the history of American liberty.

Or did it? Readers of The Times *in London were told that what was otherwise an "imposing ceremony" was "rendered ludicrous by some of the luckless sallies of that poor President Lincoln."*

You cannot, as even the victors at Gettysburg discovered, win them all.

---

*You could see less elegant versions of this sort of rhetorical maneuver, incidentally, taking place in the aftermath of the coalition's invasion of Iraq. When the WMD, the original casus belli, failed to materialize, supporters of the war were to be heard retrospectively claiming the incident for a liberal intervention against tyranny, or talking up supposed links between Saddam and al-Qaeda.

**Some of them noticed, too. "The cheek of every American must tingle with shame as he reads the silly, flat and dishwatery utterances of the man who has to be pointed out to intelligent foreigners as the President of the United States," reported the *Chicago Times*, adding: "It was to uphold this constitution, and the Union created by it, that our officers and soldiers gave their lives at Gettysburg. How dare he, then, standing on their graves, misstate the cause for which they died, and libel the statesmen who founded the government? They were men possessing too much self-respect to declare that negroes were their equals, or were entitled to equal privileges."

THE FOURTH PART OF RHETORIC

Memory

MEMORY? I HEAR YOU ask. Eh? What's *that* got to do with it? Well, historically, it has rather a lot to do with it. Before the age of the teleprompter and the earpiece and the PowerPoint demonstration—before, indeed, the age of cheap paper and pencils on which a speaker might make notes, let alone write a whole script—memory was vital to the orator's art.

If you couldn't remember what you were going to say, how were you to say it? We've all witnessed with embarrassment the off-the-cuff speaker crashing and burning at a wedding, or the panicky TV presenter "drying" on air.

We're pretty impressed these days if someone can speak fluently without notes for half an hour—David Cameron's decision to abandon his notes for his first address to Conservative Party Conference as leader, for instance, was reported with some reverence.

But in centuries past, pulpit preachers, rabble-rousers at political rallies, parliamentarians, and lawyers would be expected

to thunder on—sometimes literally for hours—without a shred of a note.

In the first place, the very fact that we're impressed when people speak without notes is a recommendation for the art of memory. Even if you have an autocue or a fistful of notes, the point at which you appear to abandon them is the point at which you capture your audience: you appear to be speaking to them, rather than at them.

Sprezzatura—that quality of life and spontaneity in a speech—is the thing to aim for. And it is seldom achieved without practice. So memory, as it matters in rhetoric, is not simply about rote learning any more than oratory is about recitation. It is about allowing the elements of the speech, and the ideas behind it, to inhabit your mind so that what's being delivered arises freshly and naturally from your thoughts.

A command of the material—including the arguments against as well as for his or her own position—is what allows the speaker to adapt a speech to the mood of the audience, to engage with counterarguments that are raised, and to move from one point to another with the ease of someone traveling through well-known territory.

Public speaking, like writing, is in many ways a confidence trick. Why do so many people—capable of delivering whole paragraphs of coherent argument in one-on-one conversation—falter when asked to speak in public? "My mind's gone blank," they say.

If you've ever delivered a speech yourself, you'll know that it's in the first few moments that you know if it's going to work. As the audience digests your first few words, and you relax into it, you realize that the rest of the speech is at your command. It is *available* to your memory. The first step shows you the second; the second the third; and by the time you've hit the third,

you can see the fourth and fifth clear ahead of you in sequence. You'll feel free to ad-lib in the confidence that you can return to your thread.

But when it goes wrong, the feeling is not one of incompetence, but of blankness: panic begets panic, and you turn away from the audience and into your own head, trying to find the words—your mind churning at the active attempt to recall and recite when, with confidence, what you know you need to say could and should spring to mind without conscious effort.

Not for nothing was Mnemosyne, the goddess of memory, regarded by the ancients as the "mother of the muses."* We don't make art or literature from nothing, but from the memory of all the art and literature we've encountered, filtered through an individual consciousness that is, itself, little more than the sum of a set of memories. Memory is not a dispensable resource that can be outsourced to USB sticks or even libraries; memory is the stuff we think with.

The poet Robert Lowell, giving a reading, once said, "Memory is genius"—and if we allow our understanding of "genius" to encompass not just its thin modern sense of "brilliance," but the idea of a presiding spirit, as in *genius loci*,** I think his words take on an even more valuable resonance.

That idea of genius loci—the spirit of a place—comes as a happy accident. For how do we think of memory? Overwhelmingly, our metaphors are spatial. Even in the paragraphs above, for instance, it seemed natural to talk about traveling through a speech "step by step," or of traveling through "well-known territory."

---

*That wasn't a figure of speech—or wasn't just a figure of speech. In mythology, she gave birth to the nine muses after nine consecutive nights of passion with Zeus.
**The "spirit of a place" is how the phrase is usually translated.

When we can't remember something, we say, "I've lost it" or "Sorry, it's gone."

Invention, as I mentioned above, has as its etymological root the idea of "coming upon" the available grounds for argument. And there again—"grounds." The "topics"—*topoi* in the Greek—are, literally, *places*. No translation is required, either, to see the spatial implications of "commonplaces."

This seems to reflect something about how the mind actually works.

Have you ever noticed how, if you're trying to find a quotation in a book you've read, you may have no idea which section it came in or where it figured in the flow of the discussion, but you will almost always have a sense of where it was on the page, and whether on a left- or a right-hand page? Playing the game of Pelmanism—where players are asked to remember the positions of particular cards in a pack spread out facedown—you can be surprised by how quickly you are able to remember where a given card is. A fascinating 1978 study[1] by two neuroscientists seemed to point to how this might be. The seat of memory, they argued, was the same part of the brain that dealt with spatial awareness: the hippocampus.

The ancients weren't big on neuroscience. But they were big on memory—and the idea of using spatiality as a way of training memory goes all the way back to them. The Elder Seneca, it was said, could reel off two thousand names he'd just heard, and recite two hundred random lines of verse backward—feats no doubt corroborated at the time by someone who had grown bored waiting for the invention of daytime television.

Lucius Scipio knew the names of all the Roman people, and King Cyrus of Persia could name all the soldiers in his army—which as well as being an impressive feat of memory (he had a

big army) was an ethos-enhancing party trick that retains its value to this day. When a politician shakes your hand (and, in all probability, grips your elbow with his other hand), he'll use your name a bit more than is quite comfortable.

There was a philosopher called Charmadas who, it was said, could recite the contents of any volumes in libraries that anyone asked him to quote, just as if he were reading them. It was of Charmadas that Cicero reported, "[He] used to say that he wrote down things he wanted to remember in certain 'localities' in his possession by means of images, just as if he were inscribing letters on wax."[2]

Even given the elements of exaggeration and myth-making in these accounts, it's clear what a premium was placed on the training of the memory. It is memory, says Quintilian, that has "exalted eloquence to its present luster."[3]

The original Mr. Memory—at least according to the ancient sources—was Simonides of Ceos, who lived circa 556–468 BC and is credited by both Quintilian and Cicero with being the first to teach an "art of memory." Simonides was a poet for hire, who had been commissioned to sing an ode in celebration of some high-up or other—Cicero has it as a Thessalonian nobleman called Scopas, though Quintilian simply has it as an anonymous "pugilist" who'd just won a famous victory. He showed up as promised, and delivered his panegyric—but in the course of it, he included a decorative digression, as might have been quite normal practice, in praise of the twin demigods Castor and Pollux.

Rather than being flattered by his association with Castor and Pollux, Scopas (or whoever it was) used this as an excuse to withhold half of Simonides's fee. He maintained that since he'd had to share his praise-poem with the twins, if Simonides wanted the

balance, he could apply to them for it. One imagines a lot of guf-
fawing from his drunken, boorish guests.

Anyway, a bit later the dejected poet received a message that
there were two men waiting for him outside the party. Off he
went to find out what they wanted—but when he left the house,
the two men were nowhere to be seen. While he was outside,
however, in a development that can be regarded either as divine
intervention or poetic justice,* the roof over the banqueting hall
collapsed, crushing Scopas and all his guests to death.

When the time came for the relatives of the dead to bury them,
there was a certain amount of confusion—what with all the man-
gled body parts and unidentifiably squished faces (squished, presumably, into the position of quite literally laughing on the other
side). But Simonides, gracious in vindication, was able to help out.
He was able to recall the exact position at which every single person at the banquet had been sitting—and so was perfectly able to
reunite the bodies and parts of bodies with their grieving relatives.

Cicero reports Simonides realizing that "the best aid to clear-
ness of memory consists in orderly arrangement . . . that persons
desiring to train this faculty must select localities and form mental images of the facts they wish to remember and store those
images in the localities . . . and we shall employ the localities
and the images respectively as a wax writing tablet** and the let-

---

*Quintilian's version remarks drily that "the deities were not ungrateful to him."
**The idea of memory as a wax tablet, incidentally, isn't original to Cicero. It
was first suggested by Plato in his *Theaetetus*: "Let us suppose that every man
has in his mind a block of wax of various qualities, the gift of Memory, the
mother of the Muses; and on this he receives the seal or stamp of those sensa-
tions and perceptions which he wishes to remember. That which he succeeds
in stamping is remembered and known by him as long as the impression lasts;
but that, of which the impression is rubbed out or imperfectly made, is forgotten, and not known."

ters written on it." What he is describing is what gets called the "method of loci" or, colloquially, the "memory palace": which is, with only a few variations, the canonical method for fixing the artificial memory from that day to this.*

And there's a significant point to be noted in Cicero's description. The notion of the wax tablet indicates that the would-be mnemonist uses a fixed structure—a locality real or imagined, but instantly and intimately available to the mind's eye—as its background and that the exercise of memory depends on juxtaposing the temporary thing to be remembered with that.

The figures in the foreground—ideally, vibrant images that have a strong symbolic connection to the phrases or ideas they are intended to evoke—come and go as required. The memory palace is a set of hooks, on which memories are deliberately hung as required and removed when done with.

Since the palace is the permanent thing, Quintilian says you need to get it right. You should choose a space of "the greatest possible extent, diversified by considerable variety, such as a large house, for example, divided into many apartments," for the rather obvious reason that you don't want to run out of space.

A detailed classical treatment of the method of loci is to be found in *Ad Herennium*, and it expands on this point—making a clear distinction between the background and foreground images and explaining the relation between them.

Memory, which the book's author describes as "the treasure-house of the ideas supplied by Invention . . . the guardian of all

---

*A 2009 paper in the neuropsychology journal *Neurocase*, "A Slice of Pi: An Exploratory Neuroimaging Study of Digit Encoding and Retrieval in a Superior Memorist," described tests on a subject who had used the method of loci to memorize π to more than 2^{16} decimal places. That's 65,536 decimal places—but they only put him in the MRI scanner for the first 540 . . .

the parts of rhetoric,"[4] is treated as Aristotle treated eloquence: a faculty of nature that is capable of being improved by art.

> The artificial memory includes backgrounds and images. . . . We shall need to study with special care the backgrounds we have adopted so that they may cling lastingly in our memory, for the images, like letters, are effaced when we make no use of them, but the backgrounds, like wax tablets, should abide.

Ad Herennium is actually—and, to me, fascinatingly—almost insanely specific about how these backgrounds should be arranged in the mind's eye. The author wants something uncluttered. He favors a deserted area to a populous one, so as to avoid passersby crowding and weakening the images—as if to suggest that if you were to choose Times Square for your memory palace, the crowds in the real Times Square would somehow impinge to damage your memory.

He seems to prefer clean lines, but warns that the backgrounds should nevertheless differ in shape and form (a series of intercolumnar spaces—I imagine a long cloister, from his description—will provoke confusion because too alike), and suggests that confusion can be avoided by marking off every fifth background space with a golden hand, and having "an acquaintance whose name is Decimus" loiter in every tenth one.

The next bit—because it seems to me to speak of an inner eye so well developed as to be different in kind from our own— is worth quoting in full:

> These backgrounds ought to be of moderate size and medium extent, for when excessively large they render the images vague,

and when too small often seem incapable of receiving an arrangement of images. Then the backgrounds ought to be neither too bright nor too dim, so that the shadows may not obscure the images nor the lustre make them glitter. I believe that the intervals between backgrounds should be of moderate extent, approximately thirty feet; for, like the external eye, so the inner eye of thought is less powerful when you have moved the object of sight too near or too far away. [5]

Yow! Stage lighting? Camera positions for the inner eye? Measurements in feet? I think this is just astonishing—because it is offered as the sort of practical stage-management advice that a modern person would never think of applying to something entirely imaginary.*

Anyway, the anonymous author—long thought to be Cicero,** but you knew that already—goes further in coming up with a f'rinstance. Again, I'll give you the passage straight:

---

*Except, oddly enough, to people like the team at Pixar making computer-generated 3-D movies. They use virtual cameras—imaginary cameras, essentially, made of math; shooting imaginary characters, also made of math—whose lens physics is faithful to the real world.

**There was a textual mare's nest for scholars to unpick thanks to this: centuries of convention and scholarship rested on the medieval conviction that *De Inventione* and *Ad Herennium* were the *First* and *Second Rhetorics of Tullius*, and that you could therefore read across and synthesize them. Worse, because Cicero includes memory under "Prudence" in *De Inventione*, and this gets picked up by Thomas Aquinas who relates it to the cardinal Christian virtue of Prudence, mnemotechnics gets folded into a whole Christian moral schema—which leads some scholars to wonder whether Dante's circles of Heaven and Hell were, in fact, memory palaces. All of this is a salutary lesson in the way tottering edifices of theology can be built on a small textual misunderstanding. Aquinas Christianized *Ad Herennium*, partly misunderstood it—misreading "solitude" for "solicitude," thus accidentally discovering a devotional aspect in it—and became the patron saint of medieval mnemotechnics.

For example, the prosecutor has said that the defendant killed a
man by poison, has charged that the motive for the crime was
an inheritance, and declared that there are many witnesses and
accessories to this act. If in order to facilitate our defense we
wish to remember this first point, we shall in our first background form an image of the whole matter. We shall picture
the man in question as lying ill in bed, if we know his person. If
we do not know him, we shall yet take someone to be our in-
valid, but a man of the lowest class, so that he may come to
mind at once. And we shall place the defendant at the bedside,
holding in his right hand a cup, and in his left tablets, and on
the fourth finger ram's testicles. In this way we can record the
man who was poisoned, the inheritance, and the witnesses.[6]

Wha—? Ram's testicles? Balancing on his finger? Naww . . .

More scholarly commentators than me have suggested an
explanation. "Ram's testicles" is a Roman pun—*testes* refers to
the witnesses in the case—while the cup suggests poison and
the tablets a will. The reason they're balanced on the fourth
digit like horrible finger puppets—and here I can do no more
than repeat what I'm told—is that some classical anatomists believed that a nerve extended from the heart to the fourth finger
of the left hand, known as the *digitus medicinalis*.

This bizarre image—it is, we'd have to admit, memorable—
was splendidly misunderstood by the time it reached the Middle Ages. The great theologian Albertus Magnus (c. 1193–1280)
repeated it in the manner of a man half-remembering something while tipsy:

For example, if we wish to record what is brought against us in
a law-suit, we should imagine some ram, with huge horns and

testicles, coming towards us in the darkness. The horns will
bring to memory our adversaries, and the testicles the disposi-
tions of the witnesses.

And in his *De Memoria Artificiali*, Thomas Bradwardine,
mathematician, theologian, and (for all of about a month before
he dropped dead in 1349) Archbishop of Canterbury, had a similar problem with (forgive me) bollocks:

> Suppose that someone must memorize the twelve zodiacal signs:
> that is the ram, the bull etc. So he should make for himself in the
> front of the first location a very white ram standing up and rear-
> ing on his hind feet with (if you like) golden horns. Likewise one
> places a very red bull to the right of the ram, kicking the ram
> with his rear feet; standing erect, the ram then with his right foot
> kicks the bull above his large and super-swollen testicles, causing
> a copious infusion of blood. And by means of the testicles one
> will recall that it is a bull, not a castrated ox or a cow.

If things got a bit hinky in the Middle Ages, then, they nevertheless kept memory front and center. St. Augustine—who in
his *Confessions* writes, "I came to the fields and spacious palaces
of memory"—gave memory the honor of being one of the three
faculties of the soul. Memory, Understanding, and Will, he said,
were the image of the Trinity in man.

Thomas Aquinas, who studied under Albertus Magnus and
was renowned for having a word-perfect recollection of everything he read, outlined four precepts for memory:

1) Invent a "convenient similitude" of the things to be
   remembered

2) Put them in a considered order
3) Cleave with affection to them*
4) Meditate frequently on them

It's plausibly suggested that mnemotechnics may have had an influence on medieval paintings—in terms of the artificial arrangements of figures and the extensive use of personification—and on the use of illuminated manuscripts. Hugh of St. Victor, in the twelfth century, said that "it is a great value for fixing a memory-image . . . the color, shape, position and placement of the letters." It's even proposed that the grotesques in medieval art may have been influenced by *Ad Herennium*'s advice on the use of outlandish images to nail an idea in memory.

Going into the Renaissance, artificial memory continued as big business. A fabulous huckster and self-publicist called Peter of Ravenna—trained as a jurist in Padua—claimed to know by heart two hundred speeches of Cicero, three hundred sayings of philosophers, and 20,000 legal points, as well as the whole of the canon law, both text and gloss.

It's worth saying that locative memory—though most startling in its results and most intriguing in the hints it gives about neuropsychology—isn't the only game in town. The number of modern actors who use a formal method of loci to remember their lines, I daresay, isn't that high, for instance—and not everyone in the ancient world went along with it.

---

*Here we seem to see the "solitude"/"solicitude" error in action. You weren't to go somewhere quiet to memorize your lines; you had to love them. And yet there again, the *Neurocase* paper I cite above on the prodigious memorizer of π describes how the subject's "self-report indicates that imagining affective situations and high emotional content is critical for successful recall."

Quintilian, even as he tips the hat to loci, expresses reservations—wondering whether, being so visual, it was quite so useful for memorizing ideas as it was for objects. He prefers mnemonics "of a simpler nature" for learning speeches—advocating something closer to rote learning, though in manageable chunks: "It will be of advantage to learn it in parts, for the memory sinks under a vast burden laid on it at once." He adds that hard work is involved—"the tedium of going through what has often been written and read, and of masticating repeatedly, as it were, the same food."

The scholar of memory Frances A. Yates—a firm Quintilian fan, who praises him as "an eminently sensible man and a very good educator"—is amusingly cynical about mnemotechnics:

> The objection to the classical art which was always raised throughout its subsequent history—and is still raised by everyone who is told of it—was voiced in antiquity. There were inert or lazy or unskilled people in Cicero's time who took the common sense view, to which, personally, I heartily subscribe—as explained earlier I am a historian only of the art, not a practitioner of it—that all these places and images would only bury under a heap of rubble whatever little one does remember naturally.[7]

Her analysis is, implicitly, backed up by the commonsense advice of Gyles Brandreth, author of the twentieth-century rhetorical handbook *The Complete Public Speaker* (Sheldon Press, 1983). He recommends the use of notes, but says that "by the time you rise to make your speech you will be so familiar with what you want to say that you won't need to read it. You may

need notes to keep you on the right track, but they should only consist of bald headings."

He adds that the memory will improve with practice at public speaking—and quotes A. P. Herbert by way of consolation for the speaker who has reached the end of his speech and forgotten one of his main points: "If you forget what you are going to say, it may be a good thing."

The useful advice most commonly given to the inexperienced public speaker, after that business about imagining your audience in their underwear, is: write out your speech; read it over and over; break it down into sections a paragraph or two long; give each section a bullet-point heading and write those headings on a card or a series of cards. Deliver the speech, in a practice run, from the cards. Then for the main event carry the cards. Don't use them unless you have to.

Nevertheless, the idea of using loci for artificial memory was at the center of formal education in rhetoric for centuries. And if all the preceding seems remote from the present day, it need not be. The Internet, aspiring as it does to store all human data in linked "sites," can easily be seen as a sort of communal memory palace of marvelous efficiency and range: an imaginary geography of knowledge to which we all have access.

The method of loci isn't a museum piece on the personal level either. The distinguished historian Tony Judt, who died in mid-2010 of motor neuron disease, used it to compose essays after his degenerative disease robbed him of the ability to move. He created a "memory chalet"—using as his background the layout of the chalet in Switzerland where he stayed on skiing holidays with his parents as a child.

To honor Tony Judt's memory, so to speak, let's build a memory palace right here. Let's say you want to remember ten ani-

mals: elephant, giraffe, cow, duck, bison, echidna,* sheep, praying mantis, ladybug, and tabby cat.

Think of your own house. Picture it in your mind's eye. Fish your keys out of your pocket and open the front door. Walk in. Close it behind you. Now, plop that elephant down there behind it, just on the scuffed bit where the door opens.

Move down to where you normally leave your coat. Hang up the giraffe—its chin will go over the hook comfortably enough. Right. Wave it goodbye and go into the kitchen. The cow will go in the fridge—top compartment in the door, where you're supposed to put eggs but never do. And . . . yes, pop the duck just under the kitchen sink. Move those bottles of bleach out of the way. Ignore its irritable quacking as you close the cupboard door.

Let's back out and go up the stairs, dropping the bison on the half-landing as you go past. It can patrol there with its big old horns, deterring burglars and such. Now, up and on. Bathroom first. Pictured it in your head? Where better for an echidna than in the bath? Watch it curl up into a little ball at the tap end. What if it's cold? Let's leave it the sheep for company.

Right! Out! Give them some privacy, for crying out loud. Go into your bedroom. Pick the praying mantis up, very carefully—respecting his dignity—and place him on top of the vanity mirror on the dressing table, looking out into the room, rubbing his green arms together as he surveys the scene.

The ladybug's tiny, so easily lost. Place her on your white pillow, where her red-and-black wings will stand out. And, finally, hoof the tabby cat right into the middle of the duvet where, happy as a cat can be, she'll turn three times round before settling in to sleep with a purr of satisfaction.

---

*Also known as a spiny anteater.

Now, snap your fingers and magic yourself back out to the street in front of the house. Can you remember those ten animals? I bet you can. If you're having trouble, just walk yourself back through the house. Now—wax-tablet-style—wipe it clean.

Vanish the animals—and go through this time putting in those particular places the numbers one to ten, or members of your family, or favorite Bob Dylan albums, or points you want to make in your defense at your forthcoming sentencing hearing. Walk back through. Is that *Blood on the Tracks* sharing the bath with *Shot of Love*? Why, so it is.

There. You've built your own memory palace—or "memory semi," as I'd urge you to think of it. At any rate, you are on the memory property ladder.

CHAMPIONS OF RHETORIC IV

Hitler and Churchill

APPLYING THE PRAISE-WORD *"champion"* to Adolf Hitler feels a bit odd, and I don't wish to be needlessly provocative. But given that men whose evil intentions meet or even outstrip that of the Nazi leader can be found all over the place, we ought to ask what it was about him that sent him rocketing to his current place in the league table: how did those intentions come to be put so horribly into effect?

The answer, as historians tell us, has to do with a perfect storm of place, time, personality, and luck: but it also has to do with his brilliance as an orator. That Hitler fits snugly with his nemesis Winston Churchill is a historical accident. But then, historical accident comes into their story. Churchill's preeminence,

too, was a product of place, time, personality, luck, and oratorical command. And both men had, in one sense, the same job. For a political leader to rally his country during wartime is one of the ultimate tests of the ethos appeal.

The recognition of this suffuses the speech note Churchill wrote for a Secret Session of the Commons in June 1940: "Lastly, say a word about ourselves. How the new government was formed. Tell the story Chamberlain's actions. Imperative there should be loyalty, union among men who have joined hands. Otherwise no means of standing the shocks and strains which are coming. I have a right to depend loyalty . . . "*

As a wartime leader, you need to make yourself both of and above your audience. You need to stress the identity of their interests with yours, to create unity in a common purpose. You need, therefore, to cast yourself as the ideal exemplar of all that is best and most determined and most courageous in your people.

Churchill

By the end of his career, the story of Churchill's oratory—as set out in David Cannadine's introduction to a collection of Churchill's speeches[1]—can be told in statistics and lists. The full edition of his speeches runs to eight volumes and more than four million words. Between 1900 and 1955, he gave, on average, one speech a week.

Among the phrases he minted were "blood, toil, tears, and sweat," "their finest hour," "the few," "the end of the beginning," "business as usual," "iron curtain," "summit meeting," and "peaceful coexistence."

---

*Churchill's words have the crunched syntax of a note to himself.

But even if, as Cannadine contends, "Speech was the very fibre of his being," that's not to say that it proceeded in any natural way from that being. He never learned to speak off the cuff—and when he tried, at the age of thirty, the occasion was an unmitigated disaster. Churchill was not a "natural orator" any more than Cicero was. As F. E. Smith unkindly put it, "Winston has spent the best years of his life writing impromptu speeches."

Churchill's mastery was the product of determined hard work. His orotund style was rooted in a classical world refracted through the English historians of the eighteenth and nineteenth centuries: the expansively melodious sentences of Gibbon and the sharp contrasts of Macaulay, both of whom he had read while soldiering in India. As he recalled in My Early Life, "I got into my bones the essential structure of the ordinary British sentence— which is a noble thing."

To shape himself as an orator he learned by heart the speeches of Disraeli, Gladstone, Cromwell, Burke, and Pitt. Churchill combined their example with his father Randolph's gift for invective. But he added something of his own—and it was this that helped tether his high style to something more conversational. He was a master of the sudden change of register—a joke, or a phrase of unexpected intimacy.

As Harold Nicolson put it, he had a combination of "great flights of oratory with sudden swoops into the intimate and the conversational." One sure way to keep your audience engaged is to surprise it—and, when you have been thundering at it from a podium, to surprise it by descending to give it a gentle tug at the sleeve is the mark of a virtuoso.

He spent hour upon hour working on drafts of his speeches— indeed, he devoted fully six weeks to preparing his first major

speech in the House of Commons. His scripts—for that is what they were—were meticulously detailed, and came complete with stage directions. His drafts look almost like poetry—broken up with line breaks indicating where to pause.

Nervous to the point of nausea before addressing an audience, Churchill consulted specialists as a young man in the hopes of ridding himself of his speech defects. He had both a stammer and a lisp, and was set to reciting, "The Spanish ships I cannot see them, for they are not in sight" in order to overcome them.

He rehearsed his speeches—gestures and all—in front of a mirror until he got them right. When, one day, his butler overheard him thundering away from his bathtub, he approached to see what the matter was. "I wasn't talking to you," said Sir Winston irritably, "I was addressing the House of Commons." (One likes to imagine him pressing home his point with a well-aimed rubber duck.)

"The flowers of rhetoric were hothouse plants," Churchill wrote in his 1899 novel Savrola, *and he included in that book an account of a politician preparing a speech that seems closely to anticipate his own practice:*

> *Instinctively he alliterated. . . . That was a point; could not tautology exaggerate it? . . . What a game it was! . . . Presently he rose, and, completely under the influence of his own thoughts and language, began to pace the room with short strides, speaking to himself in a low voice and with great emphasis. Suddenly he stopped, and with a strange violence his hand descended on the table. It was the end of the speech.*

That sense of inward concentration, of a rapture "completely under the influence of his own thoughts," gives something of

the idea of how a speaker might inhabit, or be inhabited by, his speech. Churchill liked to play martial music while he prepared speeches, the better to kindle that vital emotion in himself that he hoped to communicate to the crowd.

What Disraeli said of Gladstone was also true of Churchill: he was "a sophisticated rhetorician, inebriated with the exuberance of his own verbosity." More dangerously, it was felt by many that the exuberance—the sheer play of language—could overcome the less thrilling but more valuable quality of judgment. In this, if you want to look at it in a certain way, you could say that the mix of epideictic to deliberative, like the mix of whisky to water, strayed on the high side with Churchill. The liberal politician Charles Masterman warned that "he can convince himself of almost every truth if it is once allowed thus to start on its wild career through his rhetorical machinery."

His rolling periods impressed his audiences, but if the chief object of rhetoric is to persuade, Churchill's didn't—much of the time—do that. When he was an MP in 1935, his colleague Herbert Samuel reported, "The House always crowds in to hear him. It listens and admires. It laughs when he would have it laugh, and it trembles when he would have it tremble . . . but it remains unconvinced, and in the end it votes against him."

What was it that didn't work? Perhaps that he did not always seem to judge his audience right—a failure of ethos. The House of Commons gives itself to a dialogic style—to, at its best, a deft pattern of call-and-response across the despatch box. Churchill came in with the equivalent of a loudhailer: delivering clumping great set pieces that occasioned Balfour's famous taunt that his artillery was "powerful but not very mobile." He was, if you like, presidential where he should have been parliamentary—a complaint that

has not infrequently been made of his successor, the great wartime premier Tony Blair.

Of course, there are times when powerful fixed artillery is just what you need. The thing about Churchill was that, like the stopped clock that's right twice a day, he occupied one position and waited for the world to come to him. He spent much of his political career predicting the imminent end of Western civilization—and it was only by the damnedest good luck that it happened to be on his watch that it suddenly appeared to be coming about. If not, he might have been remembered as a self-aggrandizing windbag with an old-fashioned speaking style and a love of the sound of his own voice.

But when the country really was under threat, Churchill's fierce certainties were what an anxious audience wanted, while his style—steeped in the language of the previous centuries— seemed to encapsulate the very traditions that he was exhorting them to fight for. What at another time might have been faults became rhetorical strengths. That, you could say, is kairos *writ large.*

Churchill consciously marshaled, as the best orators will, not only the language of the past but its history to his cause— invoking Drake and Nelson as exemplars and, implicitly, allies in the struggle. Churchill's Elizabethanism was, surely, comforting in the context of war and a national identity under threat: it evoked what was at stake, but also conveyed the idea (one with which Churchill was personally intoxicated) that here was an actual turning point of history, the meeting of great historical forces in a fight to the death.

One of the ways of harnessing that feeling of connectedness to history, as we'll see later in the discussion of American political

rhetoric, is to borrow and repurpose the resonant phrases of the past. This differs from ordinary plagiarism in that to be detected— subliminally at least—is half the point. Echoes of orators past are a way of taking possession of them—of implying that you are channeling those orators and all they represent.

So when in 1940 Churchill told Parliament that "never in the field of human conflict was so much owed by so many to so few" he was quoting himself—the phrase was one that he was reported to have used, in the grip of considerable emotion—after visiting an RAF operations room during the Battle of Britain a few days beforehand. But as the historian Andrew Roberts has pointed out,[2] he was also adapting and improving, whether consciously or not, Sir John Moore's line on the capture of Corsica in 1793: "Never was so much done by so few men."

That process continued. George W. Bush is known to have installed a bust of Churchill in the Oval Office.* It wasn't all he installed. When in October 2001, Bush announced the commencement of the war in Afghanistan with the words, "We will not waver, we will not tire, we will not falter, and we will not fail," he was adapting himself. In his address to Congress on September 20, he had said: "We will not tire, we will not falter, and we will not fail." Both of those phrases, though, go back to Churchill— and the climax of the 1941 radio address in which he declared, "We shall not fail or falter; we shall not weaken or tire . . . Give us the tools and we will finish the job."

Bush, or his speechwriters, drew resonance from Churchill's phrase but adapted it to their own purposes. Bush is anaphoric where Churchill favors parallelism. "Fail," "falter," "weaken," and

---

*The bust was removed by his successor, Barack Obama.

"tire" work more or less as synonyms,* meaning the usage is an instance of the pleasingly named figure called synathroesmus, or what Puttenham calls the "Heaping Figure." Bush's first bash at it was a tricolon; the second a four-part construction—and note the added force given the construction by pleonasmus, the grammatically superfluous repetition of "will not . . . will not . . . will not . . . will not."

David Cannadine describes very well the way Churchill's style conveyed his ethos—and in doing so implicitly makes a good point about the wider issue of naturalness. You can be, and Churchill often was, off-putting to your audience by being yourself. But you will find it very hard indeed to pretend to be someone else entirely. The orator works with what he's got, and being convicted of bad faith is far more damaging than being unconvincing in good faith.

"He . . . spoke in the language he did," Cannadine writes, "because it vividly and directly reflected the kind of person he himself actually was . . . a character at once simple, ardent, innocent, and incapable of deception or intrigue, yet also a character larger than life, romantic, chivalrous, heroic, great-hearted, and highly colored."**

---

*If you're going to look really closely at it, you could note that Churchill uses the term "fail" differently than Bush. Its position at the beginning of the list of terms suggests he's using it in the sense of "failing strength," rather than in the sense of failing to accomplish an objective. In Bush's formulation "fail" gets an additional torque from its connotative congruence with the previous terms— but where they describe the determination of America's forces, it seems to talk about their effect in the world. Churchill's rhetoric here is primarily about endurance; Bush's about the implacable projection of force. Watch out, baddies.

**There are dissenting views to this account of Churchill's character, it should be said. His enthusiasm for using poison gas on restive colonials and his contemptuous dismissal of Gandhi count against him in the chivalrous and heroic stakes.

This was the character that, it seems, Britain wanted to both lead and incarnate its resistance to Hitler. But even then, things weren't quite as clear-cut as posterity would have it. The initial reaction to even some of his most celebrated speeches was muted or hostile.

In May 1940, the civil servant Jock Colville recorded in his diary how one of the private secretaries at Number 10 Downing Street responded to the "fight on the beaches" speech. "Blasted rhetoric," he complained. "He is still thinking of his books." Again, he gives shape to the idea that Churchill had an eye on posterity and a wider literary audience, rather than the Commons: that he was, effectively, pleasing himself.

After the "finest hour" speech, the Tory politician Charles Waterhouse reported, "He was not on his best form. He was inclined to be hesitant to start with and introduced some rather cheap jibes and jeers which seemed to me ill-suited to the gravity of the moment."

The story is told—no doubt Waterhouse would have loved it—that after "fight on the beaches," Churchill had continued, "We'll throw bottles at the bastards, it's about all we've got left," but that the censor buzzed it out.

One of the virtues of Churchill's wartime rhetoric, however, was that whatever his peers in the House of Commons thought, he was able to speak—as politicians a generation before had not been able to—directly to the public through the wireless.

After delivering many of his key speeches in the Commons, Churchill read them out on the radio. Here, that presidential style—all that gruffness and avuncularity, all those rumbling climaxes—was able to take full effect without being interrupted by rustling order papers and barracking Opposition MPs. He was pure voice.

Hitler

In private, Hitler was an awkward and unprepossessing character. He had the peculiar quirk of some accomplished public speakers of finding it nearly impossible to address two people in a private room, but the easiest thing in the world to appear in front of tens of thousands at a rally.

He was under no illusions, though, of the value of doing the latter. When Churchill said, "Words are the only things which last forever," he and Hitler were in broad agreement. Churchill seems to mean that the words themselves will last forever, to redound to his own glory. Hitler was an instrumentalist—and in that, perhaps more of a rhetorician. The words were a means to an end. He wanted what the words would bring about, that is, his Reich, to last forever—or at least a thousand years.

He was quite plain about it in Mein Kampf:

> *The power which has always started the greatest religious and political avalanches in history has been, from time immemorial, none but the magic power of the word, and that alone. Particularly the broad masses of the people can be moved only by the power of speech. . . . Only a storm of hot passion can turn the destinies of peoples, and he alone can arouse passion who bears it within himself.*

In a way, as with Churchill, his public voice at the peak of his accomplishment was no more than the harnessing and turning outward of a private style. The tirade was Hitler's dominant note. Where Churchill rumbled—with occasional sharp interventions of humor or domesticity—Hitler shouted. But shouting in itself is

an appeal both to ethos and pathos—it betokens a conviction that overwhelms the speaker's control; it throws him, weirdly, on the mercy of his audience because it creates the impression that artifice has evaporated under the pressure of feeling. A high-risk strategy, but one that can be thrillingly effective if the audience buys it: if you can fake sincerity, as the man said, you got it made.

Hitler was a ranter from way back. In 1920, during his bohemian phase, he was a party guest at the Munich house of a composer, Clemens von Franckenstein. He showed up in a floppy hat, and carrying a riding whip (it was a prop: he didn't know how to ride), which he cracked on his boots from time to time to impress the other guests. It didn't work. One of them described him as looking like a waiter.

When he started conversing though, "He went on at us like a division chaplain in the army. I got the impression of basic stupidity." Soon, those present recalled, the prevailing feeling was of being stuck in a railway carriage with a lunatic. Unfortunately—and in much the same way as Churchill, though it may be bad taste to insist on the parallel—by the mid-1930s that lunatic's time had come.

His rants, too, were somewhat more under control than they might have looked. He wrote his own speeches in the early years—but later moved on to dictating them to secretaries. Those secretaries were expected to get them down verbatim, while he delivered them as he would to an eventual audience. Traudl Junge, the young secretary whose memoir of the last days in the Fuhrerbunker formed the basis for the film Downfall, recalled him composing the speech he gave to mark the tenth anniversary of his dictatorship. He started out mumbling almost inaudibly, and pacing up and down, but by the time his speech reached its crescendo he had his back to her and was yelling at the wall.

These drafts would be worked over and over until he was happy with the whole performance. Like Churchill, he would practice his speeches in front of a mirror, and he was near-obsessive about choreographing every detail in advance—right down to scouting the acoustics of the venue. And as every school-child knows, he was deeply interested in the theatrics of setting, too: flags, massed ranks, dramatic lighting, and martial music. He would be the centerpiece, but the flummery surrounding him was vital to the whole effect.

The American journalist Virginia Cowles described his arrival at a rally:

> As the time for the Fuhrer's arrival drew near, the crowd grew restless. The minutes passed and the wait seemed interminable. Suddenly the beat of the drums increased and three motorcycles with yellow standards fluttering from their windshields raced through the gates. A minute later a fleet of black cars rolled swiftly into the arena: in one of them, standing in the front seat, his hand outstretched in the Nazi salute, was Hitler.

Hitler was, as is well known, a genius at the rhetorical use of not talking. The typical opening to a really corking Adolf Hitler speech is " . . . " It could go on for anything up to half a minute, which is (you'll know if you've tried it) a very, very long time to stand on a stage without saying or doing anything. When he started—which he'd typically do while the applause was still fading out, causing the audience to prick up its ears the more—he would do so at a slow pace and in a deep voice. The ranting was something he built up to, taking the audience with him.

He preferred to speak in the evening, believing that "in the morning and during the day it seems that the power of the human

will rebels with its strongest energy against any attempt to impose upon it the will or opinion of another. On the other hand, in the evening it easily succumbs to the domination of a stronger will." Thus speaks a man who got his start launching his Putsches *from beer halls.*

He's said to have picked up acting tips from a favorite Bavarian comedian, Weiss-Ferdl.* He learned to turn his distinctive accent and strident, harsh voice to advantage, and—though he was quite capable of genuine hysterical rages—he also had the trick of turning them on and off at will. There's a telling story from Ribbentrop's secretary, Reinhard Spitzy, about an occasion when, while entertaining guests, Hitler learned that a British diplomat had arrived to see him. "Don't let him in yet," Hitler told the servant who had answered the door, "I'm still in a good mood." Before the eyes of his guests, Hitler worked himself up into a purple-faced rage, then made his excuses and went to meet the diplomat. He returned to the room in due course, full of smiles and chuckles. "He thinks I'm furious!" he told them.**

Hitler combined a mesmeric power over crowds with a profound contempt for them. "The masses are like an animal that obeys its instincts," he is claimed to have told Hermann Rauschning. "They do not reach conclusions by reasoning. . . . At a mass meeting, thought is eliminated."

But the importance of understanding that instinctive animal—of aligning yourself with it—was something he didn't underestimate

---

*Weiss-Ferdl had a sense of humor about the Fuhrer too. In the course of his cabaret act in Munich, he would produce a whole armful of framed portraits of the Nazi leadership and muse aloud, "I don't know whether to hang them or put them up against the wall."

**Churchill, though in rather a less alarming way, permitted himself the same sort of wink at the wings. After one particularly stirring speech, he's said to have muttered, "That got the sods, didn't it?"

either. He once commended Lloyd George on his *"positively amazing knowledge of the broad masses of the people,"* and aspired to the same thing himself. While other senior Nazis went about festooned with ribbons and medals,* Hitler always dressed in a plain uniform, the only adornment being the Iron Cross First Class that he had won in 1914. That medal, let it be noted, is a token of bravery, not of rank.

Here's how he opened his address to laborers at the Siemens Dynamo Works in Berlin in 1933:

> German compatriots, my German workers, if today I am speaking to you and to millions of other German workers, I have a greater right to be doing this than anybody else. Once I stood amongst you. For four and a half years of war, I was in your midst. And through diligence, learning—and, I have to say, hunger—I slowly worked my way up. Deep inside me, I always remained what I had been before. . . .
>
> They [Germans] should see that what I am saying is not the speech of a Chancellor, but that the whole people stands behind it as one man, man for man, woman for woman. What is bound together today is the German people itself. . . . You can see me as the man who does not belong to any class, to any caste, who is above all that. I have nothing but a connection to the German people.

That is a virtuosic ethos appeal—and one carefully directed at an audience that might be assumed, being made up of blue-collar

---

*A mistake other dictators never seem to learn from. Just look at the late Colonel Gaddafi. Ugh. Kim Jong-il, in his funny little jumpsuit, was probably as savvy as they get.

workers, to be natural sympathizers with trade unions and parties of the Left: a hostile audience, in other words.

But here Hitler addresses them in a way that is a mixture of the paternal and the fraternal. He has fought alongside them, suffered alongside them—"hunger" calls to mind the food shortages—and now he is there as their leader and protector. He openly asserts his right to speak, and the indivisibility of their interests from his. The idea that there may be competing class interests within the German polity—the sort of idea that Marx might have promulgated—is firmly nixed.

The Nazi commonplace "Ein Volk, ein Reich, ein Fuhrer"—*"One people, one nation, one leader"—is a rhetorical maxim as well as a more narrowly political one. What, after all, is an orator trying to do but corral his audience into unanimity: to make them one?*

Compare Elizabeth I's speech to her troops at Tilbury in 1588, as they prepared to face the Spanish Armada. She makes a point of inverting her relationship with her audience, casting herself as dependent on her people: "Let tyrants fear; I have always so behaved myself that, under God, I have placed my chiefest strength and safeguard in the loyal hearts and good will of my subjects." That speech ends with a great set of rhetorical fireworks leading up to a ringing tricolon—and one that asserts the organic unity of the nation under God:

> *Not doubting by your obedience to my general, by your concord in the camp, and by your valor in the field, we shall shortly have a famous victory over the enemies of my God, of my kingdom, and of my people.*

It's notable that some people took the view that the Fuhrer was possessed by that other expert orator, the devil. Two British

attendees at a 1934 stadium rally in Berlin, seated just behind Hitler, reported that he was whipping his audience into the usual spittle-flecked frenzy when "an amazing thing happened. . . . [We] both saw a blue flash of lightning come out of Hitler's back. . . . We were surprised that those of us close behind Hitler had not all been struck dead."[3] It was, after a considered post-match discussion, the opinion of these observers that this was no mere epiphenomenon of his apocryphally vegetarian diet: the German Reichskanzler was indeed, from time to time, in the thrall of Satan. In ordinary life, as Wyndham Lewis remarked, "a more prosaic person it would be difficult to find."

Strive though theorists have since ancient times to naturalize the connection between oratory and civic virtue, Hitler is a good instance of the extent to which they have failed. Rhetoric's effectiveness is, in the final analysis, independent of its moral content or that of its users. And this is one reason why the more good guys get clued into how it works, the better off we will all be.

THE FIFTH PART OF RHETORIC

Delivery

THE PROOF, AS WE all know, is in the pudding, and the show isn't over until the fat lady sings. Delivery is the pudding, the singing lady, of the rhetorical world. Here is where the carefully crafted piece of rhetoric—rock-solid in ethos, sinuous in logos, heart-tugging in pathos—actually meets its audience. And everything is still in the balance. Anyone who's seen a bad actor butcher Shakespeare or a good one breathe life into the most leaden of sitcom dialogue knows that a text doesn't live until it's spoken.

I'll for the most part be referring, in this chapter, to spoken rhetoric. But let it not be thought that delivery isn't important to rhetoric on the page. If your Dear John letter is printed in purple Comic Sans and sent by second-class post, it may not have quite the same effect on its heartbroken recipient as if it is written by hand—or, for that matter, spoken in person with a kindly and regretful tone.

Everybody involved with the printed word knows how enormously the details of font, type size, and pagination affect how readable a piece of writing is, what tone it conveys to the eye, and what sort of ethos it projects.

The dense type in the small print of a contract both conveys authority and discourages scrutiny. The letter written to a newspaper—as the cliché rightly has it—in green ballpoint pen on file paper inclines an editor to think the sender loony, while the self-same text typed on creamy paper and signed with a fountain pen will like as not whistle into the lead slot of the letters to the editor. The *samizdat* look of a photocopied and home-designed flyer for a band conveys a certain message to the hipster into whose hand it is pressed.

I have long nursed a pet theory that the very profitable and successful satirical magazine *Private Eye* continues to be printed on flimsy paper because it helps to connote the antiestablishment, homemade spirit in which it was founded . . . and because it subliminally discourages libel plaintiffs by giving the impression that there's no money there to be had in damages.

In most cases, with written rhetoric, the writer is remote from his or her audience so the dialogic aspect of the exchange is different. The audience's reaction is anticipated and hopefully shaped by the writer, but it can't be taken into account during the event. A writer "reads" his audience in advance, not in real time. So if you're nodding off at this point, there's nothing I can do about it. Likewise, if a particular joke makes you laugh, I can't decide extempore to riff on it further.

For someone giving a speech in person, however, reading the audience is a constant process. Where do they laugh? Do they look bored? Am I going too fast? Can they hear me? Did someone just walk out? Is my ex-wife here? *Yikes*, my ex-wife *is* here! And so on.

Cicero's first oration against Catiline, discussed in my chapter on Cicero, offers a master class in using the situation of the speech for the stuff of it: he addresses half the speech to Catiline himself, and he uses the audience's reaction—its embarrassed silences and its reluctance to sit next to the guilty man—as the fuel for his attack. But even where you aren't interacting with the audience as directly and dynamically as that, you need constantly to remember that you are talking *to* an audience or *with* an audience, never *at* an audience.

Though Aristotle doesn't include a detailed study of delivery in his *Rhetoric*, he does note its importance—greater, in his account, than both the style and the substance of a speech. Experts in the arts of delivery, he says, "more or less carry off the prizes at the contests, and just as in the case of tragedy actors now have more effect than the poets, so it is also in political contests, through the baseness of the citizenry."

Just as he wishes that logos alone, among the persuasive appeals, were effective, Aristotle acknowledges the overriding importance of delivery only as a regrettable fact of the world as we find it. But since rhetoric is a *technè*—an instrumental skill designed to bring about results—he knows that it deals with the world as we find it, not as we would like it to be.

The most eminent Attic practitioners were in agreement. According to Quintilian, when Demosthenes was asked what the most important skill was in the whole art of oratory, he said, "Delivery." Asked what came second, he said, "Delivery." In third place? "Delivery."*

---

*This is what might be called the "Fight Club joke," after the first and second rules of Fight Club in the book of the same name.

The question of delivery—it's called *actio* in Latin and *hypokrisis* in Greek—is traditionally subdivided into control of the voice and control of physical gesture. For most of history, where amplification was impossible and speeches were expected to go on for much longer than they do now, being in control of your voice was not simply a question of mastering your intonations. An orator's voice needed to be trained and looked after no less carefully than an opera singer's.

Once the voice is properly trained—capable of sustaining volume and clarity—it needs to be modulated with judgment. Cicero warns in *De Oratore*, "I would not have the letters drawlingly expressed; I would not have them negligently slubbered over; I would not have words dropped from one in a dry, spiritless manner; I would not have them spoken with puffing and swelling."

The difference that delivery can make to a speech is attested to by Philip Collins, a former speechwriter for Tony Blair. Writing in *The Times*,[1] he compared John F. Kennedy's inauguration speech with Barack Obama's address in Tucson, Arizona, after the attempted assassination of congresswoman Gabrielle Giffords.

> Read JFK's 1961 text out loud and it will sound pretty good. Now try the same with Mr. Obama's Tucson speech. Unless you can emulate the way that Mr. Obama lets his consonants slide before hitting the crucial word, it will sound flat. Mr. Obama's public speaking is much more like singing than it is like talking. It's an idiom directly out of the black American churches.

A nice way with sliding consonants has been a winner since before the birth of Christ. The handbook *Ad Herennium*, for instance, advises careful control of pace and variation of tone:

Pauses strengthen the voice. They also render the thoughts more clear-cut by separating them, and leave the hearer time to think. Relaxation from a continuous full tone conserves the voice, and the variety gives extreme pleasure to the hearer too, since now the conversational tone holds the attention and now the full voice rouses it. Sharp exclamation injures the voice and likewise jars the hearer, for it has about it something ignoble, suited rather to feminine outcry than to manly dignity in speaking.

Just as style may vary according to where you are in the speech, so will the delivery. *Ad Herennium* recommends "for the Introduction a voice as calm and composed as possible," for instance. Under the heading of "Flexibility" it divides the registers of voice into "Conversational Tone" ("relaxed and close to daily speech"—suitable for your exordium and digression), "Tone of Debate" ("energetic, and suited to both proof and refutation") and the "Tone of Amplification," which "either rouses the hearer to wrath or moves him to pity."

There follow several pages of splendidly detailed discussion of the different aspects of each, in terms that will be quite recognizable to the modern reader. But the idea that you begin calmly and build up—think of the way an epic ranter like Hitler started slowly before cranking himself into a frenzy—is little more than common sense. The metaphor that you want to "take the audience with you" is an apt one: the laws of inertia say that anything as big and heavy as an audience accelerates from a standing start slowly; but when it really gets moving, there's no stopping it.

Likewise, that tone should vary without clashing and be euphonious without being soporific is pretty unexceptionable advice. To this we could add that the bald lies ("I shall be brief")

and uncomfortable truths ("Unaccustomed as I am to public speaking") with which most amateur oratory is prefaced are best dispensed with.

For most of those of us who really are unaccustomed to speaking in public, probably the single most important point about delivery is *pace*. Most people, particularly when nervous, talk too fast. Slowing . . . it . . . down . . . until . . . it's . . . on . . . the . . . verge . . . of . . . feeling . . . unbearable . . . is just about the way to go. A key expositor of the modern-day handbook tradition, Gyles Brandreth,[2] identifies "a comfortable speed" as 110 words per minute—"just a shade slower than in ordinary conversation," though it's as well to bear in mind that what to the audience will sound "a shade slower" probably *feels* positively treacly to the speaker.

When it comes to physical gestures, Brandreth has sensible advice for the modern rhetor too. "Most of us take little notice of our hands," he writes, "until, that is, we have to speak in public, and then they appear uncommonly large and obtrusive." He counsels against the folded arms and hands-in-pockets look, and recommends instead resting one's hands lightly on either side of the podium (if there is one, and it's at chest-height), or—if at a table or on a stage—clasping them lightly together in front of the waist.

He advises, contra accepted wisdom, that letting your hands hang loosely by your sides "looks too false" (we might add that it feels almost unbearably unnatural, and that the attempt to hold them there will almost certainly result in some involuntary swinging back and forth better suited to the diving board than the board meeting), and that only Prince Philip can really get away with clasping his hands behind his back (*nota bene*, Prince Charles).

As for mannerisms, he says, "the basic rule is . . . *avoid them altogether.*" Fiddling with props, twiddling a cuff-button, rotating a wedding ring, or tugging at an earlobe will all distract the audience from what you're actually saying. If these are unconscious, they need to be consciously expunged. If they are deliberate . . . well, it's time to deliberate again.

If this sort of detailed consideration of how the speaker physically positions himself seems over the top, it is as nothing to the efforts of quite my favorite theorist of gesture, John Bulwer.

Bulwer (c. 1606–1656) was the first person to make a systematic attempt to catalogue and explain hand gestures: to produce, if you like, a dictionary and grammar of them. His masterwork was 1644's *Chirologia . . . Chironomia.*[3]

Believing that sign language is universal (he was wrong about this, as it happens) Bulwer wrote that "being the only speech that is natural to Man, it may well be called the Tongue and generall language of Humane Nature, which, without teaching, men in all regions of the habitable world doe at the first sight most easily understand."

Bulwer was of the firm view—and it is one entirely in line with what the classical authorities have to say about style and delivery—that what nature provides, art can improve. Scorning the idea that "gestures are perfect enough by nature," he writes, "we see many in both sacred and profane places so preposterously and ill-favoredly expressing their minds that 'tis a wonder how any eye can behold them with attention. Certainly, men polished with humanity cannot, without loathing, behold the prevarications of such dirty and slovenly orators."

So he embarked on a heroic if slightly demented attempt to systematize the whole range of human gestures, from the highest to the most earthly—and he did so in a formidably scholarly

way. *Chirologia*, the first book, was—as it were—analytic: it sought to describe and analyze the hand gestures found in nature. Its companion volume, *Chironomia*, is a handbook* of sorts, setting out to show how gestures might be turned to rhetorical use through art.

Bulwer, as I say, is some scholar. He cites works from 158 historians, poets, and rhetoricians in support of his arguments. *Chirologia* navigates by the Bible, Plutarch, Tacitus, and Xenophon, while *Chironomia*'s guiding lights are Quintilian, Cicero, and the Bible (again). Bulwer favors classical sources, though not slavishly. And what is, to my mind, utterly brilliant about his book is that it is *illustrated*.

It is one of the standing tragedies of Western letters that Bulwer died before he was able to complete his proposed sequel: a two-part magnum opus, to be entitled *Cephalelogia . . . Cephalenomia*, on the gestures of the head. That he left us *Dactylogia* ("The Dialects of the Fingers") is a shred of comfort, at least.

Chironomia—which, being the hands-on** part, is the one that concerns us most—is divided into four parts:

1) "The Canons of Rhetoricians Touching the Artificial Managing of the Hand in Speaking." In this section Bulwer looks at the larger gestures conveying the gross emotions: shame, refusal, demandingness, etc. He identifies no fewer than forty-nine gestures, of which twenty-four are illustrated.
2) "Indignatio: Or, The Canons of the Fingers." Here come the more refined concepts for which finger work is

---

*Ha ha!
**Ha ha!

necessary—the numbering off of arguments, the contrasting of points, and so forth. There are thirty-four such gestures of which, again, twenty-four are shown in the accompanying woodcuts.

3) "The Apocrypha of Action: Or, Certain Prevarications Against the Rule of Rhetorical Decorum." This is Bulwer's blooper reel—a compendium of instances of What Not to Do. Naturally, it is the most compelling of the lot. He firmly cautions against gesturing with the elbows, clapping the hands ("a gesture too plebeian and theatrically light for the hands of any prudent rhetorician"), or waving the arms wildly. "The trembling hand is scenical and belongs more to the theatre than the forum," he sniffs. "To denounce with a high hand, or to erect a finger to its utmost possibility of extension is a blemish in the hand of an orator," he rebukes us.

4) "Certain Cautionary Notions" is a section in which Bulwer points* to a few basic principles—much as discussions of vocal delivery tend to do—such as aptness, timing, variety, and so forth.

Bulwer, as well he might be, was a fantastic cheerleader for the efficacy of the hand gesture. The hand, he writes, is "the substitute and viceregent of the tongue" and "the spokesman of the body." Gesture, he tells us, is "the very palm** and crown of eloquence"—as anyone who has ever been saluted by a disgruntled commuter on a Los Angeles freeway will know.

---

*Ha ha!
**Boom boom!

When you actually look at the hand gestures described with such precision by Bulwer, you see an awful lot that is recognizable and familiar. Take this, for instance: "To bring the hand to the mouth, and having kissed it, to throw it from us . . . their expression who would present their service, love and respect to any that are distant from them." That is the blowing of a kiss, isn't it? Or this: "The middle finger put forth and brandished in extent is an action fit to brand and upbraid men with sloth, effeminacy and notorious vices . . . vulgarly *Higa* . . . the putting forth of the middle finger, the rest drawn into a fist on each side . . . a natural expression of scorn and contempt." That is what we now call "flipping the bird."

As well as being so abundantly charming, *Chirologia . . . Chironomia* has a properly interesting place in the history of rhetoric, and sensible things to say about it. For, much as an encyclopedic catalogue of gestures sounds contrived, its founding idea is quite the opposite: that art can do nothing if it doesn't have nature as its foundation. "Shun affectation," wrote Bulwer, "for all affectation is odious; and then others are most moved with our actions when they perceive all things to flow, as it were out of the liquid current of nature."

That is not, I would suggest, simply good advice when it comes to hand gestures. It is as much as to affirm that when delivering anything from a State of the Union address to a show-and-tell in your primary school science lesson, you need not only to fit your delivery to your audience, you need to fit it to yourself. Bad faith, insincerity, playacting, or—yes—"rhetoric" will always torpedo your connection with an audience. Work with what you've got. Be yourself.

That the Greek word for delivery, *hypokrisis*, is also the word for acting, points us back to Bulwer's insight. Both rhetoric and

acting are nature by art modified. The "method" school of acting has always asked its practitioners not to impersonate the
characters they portray, but to inhabit those characters. Rhetoric likewise: Tony Blair's effectiveness as a speaker came from
the overwhelming impression that, even when he contradicted
himself, at the moment he spoke a given sentence, he believed it
in his very sinew. When Bill Clinton said, "Ah feel your pain," he
made you think he truly believed it—even if nobody else did.
This is at the root of the most optimistic accounts of rhetoric:
that the ideal orator is a man in whom eloquence is the conduit
of true feeling and good intention.

The idea, then, that the connection between oratory and acting is in some way disreputable—that the orator is a fraudulent
wearer of masks—gets things a little upside-down. The two have
always had a relationship—and the best of both spring from a
common source.

To all the rules you might devise for delivery, there are exceptions. "Never laugh at your own jokes" is usually good advice.
The Scottish comedian Billy Connolly, with magnificent success,
defies it: he can scarcely deliver the punch lines of some of his
jokes, so speechless with mirth is he, but he has the quality of
laughing genuinely and infectiously, and he takes the audience
with him.

And remember: even the professionals die on stage from
time to time. According to Diogenes Laertes, when Plato first
read his dialogue "On the Soul," every single member of the audience got bored and left except for Aristotle.* And as a young

---

*This is, when you think about it, a bit like the theory that only about three
people bought the Velvet Underground's first album, but that everyone who
did started a band.

man, the future emperor Claudius had trouble getting through his first public reading because a fat man crashed through several benches and gave Claudius the giggles so badly he kept interrupting his own speech.

The best advice remains: be yourself—but that injunction, as the commerce between rhetorical delivery and acting suggests, can be unpacked. The good speaker *plays* himself—and does so using the total immersion technique of a dedicated method actor. "Good delivery," as the author of *Ad Herennium* tells us, "ensures that what the orator is saying seems to come from his heart." Fool yourself first, and the audience will follow.

Finally, be mindful that, though nobody wants to hear you announce, "I shall be brief," they will want you actually to *be* brief.

The American preacher Jenkin Lloyd Jones warned, "A speech is a solemn responsibility. The man who makes a bad thirty-minute speech to two hundred people wastes only a half hour of his own time. But he wastes one hundred hours of the audience's time—more than four days—which should be a hanging offense."

The late Lord Mancroft put it more succinctly still: "A speech is like a love-affair—any fool can start it, but to end it requires considerable skill."

THREE BRANCHES
OF ORATORY

THE FIVE CANONS OF rhetoric, as I've just outlined them, provide a fairly thoroughgoing toolkit for all rhetorical writing or speech. They take you step by step from the first germ of an idea in the head to the last syllable of the delivery. Which particular instruments you'll need to grab from that toolkit for a given occasion depends substantially on what the occasion is.

Let's take a step back to look, then, at the types of occasion that most commonly arise—and the particular forms of rhetoric that address them. Aristotle said there were three types of rhetoric—widely known now as the three branches of oratory—and his distinction between them remains a useful one. One type seeks to persuade people about a course of action in the future, one seeks to persuade people of a version of events in the past, and one seeks to delight and impress in the present. By now, it

should more or less go without saying that the distinction isn't an absolute one. The three branches grow from a common trunk, and their foliage tangles and overlaps, making the tree of rhetoric an especially umbrageous and pleasant spot for a picnic. Thus, Aristotle:

> The genres of rhetoric are three in number, which is the number of the types of audience. For a speech is composed of three factors—the speaker, the subject and the listener—and it is to the last of these that its purpose is related. Now the listener must be either a spectator or a judge, and, if a judge, one either of the past or of the future. The judge, then, about the future is the assembly member, the judge about the past is the juror, and the assessor of capacity is the spectator, so that there must needs be three types of rhetorical speech: deliberative, forensic and display.

That seems to me fairly close to being self-explanatory. The "assessor of capacity" isn't an officer from the inspectorate of weights and measures, by the way—he is the member of an audience admiring (or otherwise) the rhetorical capacity of someone delivering an epideictic or display oration.

Aristotle goes on to subdivide these three branches into two types apiece. Deliberative speech has to do with exhortation and deterrence; forensic (or judicial) speech has to do with prosecution and defense; epideictic to do with praise or denigration. (Epideictic rhetoric is slightly the odd one out, as we'll see later. But let the distinction stand for now.)

These, as Aristotle argues, are the central points of each sort of rhetoric. Ancillary issues can be argued either way, but these

are the irreducible core of each sort: a litigant might not dispute that a given occurrence had taken place, but would never concede that he was in the wrong; a political orator might concede some aspects of his claim, but will never argue that the course of action he advocates is discreditable or disadvantageous.

This understood, let's look at them—as with the canons—one by one.

DELIBERATIVE RHETORIC

IT IS DELIBERATIVE RHETORIC, rather than either of the other types, that probably first comes to mind when you think of oratory. A "stirring" speech is so called because it stirs its audience to action. Francis Bacon's definition of rhetoric goes to exactly that: "The duty and office of rhetoric is to apply reason to imagination for the better moving of the will."

As I have mentioned, each of the three branches of rhetoric is associated with an orientation in time. Deliberative rhetoric is associated with the future: to act or not to act. In terms of Cicero's identification of the three offices of oratory—to teach (*docere*), to delight (*delectare*), and to move (*movere*)—deliberative rhetoric has as its prime task the latter. Persuading somebody to believe something (as a preacher might) or persuading somebody to do something (as a leader might) is the essence of the deliberative mode.

Aristotle identified two basic lines of attack: virtue or vice, and advantage or disadvantage. You can try to persuade your audience, in other words, that a given course of action is the

right thing to do; or you can try to persuade them that it's in their interests. If you can press the case in both respects, so much the better.

Here's *Ad Herennium* on the subject:

> If it happens that in a deliberation the counsel on one side is based on the consideration of security and that of the other on honor, as in the case of those who, surrounded by Carthaginians, deliberate on a course of action, then the speaker on security will use the following topics: Nothing is more useful than safety; no one can make use of his virtues if he has not based his plans on safety; not even the gods help those who thoughtlessly commit themselves to danger; nothing ought to be deemed honorable which does not produce safety. One who prefers the considerations of honor to security will use the following topics: Virtue ought never to be renounced; either pain, if that is feared, or death, if that is dreaded, is more tolerable than disgrace and infamy; one must consider the shame which will ensue—indeed neither immortality nor a life everlasting is achieved, nor is it proved that, once this peril is avoided, another will not be encountered; virtue finds it noble to go even beyond death; fortune, too, habitually favors the brave; not he who is safe in the present, but he who lives honorably, lives safely— whereas he who lives shamefully cannot be secure forever.[1]

As the prosecution of the War on Terror over the last decade has shown us very starkly, the very same topics of persuasion remain at the heart of governmental decision-making and public debate over policy.

Those in favor of the extrajudicial internment of "enemy combatants" in Guantanamo Bay, and the coercive forms of in-

terrogation they underwent there, represented their arguments as pragmatic: these techniques, while bending the principle of the presumption of innocence, were the only way the US government could be sure of preventing future terrorist attacks. Among the more robust voices on the American Right, there was also— stated or implied—a moral case: the belief that foreign nationals picked up on the field of battle or otherwise linked to militant Islamism deserved harsher treatment than the Geneva Convention allowed for.

Their opponents argued that torture and internment were in themselves morally wrong—and on a pragmatic line, that far from preventing future attacks, they would have the effect of radicalizing the prisoners' coreligionists, and damage the moral standing of America in the world. The two lines of attack are neatly knotted in an apothegm, originally attributed to Benjamin Franklin, much repeated in various forms at the time: those who would give up liberty for security deserve neither, and will lose both.

Let's start by shooting back to see the same topics working in ancient Athens. The oratorical reputation of Demosthenes (c. 383– 322 BC) in the ancient world was without rival, and in their different eras, both Dr. Johnson and Sir Philip Sidney regarded him as a paragon. Much of his early career was spent attempting to rouse his countrymen to action against Philip II of Macedon, a neighboring tyrant with whom Athens was at war and whom Demosthenes regarded as the greatest threat to the city's security.

In 351 BC, Demosthenes delivered what became known as the First Philippic*—in which he argued that the Athenians, overconfident of their own superiority, were in danger of being

---

*The term "philippic"—for the political equivalent of an air strike on a particular enemy—comes from Demosthenes.

caught with their trousers down. He argued for a major military fundraising drive—the same argument rumbling on at the time of writing about whether Britain needs to renew its nuclear deterrent.

Demosthenes began by justifying his decision to speak first:

> If the question before us were a new one, men of Athens, I should have waited until most of the regular speakers had delivered their opinions, and if satisfied with any of their proposals, I should have remained silent, but if not satisfied, I should then have tried to express my own views. Since, however, it is our fortune to be still debating a point on which they have often spoken before, I can safely claim your indulgence if I am the first to rise and address you. For if in the past their advice had been sound, there would be no need for deliberation today.

Already, Demosthenes has placed his opponents firmly in a box marked: "Had Their Chance: Proved Wrong." He has introduced an element of urgency to the question—we've been here before, and the problem is still not solved. And he has established his own credentials to speak—painting himself as one whose natural humility would incline to keep silent, but whom necessity now compels to speak up.

The line of argument in the speech that follows is carefully trodden. We all know that, proverbially, "Politics is the art of the possible." The territory of political rhetoric is, accordingly, that of possibility. It works both ways: politicians like to present their favored course of action as necessary or inevitable; yet against the suggestion that the contrary course of action is irresistible, almost limitlessly to push the power of human agency.

When history's on your side, in other words, it is an irresistible force; when it's against you, man is the master of his destiny.*

Demosthenes needs to persuade his audience, on the one hand, that Philip is a serious and powerful threat, but on the other that he is a threat Athens has every chance of seeing off. He needs to alarm the complacent and reassure the quietistic. So he begins: "Now in the first place, Athenians, there is no need to despair of our present position, however hopeless it may seem."

His line is, ingeniously, that the present gloomy state of affairs—Philip having conquered substantial Athenian territory—is what offers the best hope for its restitution. Since (in Demosthenes's account of it) it is Athenian complacency that yielded Philip his victory, Athenian action can rob him of it again. "Do not believe that his present power is fixed and unchangeable like that of a god," he says later. Anything Philip has done, we can do better. And at present, he rebukes the audience: "Your affairs are in this evil plight just because you, men of Athens, utterly fail to do your duty."

Demosthenes's vamping with modes of address is one of the most effective devices running through this speech. When the question of advantage comes up, we are generally in the first person plural: Demosthenes identifies himself with his audience as it heads for the sunlit uplands. "We" need not despair; "we" beat the Spartans; "we" used to hold all this territory. But he shifts to the second person plural to rebuke and exhort—the rhetorical

---

*Classic Marxism always seems to me to embody this contradiction—or, looked at another way, to make naked use of compulsion as a rhetorical strategy. If Marxists had absolute faith in the doctrine of historical immanence and the inevitability of capitalism bringing about its own demise, they wouldn't need to bother agitating for a revolution.

equivalent of grabbing his listeners by the lapels and shaking them.

What links this pronominal shuttling back and forth is the constant refrain "men of Athens . . . men of Athens . . . Athenians . . . Athenians." The audience is reminded again and again of its civic allegiance—and by implication, its civic duty. When the men of Athens start acting like men of Athens, there will be no "you"; there will only be "we." By acting on what he learnt from the Athenian example, Philip has conquered what belonged to them; so only by acting as Athenians will they get it back.

In a pithy formulation that marries *chiasmus* and *antithesis*, he puts the nub of his argument: "I want you to know and realize that, as no danger can assail you while you are on your guard, if you are remiss no success will attend you."

If the ostensible topic of the speech is advantage, its rich bass note is that of virtue: "For a free people there can be no greater compulsion than shame for their position." The two are made to mesh: by doing your patriotic duty and being true to your Athenian identity, you will secure the good of the state.

The topic of possibility is raised repeatedly—and Demosthenes artfully rides two horses. He wants the Athenians to arm against Philip because his territories are up for grabs, and what he did against us can be as easily done against him; but he also says that so great is Philip's insolence that "he leaves you no choice of action or inaction," and that "our business is not to speculate on what the future may bring forth, but to be certain that it will bring disaster, unless you face the facts and consent to do your duty."

As it turned out, history was on the other side and most of Greece was overrun by Philip. But you can't say Demosthenes didn't try.

The classic instance of deliberative rhetoric is, as above, politics (it's also sometimes called "legislative" oratory), but it is by no means confined to that sphere. Any exhortation to act or not to act in the future is deliberative in nature. The football coach's halftime pep talk is deliberative. The pitch for an account in a client meeting is deliberative. The television advertisement is deliberative.

And more often than not, the opinion pages of newspapers are in the deliberative mode. "Leaders," or "leading articles," are so called because they seek to lead. Columnists spend most of their time telling you what they think ought to be done, or, even more often, denouncing as folly the policy of the government—which adds up to telling you what ought not to be done.

Simon Jenkins is an elegant expositor of the straight-up deliberative essay. An article in the *Guardian* in February 2010[2] shows him on good form and makes, it seems to me, a nice contemporary contrast to Demosthenes. If that was a philippic, this could be called an argie-ment.

The old dispute between the United Kingdom and Argentina over ownership of the Falklands had heated up again—in this case, because plans for British companies to prospect for oil off the Falkland archipelago were described as a "breach of sovereignty" by the Argentinean government, who continue to assert title over the islands they call "Las Malvinas." Sir Simon used the occasion—*kairos*, if you like—as the opportunity to argue that the Falklands should (and will) be ceded to Argentina.

Sir Simon's exordium was grabby: he set out the parallels between the present moment—commercial dispute; Argentina complains to the UN; British government doesn't take the threat seriously—and the prelude to the 1982 war.

Then, continuing a little run of antitheses hinged on "now" and "then," he set out the differences between the cases.

> Then it took nine weeks of counterinvasion, with a thousand deaths and £3 billion spent, for Britain to restore the status quo ante. The Falklands war was a catastrophic failure of diplomacy and deterrence. Now, at least, war is unlikely. Britain has almost as many troops on the islands, 1,200, as there were islanders at the time of the invasion. It is on guard and the latest row with Argentina is merely over the arrival of an oil rig, the *Ocean Guardian*, in waters north of Port Stanley.

Sir Simon's stance in this article accords quite happily with the precepts Aristotle sets out for deliberative oratory in *Rhetoric*. "In the matter of revenue, the would-be orator must know the nature and extent of the city's sources of income. . . . In connection with war and peace, the speaker must know both the present and potential strength of the city. . . . In connection with the defense of the realm, the speaker must not be unaware of how the city is defended. . . . For national security, it is necessary to be able to consider all these matters, but no less should the orator have expertise about legislation."

His argument proper begins with an apothegm. Noting that Argentina's defeat in the 1982 war did not settle the legal question of the islands' ownership, he stated, "Military conquest does not establish legal title." In this part of the article, he's concentrating ostensibly on the topic of virtue: who is the rightful owner of the islands.

His ethos appeal, it may be worth mentioning, is largely made through implication. Like all newspaper columnists, a

prominent position in a newspaper of established reputation—
mug shot, name in big letters at the top of the column, and so
on—provides a *locus standi* as a sort of given. Those are the ty-
pographical equivalent of, say, a lectern and a backdrop bearing
the logo of some organization or other. When he writes, "Anyone
who studies the tortuous history and law of the Falklands will
know . . . " he implies that he is among those who *have* studied
them (in fact, he coauthored a 1982 book about the Falklands
with another distinguished journalist, Max Hastings), and that
what he has to say therefore carries a certain authority.

He sketches out the history of the islands, and the "crude act
of imperial aggression" in 1833 that secured them for the UK—
evoking the basic judicial topic that what's bad in the root will
be bad in the fruit. He then appeals to authority—noting that
thirty-two Latin American countries have supported Argentina's
title to the islands in the week that his article appeared, and that
the United States has "conspicuously" failed to side with Britain
on the matter.

He then sets out the argument in favor of Britain's retention,
one of "prescription"—essentially, that possession is nine-tenths
of the law: British colonists have been there uninterrupted since
the 1830s. He notes that these considerations are "strong, if not
overwhelming in international law."

Here is a little sleight of hand. "But legal title is not all," he
writes—implying by the shape of the sentence that the claim of
"prescription" has been refuted. Actually, it has been moved on
from. He shifts his ground to the question of practical advantage, arguing that the Falklands are a costly inconvenience to
Britain: "Continuing to garrison and supply them from Britain
was an expensive legacy of empire."

Analogy comes next: he points out that at the very time that Britain was fighting Argentina over the Falklands, it was arranging to hand Hong Kong back to China "on similar grounds of expediency."

His article—addressed, notionally, to the liberal internationalist Britons who read the *Guardian* newspaper—goes on to make a subtle audience-shaping move. One of the prime objections to giving Argentina the Falklands is that the islanders themselves wish to be British. In this article, the islanders are not part of Sir Simon's notional "us." They are very much "them": "Intransigent in their response to the Ridley negotiations [for a compromise settlement with Argentina] and backed by neo-imperialist rightwingers in the House of Commons, the islanders demanded and got their rescue by the 1982 task force and extravagant support ever since. They have rebuffed all efforts by later Buenos Aires mediators to re-establish contact."

Here's an *argumentum ad populum*—"neo-imperialist rightwingers" are dog-whistle boo-words to *Guardian* readers—and a firm attempt to establish the islanders as unreasonable and intransigent. This line of attack also seeks to establish a divergence between the interests of the islanders and the interests of their UK-dwelling compatriots: he nixes the islanders' claim to the oil ("no more belongs to them than the revenue of North Sea oil belongs to the Orkneys"), and states that "2,500 colonists cannot enjoy an unqualified veto on British government policy."

Finally, having ridden the twin horses of natural justice and political pragmatism, Sir Simon moves on to what you might call *force majeure*: the attempt to give a contingent deliberative question the aura of historical inevitability. "Distant colonies are a post-imperial anachronism. Britain will have to negotiate with Argentina because the world, either at the UN or the Hague, will

insist on it," he writes, shaping an enthymeme whose hidden premise—that "the world" always acts compellingly against post-imperial anachronisms—may not be as unimpeachable as he makes it sound.

Whether Sir Simon is right about the future of the Falklands is neither here nor there, for our purposes. Indeed, it's not that important for his newspaper either. What matters is that he is a dab hand at pulling the levers of deliberative oratory—and making his yanks of those levers just sharp enough that the reader, with indignation or pleasure, notices them being pulled.

CHAMPIONS OF RHETORIC V

Martin Luther King
Daydream Believer

"I HAVE A DREAM." *Those four words are probably now as well known as any phrase of comparable length in modern history. They were the refrain to the great speech Martin Luther King Jr. delivered on August 28, 1963, at the March for Jobs and Freedom in Washington in an attempt to bolster the passage of John F. Kennedy's civil rights bill through Congress. It's a speech that continues to be regarded as the pinnacle of twentieth-century American rhetoric.*

"Five score years ago, a great American, in whose symbolic shadow we stand, signed the Emancipation Proclamation," is how the speech begins. It invokes, as any American schoolchild will

know, the memory of Abraham Lincoln—not only with that ethos-shaping circumlocutio *"a great American,"* but indirectly through the echo of the opening words of his "Gettysburg Address," "Four score and seven years ago . . ." The archaism "score" isn't used by accident. Nor is the shadow entirely symbolic: the speech was delivered at the Lincoln Memorial in Washington. Four days before the speech, Dr. King told a journalist that he knew he needed to deliver "a sort of Gettysburg address."*

The language of the speech is a tissue of allusion and quotation, drawing on stores of common knowledge and idiom that will resonate with the several audiences to whom the speech is addressed. Its psalmic anaphoras and parallelisms in terms of form, and its quotations and near-quotations in terms of content, ineluctably evoke the Bible: Amos, Isaiah, and the Psalms. It also draws on the languages of the Constitution ("we hold these truths"), patriotic anthems ("let freedom ring"), and—particularly in its extraordinary and musical peroration—on the language of the Negro spiritual ("Free at last"). It is deeply wired, in other words, into a shared linguistic history. It even chucks in a nod to Shakespeare's Richard III *in its reference to "this sweltering summer of the Negro's legitimate discontent."*

To feel its main force requires nothing much more than a set of ears and a heart, but to understand Dr. King's best-known speech more fully, it helps to set it in context. The phrase "I have a dream," for instance, is not unique to that speech—and, as the speech was planned, did not even feature in its text.

---

*You might also notice how quickly the code-grooming starts: Dr. King is aligning his cause with the national cause "American."

The speech is best understood, at least in part, as a sermon—and as its dense mesh of quotations and allusions indicates, sermons in the tradition from which King comes are quasi-improvisational, self-plagiarizing (its themes, ideas, and phrases were working their ways through King's speeches for more than a decade previously), and massively intertextual.

I haven't written much in this book about religious rhetoric, which deserves (and has) whole libraries of books to itself. As I've mentioned in passing, the Christianization of the classics in the medieval and early modern periods saw some of the formal precepts of the pagan world folded into the theological schemes of Augustine and Aquinas—and rhetoric that had as its object the turning of souls to God proliferated through countless sects and traditions.

Sermons are a distinct but still recognizable rhetorical form—and their stylistic and textual resources are available to other rhetorics that seek to draw on their power. An orator's most powerful appeal remains ethos. The civil rights movement grew out of the black churches of the American South, and for its most accomplished orators, the sermon and the political speech had a common root, a common language, a common audience. On almost every occasion he was asked, Dr. King described himself simply as "a preacher."

Dr. King was speaking to a religious community as well as a political one, and his language formed a bridge between the semisacred rhetoric around the American Constitution and the expressly Biblical language of the Southern pulpit. When he warns in the speech against the "tranquilizing drug of gradualism," he is making a political point, but it is a point paralleled by the theology underpinning it. Though Dr. King asks his audience to "continue to work with the faith that unearned suffering is redemptive,"

he rejects the "compensatory religion" of the apolitical folk pulpit. Human agency and the divine plan mesh: man can and must act for justice in the sublunary world—and God will act through him.*

Scholars have argued that King's speech embodies the Christian notion of kerygma:[1] that it speaks of "realized eschatology" or the present fulfillment of scripture—that is, living through the age in which the Kingdom of God is actually coming into being here on earth. As I hope to show below, the figurative language of the speech more than bears that argument out.

There's a case, first of all, to be made for thinking more closely, though, about the mechanisms of Martin Luther King's delivery of this particular address. A shrewd and persuasive essay by Alexandra Alvarez[2] makes an in-depth case for why the conventional prose transcription of the speech is "inaccurate"—and by paragraphing it in "idea units" obscures its poetic structure and the way it functions as a performance. It's a firm reminder of the way that spoken rhetoric lives in the voice: a speech is not just an essay read aloud.

Dr. King's speech should be understood, she says, as a sermon in the Southern Baptist tradition, where the audience's antiphonal responses are a central part of the speech. When Dr. King says, for instance, "One hundred years later the Negro still is not free," that is actually spoken not as one phrase but as two:

> One hundred years later
> The Negro still is not free

---

*King also includes a thinly coded call for restraint to the "marvelous new militancy which has engulfed the Negro community" (and, he doesn't mention, threatened to split his own movement); doing nothing is wrong, but he warns too against "allow[ing] our creative protest to degenerate into physical violence."

She writes: "The response 'My Lord' followed each line. These responses are perceivable throughout the tape even though the speaker stood on a podium, on the Lincoln memorial, and the audience was standing on a lower level, far from the microphone."

This call-and-response structure, she argues, changes the dynamics of the way the speech is given and the way it is received. Instead of the speaker and audience corresponding to the sender and addressee, the speaker and audience together constitute the message's sender. It is, if you like, the ultimate form of successful ethos appeal: Dr. King doesn't just identify himself with the crowd—he actually co-opts them as orators on his behalf. In so doing he makes good his stated desire to shape, through his sermons, what he called a "beloved community."

The notion of the "beloved community" represents a development of the then largely unsystematized black theology that coalesced around the idea of communities of goodwill, through its academic analogues in the white Protestant tradition that King studied at Crozier Seminary and Boston University.[3] A key point is that, like King's theology, the beloved community includes both black and white. King used the metaphor of a soul divided against itself when talking about segregation: "America has manifested a schizophrenic personality on the question of race."

Alvarez reprints the speech divided into lines as you might tabulate poetry, and argues in support of her approach that 160 of the 193 lines she identifies end on a falling intonation, inviting a response from the audience, and she notes down those responses. Throughout the speech, members of the crowd shout out as you might hear a Baptist congregation respond in church.

"My Lord," "Yes," and "Yeah" are the main responses, in addition to frequent interstitial applause. So, for instance, the section

toward the end of the speech where Dr. King echoes the Book of Isaiah* looks like this (responses in parentheses):

> I have a dream that one day "every valley shall be
>   exalted *(Yes)*
> and every hill and mountain shall be made low, the
>   rough places will be made plain *(Yeah)*
> and the crooked places will be made straight *(Yeah)*
> and the glory of the Lord shall be revealed *(Yeah)*
> and all flesh shall see it together." *(Yes)*
> This is our hope. *(Yeah)*
> This is the faith that I go back to the South with. *(Yeah)***
> With this faith *(My Lord)*
> we will be able to transform the jangling discords of our
>   Nation *(Yeah)*
> into a beautiful symphony of brotherhood *(Brotherhood)*

No such transcription can, of course, be authoritative and final—but Alvarez points toward a very useful way of looking at the way that speech works, and one much more fruitful than setting it out as if it were a written essay.

Though oral and written rhetoric have their basic mechanisms and many of their effects in common—and for that reason I've frequently treated them as interchangeable in these pages—it

---

*Isaiah 40:4: "Every valley shall be exalted, and every mountain and hill shall be made low: and the crooked shall be made straight, and the rough places plain."
**Alvarez's transcript here omits the line "With this faith we will be able to hew out of the mountain of despair a stone of hope." I'm not sure whether a printing or a transcription error is responsible.

should always be remembered that they aren't entirely the same animal. The fractured syntax of George W. Bush, for instance, is largely effective in his speeches (indeed, were we not living in an age of recorded sound and precise transcription, all but his most bizarre manglings of the language would go unnoticed) but looks glaringly inept on the page.

The speech theorist Walter Ong identified the characteristics of "primary orality" (that is, the way language works in pre- or non-literate societies) as including "formulaic styling," being "additive rather than subordinative . . . aggregative rather than analytic . . . redundant . . . close to the human lifeworld . . . empathetic and participatory rather than objectively distanced . . . and more situational than abstract." These characteristics, it seems reasonable to suppose, survive in the oral literature of successor cultures.

As I discussed in the chapters on memory and style, the patterns of figuration or "formulaic styling" in rhetoric, as in poetry, can be seen as descending from oral culture and the demands of mnemotechnics. Likewise, in spoken rhetoric you're much more likely to encounter redundancies, repetitions, and an aggregation of effects and meanings; and in spoken rhetoric, there is nearly always—if not, perhaps, to such an extreme as in King's performance at the rally—a dynamic interaction with the audience.

The orality of this speech is everywhere in evidence. It consists of a whole series of anaphoric fugues, overlapping and building: the figure of climax on a grand scale. "I have a dream" is only one of the phrases that recurs. We also hear, repeatedly: "One hundred years later"; "now is the time" and "this is the time"; "we can never be satisfied" and "we cannot be satisfied"; "some of you have come"; "go back"; "we will be able"; "let freedom ring"; and "free at last."

The phrase "I have a dream" recurs eight times in the speech, and signals a particularly Christian enargia. Placing himself at the end of an arc of providential history that passes from Moses leading his people to the Promised Land, through Lincoln's signing of the Emancipation Proclamation, King makes the shared vision of that "dream"—"a dream deeply rooted in the American dream," he takes care to spell out—the object for the beloved community.

As I mentioned above, it isn't a phrase that King had even planned to use*—it was, if you like, a riff he happened to have in his back pocket. It's a phrase of which he had used versions here and there in speeches—including one in Charlotte, North Carolina, three years previously entitled "The Negro and the American Dream." It is a token of how in tune with his audience he was—how right Alexandra Alvarez is to stress the speech's dialogic quality, in other words—that it even came out. Folk history has it that the digression was prompted by a shout from the audience—the singer Mahalia Jackson crying, "Tell them about the dream, Martin." Dr. King didn't explicitly endorse that version of events, but did credit his interplay with the crowd as being the catalyst:

> *I started out reading the speech, and I read it down to a point, and just all of a sudden, I decided—the audience response was wonderful that day, you know—and all of a sudden this thing came to me that I have used—I'd used it many times before, that thing about "I have a dream"—and I just felt that I wanted to*

---

*Drafts of the speech were various called "Normalcy, Never Again" and "A Canceled Check."

use it here. I don't know why, I hadn't thought about it before the speech.

Improvisation was by this stage nothing unusual. "King did not so much write most of his speeches as assemble them, by rearranging and adapting material he had used many times before," according to the historian Drew Hansen.[4] That is not to say, on the other hand, that the material itself came off the cuff. In his years as pastor of the Dexter Avenue Church in Montgomery, one observer recalled that he would "devote hours to writing out and memorizing the complete text of his sermon," while his pulpit assistant John Thomas Porter recalled that King would arrive with a full text of his sermon—then leave it on a chair as he ascended to the pulpit and speak without notes.

The speech shuttles back and forth between the abstract metaphors and giant timescales of its Biblical register and the here-and-now of individual battlefronts in the fight for civil rights. The section where the speech is most concrete is bookended by a secular abstraction ("our national creed") and a theological abstraction ("the Glory of the Lord shall be revealed"). Conversely, the grand scheme of history is anchored in "nineteen sixty-three," in a "sweltering summer." The effort "to make justice a reality for all God's children" is literalized and domesticated in "my four little children," and in the "little black boys and black girls" joining hands with "little white boys and white girls."

The "hill and mountain . . . made low" from Isaiah, and the almost Blakean "mountain of despair" are established in the speech as archetypes—and then made literal in the sweeping run of anaphora on "let freedom ring": "the prodigious hilltops of New Hampshire . . . the mighty mountains of New York . . . the heightening

Alleghenies of Pennsylvania . . . the snowcapped Rockies of Colorado . . . the curvaceous slopes of California . . . Stone Mountain of Georgia . . . Lookout Mountain of Tennessee . . . every hill and molehill of Mississippi."

I don't know about you, but "molehill" is almost my favorite word in the whole thing. It is a pointer to something that is too little remarked about this speech, I think, and that is central to its power. "I Have a Dream" is not just passionate. It is also whimsical. It is not just moving. It is also funny—and deliberately so.

Look, near the beginning of the speech, at the playfulness with which Dr. King works through his extended metaphor about the promissory note. Not only does this speech fulfill the Ciceronian injunction to move and to instruct, it also knows to delight:

> *In a sense we have come to our nation's capital to cash a check. When the architects of our republic wrote the magnificent words of the Constitution and the Declaration of Independence, they were signing a promissory note to which every American was to fall heir. This note was a promise that all men, yes, black men as well as white men, would be guaranteed the unalienable rights of life, liberty, and the pursuit of happiness.*
>
> *It is obvious today that America has defaulted on this promissory note insofar as her citizens of color are concerned. Instead of honoring this sacred obligation, America has given the Negro people a bad check, a check which has come back marked "insufficient funds." But we refuse to believe that the bank of justice is bankrupt. We refuse to believe that there are insufficient funds in the great vaults of opportunity of this nation. So we have come to cash this check—a check that will give us upon demand the riches of freedom and the security of justice.*

The exhilarating quality of the "I Have a Dream" speech—delivered, let's not forget, at a time when there wasn't all that much for black Americans to be exhilarated about—comes out in its humor; and that in turn gives it force. Here is not just a statement of faith, but an enactment of it: so confident is Dr. King that his God and his people will see him right that he is able not just to stand up to the "vicious racists" of Alabama—he is able to laugh at them.

JUDICIAL RHETORIC

JUDICIAL RHETORIC, OR FORENSIC rhetoric as it is also sometimes called, is rhetoric that deals with the past: the rhetoric not so much of praise and blame but of conviction and exoneration. It seeks to establish what happened, why it happened, and whether the actors involved were at fault in terms of the moral law or the law of the land.

Judicial rhetoric has also tended to receive the most extensive treatment in rhetoric handbooks and the teaching of rhetoric. Even in the ancient world, high-level participation in politics was less common than involvement in the law courts. Edward Corbett and Robert Connors record that, in ancient Athens, "It was a rare citizen who did not go to court at least a half a dozen times during the course of his adult life."[1] So for those who made their money teaching rhetoric, it was the bread and butter of their business. And it was judicial rhetoric in which probably the most influential orator of all time, Cicero, made his name.

As the name suggests, judicial rhetoric's classic instance is the language of the courtroom—and our addiction to its rigor

and aggression, its swift reverses and baroque perorations, can be seen in the legal dramas that continue to fill our screens and theaters. But judicial rhetoric is everywhere that blame is: the post-mortem after a costly mistake in the office; the free and frank discussion you have with your no-good boyfriend after reading his text messages; or the inquiry that goes on when the sound of wailing toddlers summons you to the playroom and two tearful children simultaneously yell, "*He started it!*"

If deliberative rhetoric turns on the four special topics of advantage, disadvantage, virtue, and vice, judicial rhetoric is concerned (Aristotle tells us) with two special topics: justice and injustice. For practical purposes, however—and to extend the symmetry with the forensic branch in what I hope is a sensible manner—we could add to that pair the question of legality and illegality.

Certainly, subsequent treatments of *stasis*—broadly, the question of what exactly is at issue in a trial—have tended to imply this additional distinction even if it isn't front and center in Aristotle.*

A popular Greco-Roman scheme divides the questions of stasis into four:

1) Conjectural stasis deals with questions of fact: Did he do it?
2) Definitional stasis deals with questions of definition: What kind of thing did he do?

---

*Aristotle's discussion of judicial rhetoric centers on the notion of *adikia*, or injustice, which he defines as "voluntary illegal harm." He then divides the law into particular law (i.e., the written statutes of the state) and general law, which he defines as "those unwritten laws which are held to be agreed by all men." The two are rolled up together in the special topics of justice and injustice.

3) Qualitative stasis deals with questions of quality: Was it legal or was it just?
4) Translative stasis deals with questions of jurisdiction: Is this the right court in which to be trying the question?

Abstract and technical though this may sound (and, as you'll already have spotted, the lines between one and two, and two and three are slightly blurry in practice) it does bring some clarity to the points at issue.

To return for a moment to Jellystone Park, conjectural stasis would have us ask whether Yogi Bear was responsible for the disappearance of the picnic basket, definitional stasis whether he grabbed it and snaffled the contents, qualitative stasis whether the bylaws of Jellystone Park prohibit the theft of picnic baskets, and translative stasis whether the alleged theft should be tried in a human court or whether this thieving wild animal should be summarily shot by a park ranger.

Those Aristotelian topics are well illustrated in one of the most successful courtroom dramas of recent years—the film *A Few Good Men*. Tom Cruise plays a navy lawyer, Daniel Kaffee, acting in the court-martial of two marines accused of murdering an unpopular colleague, William Santiago, at the US naval base in Guantanamo Bay. He suspects—this film, incidentally, was made long before "Gitmo" caught the world's attention in the way it did—that the two men were acting under orders and carrying out a "code red," slang for an illegal punishment beating.

The case comes to its climax when Cruise pressures the camp commander, Colonel Jessep, to admit that he ordered the code red as punishment for the dead marine's failure to respect the chain of command. Here's the key moment from Aaron Sorkin's

fine script. We meet Kaffee, objections flying around him, angrily hectoring the colonel to answer the question.

KAFFEE: I'll ask for the fourth time. You ordered—

JESSEP: You want answers?

KAFFEE: I think I'm entitled to them.

JESSEP: You want answers?!

KAFFEE: I want the truth.

JESSEP: You can't handle the truth!

And nobody moves.

JESSEP [*continuing*]: Son, we live in a world that has walls. And those walls have to be guarded by men with guns. Who's gonna do it? You? You, Lieutenant Weinberg? I have a greater responsibility than you can possibly fathom. You weep for Santiago and you curse the marines. You have that luxury. You have the luxury of not knowing what I know: That Santiago's death, while tragic, probably saved lives. And my existence, while grotesque and incomprehensible to you, saves lives.

[*Beat*]

You don't want the truth. Because deep down, in places you don't talk about at parties, you want me on that wall. You need me on that wall.

[*Boasting*]

We use words like honor, code, loyalty . . . we use these words as the backbone of a life spent defending something. You use 'em as a punchline.

[*Beat*]

I have neither the time nor the inclination to explain myself to a man who rises and sleeps under the blanket of

the very freedom I provide, then questions the manner in which I provide it. I would rather you just said thank you and went on your way. Otherwise, I suggest you pick up a weapon and stand a post. Either way, I don't give a damn what you think you're entitled to.

KAFFEE [*quietly*]: Did you order the code red?

JESSEP [*beat*]: I did the job you sent me to do.

KAFFEE: Did you order the code red?

JESSEP [*pause*]: You're goddamn right I did.

Here is, I'd suggest, a nicely tangled set of issues around stasis. For Kaffee, the question is of conjectural stasis. His only concern is to establish a fact: "Did you order the code red?" Jessep is finally bounced into conceding that fact as an accidental by-product of angrily insisting on its irrelevance.

For him—though hitherto he has known better than to admit it to the court—the question is of qualitative and/or translative stasis: he did order the code red, but that was the right thing to do by the unwritten law and this court does not have the right to judge him for it.

But while he makes his case—essentially that he answers to a higher authority—Jessep fatally damages his own ethos appeal. His famous line, "You can't handle the truth"—as well as being, to state the obvious, a confession that his own testimony is likely to be mendacious—places the "you" of his audience firmly on the other side of a divide. His main figural position is now antithesis: "*I* have a greater responsibility than *you* can possibly fathom"; "*You* have the luxury of not knowing what *I* know"; "*We* use these words as the backbone to a life spent defending

something. *You* use 'em as a punchline"; "*I* don't give a damn what *you* think you're entitled to."

While this made for great drama, it was, of course, a terrible mistake. The basic pronominal movement of the successful orator is never toward "us and them," but away from it. As case after case shows, it is from "I" through "you" to "we."

Actually, Jessep is being truthful to himself. The whole film turns on the question of ethos: Santiago's death came about because he didn't fit into the Marine Corps, with its ethos of absolute obedience. Jessep's speech dramatizes the question of whether, in order to protect the lives and freedoms of a given polity, the defenders of that polity can separate themselves from its ethos. The marines, in Jessep's worldview, protect the American community by forming a separate, tighter, more ruthless community of their own, which protects Americans but is not, finally, answerable to them.

Kaffee's next line is a sidestep: an entire change in register, dropping into the impassive jargon of the court.

> KAFFEE: Please the court, I suggest the jury be dismissed so that we can move to an immediate Article 39a Session. The witness has rights.

In delivering that line he is asserting the identity of his ethos with the court he serves and aggressively rebutting Jessep's translative stasis. This is a court-martial, Jessep is a member of the US Marine Corps, and his goose is now well and truly cooked.

Where judicial rhetoric takes place in a courtroom or any similar formal environment (a headmaster's study, for instance), it's worth mentioning in parenthesis, much of the work of ethos

presentation is done by the trappings of the court. A witness will typically swear a public oath to tell the truth; lawyers—whose own authority is signified by the clothes they wear and the position they occupy in the formal structure of argumentation—will present evidence as to the credibility of the witnesses, and any special standing or expertise they may have.

What would be a good contemporary instance of judicial rhetoric from the real world—or a contemporary instance, at least? As it happens, one presented itself just as I was settling down to write this chapter.

It was the immediate aftermath of the January 2011 massacre in Tucson, Arizona, in which a lone gunman, Jared Lee Loughner, shot six people dead and left more than a dozen wounded, among them the Democratic congresswoman Gabrielle Giffords. In the aftermath of the shooting, many speculated that the paramilitary rhetoric that the new Right brought to American politics may have contributed to Loughner's actions.

Singled out for particular anger was the crosshairs logo with which, on her website, the Republican politician Sarah Palin had chosen to indicate that Giffords's was a target seat. Not long before the shooting, Giffords herself had complained: "We're in the *crosshairs* of a gun sight over our district. When people do that, they've got to realize that there are consequences to that action."

Though the image was removed from her website, Palin kept her counsel for four days before posting a prerecorded statement in an online video. She was pictured posing smartly dressed and carefully lit and made-up, in front of a fireplace. The boilerplate props of the American politician's ethos appeal were in place: a stars-and-stripes lapel pin and a large American

flag draped behind her shoulder, as if to suggest that this is just how the Palin living room is ordinarily decorated.

> Like millions of Americans I learned of the tragic events in Arizona on Saturday, and my heart broke for the innocent victims. No words can fill the hole left by the death of an innocent, but we do mourn for the victims' families as we express our sympathy. . . .
>
> Like many, I've spent the past few days reflecting on what happened and praying for guidance. After this shocking tragedy, I listened at first puzzled, then with concern, and now with sadness, to the irresponsible statements from people attempting to apportion blame for this terrible event.

Here is a strong attempt to fix Mrs. Palin's stance. Her silence after the shootings was explained, in this substantially Christian nation, in terms of prayer and reflection. "Like millions of Americans . . . Like many . . . " seeks to align herself and identify her interests and attitudes with those of the average American. She also advances the almost obligatory anti-rhetorical commonplace: "No words can fill the hole left by the death of an innocent." (President Obama's address in Tucson the following day offered the near-identical "There is nothing I can say that will fill the sudden hole torn in your hearts.")

That zeugmatic tricolon—"I listened at first puzzled, then with concern, and now with sadness"—seeks to give the impression that so high-minded is she, her immediate response to people attacking her was puzzlement. She places herself *above* her critics—offering them not the tribute of anger but the deliberately patronizing "sadness."

She moved on to the theme of her speech proper, which is the commonplace that criminals, rather than society, are to blame for crime. Rather than simply make that assertion herself, she quoted an authority figure, Ronald Reagan: a conservative political icon commanding respect and affection.

> President Reagan said, "We must reject the idea that every time a law's broken, society is guilty rather than the lawbreaker. It is time to restore the American precept that each individual is accountable for his actions." Acts of monstrous criminality stand on their own. They begin and end with the criminals who commit them, not collectively with all the citizens of a state, not with those who listen to talk radio, not with maps of swing districts used by both sides of the aisle, not with law-abiding citizens who respectfully exercise their First Amendment rights at campaign rallies, not with those who proudly voted in the last election.

The rest of the speech was essentially a working out of that theme—the contrastive link between the personal responsibility of the gunman and the political responsibility of the campaigner being its master figure, introduced with the words: "The last election was all about taking responsibility for our country's future."

> There are those who claim political rhetoric is to blame for the despicable act of this deranged, apparently apolitical criminal. And they claim political debate has somehow gotten more heated just recently. But when was it less heated? Back in those "calm days" when political figures literally settled their differences with dueling pistols? . . .

But, especially within hours of a tragedy unfolding, journalists and pundits should not manufacture a blood libel that serves only to incite the very hatred and violence they purport to condemn. That is reprehensible.

As those extracts suggest, her subtextual aim in this speech—in context of the appropriate bromides about evil, tragedy, senseless violence, precious lives, heroism, and so on—was to defend herself and her ideological allies against the claim that their rhetoric bore any responsibility for the attack.

Here, in terms of judicial stasis, was where she pitched her tent. Yes, she conceded implicitly, she *did* use various forms of political rhetoric and yes, they *were* aggressive. But on the qualitative and translative counts, she sought to demonstrate that her rhetoric was both just—that is, in accordance with the founding principles of the republic—and that "journalists and pundits" were not the appropriate people to pass judgment on it. Whenever you hear someone deplore "trial by media" or ask, "Who are you to judge me?" they are making a claim to do with translative stasis, and that is what is happening here. In a sense, it was rhetoric itself on trial—and, as ever, it was rhetoric that was used to defend it. That irony was redoubled: the way she chose to defend herself against trial by media was through the media; and while denying that words could be held responsible for inciting hatred and violence, she asserted that media reporting "serves . . . to incite . . . hatred and violence."

Where the speech failed, I think, was not that it was self-justifying, but that it *sounded* self-justifying. Positioning herself above her critics sounded arrogant. And complaining about the "blood libel" (leaving aside for the moment her catastrophically

clumsy use of a phrase with so specific a historical genealogy) seemed to stand out against the relatively formulaic expressions of anger and regret she produced about the actual shooting: it sounded as if she felt more strongly about being damaged politically than she did about the victims of the shootings being damaged physically.

Both Palin's and Jessep's examples show how—in judicial rhetoric as in forensic—the importance of staying in control of where you stand vis-à-vis your audience is vital if what you want to convey about the points at issue is to come across. That's the truth. Handle it with care.

CHAMPIONS OF RHETORIC VI

Barack Obama
The Audacity of Trope

IN HIS SECOND BOOK, The Audacity of Hope, *the now president credited himself with what he called "a certain talent for rhetoric." Actually, Obama has rather more than that. He is one of the most consciously and artfully rhetorical speakers in the recent history of American politics.*

Obama's high style, as I've mentioned earlier in this book, has drawn criticism from his enemies. As we've seen again and again, rhetoric that declares itself so obviously as rhetoric is vulnerable to attack: it can be made to look self-indulgent, theatrical, and insincere—all charges that have been leveled and continue to be leveled against Obama.

But Obama's showy use of rhetoric isn't just geared to persuasion in and of itself. It's doing something else. In the same way as Churchill's Elizabethanisms were geared to evoke a semi-imaginary golden age of British history, Obama's style during the presidential campaign was directly geared to positioning him at the confluence of two great oratorical traditions in American public life.

Here was a candidate who started the race as an outsider—and who would, if successful, become the first mixed-race president and, what's more, one with a Kenyan national as a father and a Muslim middle name.

A successful Obama campaign would be completely without precedent. It had not been that long since—in John F. Kennedy—the election of a Catholic as president had been seen as somewhat scandalous. So it became crucial, in what remains a highly conservative country, that Obama assert a live connection to American history. More than simply assert, he needed to establish that connection at the absolute root level, at the level of language itself. Obama sought, through his rhetoric, to embed himself in a vital American tradition.

His rhetoric, therefore, was consciously seeded with echoes of Abraham Lincoln and Martin Luther King: America's orator-hero, and the martyred figurehead of black America's liberation struggle. He positioned himself as the inheritor of their political and oratorical traditions.

Like all senior politicians in the modern age, Obama employs speechwriters. His lead speechwriter, Jon Favreau, was named by Time magazine as one of the hundred most powerful people on the planet. Favreau is a prodigy: a self-declared rhetoric geek, at the time his boss took office Favreau was only twenty-six years old. But when Obama called Favreau his "mind reader," he meant to pay him the compliment that he helps Obama to sound like himself.

*Some politicians sound like their speechwriters. But it is inconceivable that Obama does not take a strong and detailed interest in both the content and the style of his own speeches. His history is one of nonstop engagement with the persuasive arts—from his work as a community organizer in Chicago to his education in the debating halls and lecture theaters of Harvard's law school. And the written language of his books (*Dreams from My Father, *it's worth remembering, was written before he was a politician) is entirely consonant with the baseline language of his speeches. Favreau tips the hat to that when he says that writing for Obama is "like being Ted Williams's batting coach."*

Rhetoric is at the pith of Obama's nature. It doesn't, I think, stray too far into pop psychology to notice that the force of the spoken word was the young Barack's enduring impression of his father. His parents split when he was a toddler, and for most of Obama's childhood, his father lived on another continent altogether. "My father was almost entirely absent from my childhood," Obama later recalled, "having been divorced from my mother when I was 2 years old." Barack Obama Sr. lived in Kenya and visited his son only on one occasion, for a month, in 1971 when Barack was a ten-year-old boy. This is what the boy remembered:

Whenever he spoke . . . his large hands outstretched to direct or deflect attention, his voice deep and sure, cajoling and laughing— I would see a sudden change take place in the family. . . . It was as if his presence had summoned the spirit of earlier times.

Fathers who aren't there can be just as influential as fathers who are. Obama references his in the title of his memoir—and it was his father's gift specifically that he called to mind the first time he was called on to speak in public. Having become involved

*in student politics at his university in Los Angeles, he was invited
to introduce a small anti-apartheid rally.*

*The scene, as he remembered it, was one of "a few hundred
restless after lunch," and he was competing for attention with a
pick-up Frisbee game off to one side. As he waited to speak, he remembered "the power of my father's words to transform. If I
could just find the right words, I had thought to myself. With the
right words everything could change—South Africa, the lives of
ghetto kids just a few miles away, my own tenuous place in the
world." He took the podium, he wrote, "in a trancelike state."
The trance never quite abated—and the child became one of the
most accomplished public speakers of the age.*

*Let's look a bit more closely at his technique. Obama's high
style was well evidenced in his address at the Victory Column in
Berlin in July 2008 (a conscious channeling, incidentally, of the
legacy of JFK: until Angela Merkel intervened, Obama had hoped
to deliver his speech at the Brandenburg Gate, where Kennedy declared "Ich bin ein Berliner").*

*As we speak, cars in Boston and factories in Beijing are melting
the ice caps in the Arctic, shrinking coastlines in the Atlantic,
and bringing drought to farms from Kansas to Kenya.*

*The first clause gives us that alliterative double—"Boston"
and "Beijing"—which opens on to a rising tricolon whose third
term is itself doubled up. The whole lot is thick with alliteration:
"Arctic" and "Atlantic," "Kansas to Kenya." Note, too, the movement of the sentence in space: from the intimate here-and-now of
"as we speak" in an outward spiral through the industrial scale of
cars and cities to continental and global effects. That, for a single
sentence, is really doing some work.*

In March 2010, speaking after Congress voted on his cherished healthcare reforms, his opening words were similarly tightly structured:

> *Tonight, after nearly one hundred years of talk and frustration, after decades of trying, and a year of sustained effort and debate, the United States Congress finally declared that America's workers and America's families and America's small businesses deserve the security of knowing that here, in this country, neither illness nor accident should endanger the dreams they've worked a lifetime to achieve.*

Once again, this speech puts us in the here-and-now—"tonight"—and invites us to imagine that moment as a pivot, with a weight of historic significance bearing on it. His tricolon gives us "one hundred years" of this, "decades" of that, and "a year" of the other before, "finally," the moment of achievement arrived. In a country with a profoundly Puritan inheritance—whose historical rhetoric is marinated in language of election,* providential history, and Manifest Destiny (Puritans are to theology as Whigs are to history)—this way of presenting history is particularly powerful.

A second tricolon—inflated with polysyndeton *and that* pleonastic *repetition of "America's"—enacts another gentler change of scale from the individual to the collective ("workers . . . families . . . small businesses"). "Here, in this country" returns us to the moment. It's worth noting that the parenthesis "in this country" does the same work as the repetition of "America's" (and the expansive use of the full phrase "United States Congress"): Obama's desire to*

---

*I use the word in its theological sense: the Elect are those singled out by God.

expand state provision of healthcare is a bill that has been painted again and again by the American Right as socialistic and un-American. It matters deeply to Obama to brand the decision, as it were, with the Stars and Stripes.

If Obama has a signature rhetorical figure, I'd say, it is anaphora. His speech to the Iowa caucus on January 3, 2008, for instance, was absolutely thick with it. It opened: "You know, they said this time would never come. They said our sights were set too high. They said this country was too divided, too disillusioned to ever come together around a common purpose."

He went on to promise: "I'll be a president who finally makes healthcare affordable . . . I'll be a president who ends the tax breaks . . . I'll be a president who harnesses the ingenuity . . . I'll be a president who ends this war in Iraq . . . "

Then: "This was the moment when . . . this was the moment when . . . this was the moment when . . . "

And, as his speech built to its climax, "Hope is what I saw. . . . Hope is what I heard. . . . Hope is what led a band of colonists to rise up against an empire."

When Obama uses anaphora in the way he does, he is taking advantage of its historical resonance as well as its immediate rhetorical effectiveness.

To Americans literate in their own country's history, those repetitions will bring consciously or unconsciously to mind the Declaration of Independence, where the rap sheet against King George rolls out in an anaphoric fugue. "He has refused . . . He has forbidden . . . He has refused . . . He has called together . . . He has dissolved . . . He has refused . . . "

That resonance goes to the side of Obama's self-presentation that attempts to forge a connection with Abraham Lincoln. Lin-

coln, like Obama, was a lawyer from Springfield, Illinois, and it
was in Springfield that Obama chose to launch his campaign in
2007, asking in that speech what the life of "a tall, gangly, self-
made Springfield lawyer tells us." The answer he gave invoked
Lincoln as a rhetorician—"He tells us that there is power in
words. He tells us that there is power in conviction. . . . He tells us
that there is power in hope"—and talked about how Lincoln
achieved change through "his will and his words" [my emphasis].
After winning the presidency, Obama made a point of traveling to
Washington by train from Philadelphia for his inauguration—
retracing the journey that Lincoln made when he took the presidency in 1861.

What Lincoln stands for, in the constellation of meaning that
Obama's ethos appeals traces, is twofold. He was the emancipator of the slaves;* and he was the conciliator after the Civil War.
Obama casts himself in both traditions. His own color gives Lincoln's abolitionism a Mosaic fillip—Obama as emancipator of
his own people. And during his election night speech, he made explicit his identification of the bitter red versus blue divide during
the Bush years with the Civil War whose wounds Lincoln sought
to heal:

---

*History is not quite so clear-cut on this. Though he eventually signed the
Emancipation Proclamation, during the Civil War Lincoln wrote to the *New
York Tribune* to say, "If I could save the Union without freeing any slave I
would do it, and if I could save it by freeing all the slaves I would do it." He was
a pragmatist, and slavery wasn't at the top of his list of priorities. For rhetorical purposes what matters, though, is that posterity chooses to see him as un-
flinchingly anti-slavery on principle—just as it chooses to see the Civil War as
having been fought against slavery and the Second World War as having been
fought to save Jewish lives from the Holocaust.

> As Lincoln said to a nation far more divided than ours, we are
> not enemies but friends. Though passion may have strained, it
> must not break our bonds of affection.

In a rousing passage in The Audacity of Hope, Obama wrote
that to abandon our values and ideals would be "to relinquish
our best selves"—which is, surely, a conscious echo of one of the
most famous phrases in Lincoln's First Inaugural, "the better angels of our nature."

Obama also borrows some of his folksiness from Lincoln. Those
drops from the high style that made Lincoln's oratory so effective—
that sense of his coming off the podium and speaking in intimate,
everyday language—are also present in Obama. He promises to
"disagree without being disagreeable"; Lincoln's first inaugural
talked about "cheerfully" giving protection to the states.

As I mentioned above, there was a strong sense during his
election campaign of Obama locating himself not just in recent
history nor even the history of the United States, but in a millen-
nial or prophetic timescale. He'd talk about "unyielding faith,"
"impossible odds," "the voices of millions." One of the catch-
phrases of his early campaign was, "There is something happening in America."

Here's the peroration to the speech in St. Paul, Minnesota,
with which he greeted his presidential nomination in the summer
of 2008:

> The journey will be difficult. The road will be long. I face this
> challenge—I face this challenge with profound humility and
> knowledge of my own limitations, but I also face it with limitless
> faith in the capacity of the American people.

Because if we are willing to work for it, and fight for it, and believe in it, then I am absolutely certain that, generations from now, we will be able to look back and tell our children that this was the moment when we began to provide care for the sick and good jobs to the jobless. . . . This was the moment when the rise of the oceans began to slow and our planet began to heal. . . . This was the moment when we ended a war, and secured our nation, and restored our image as the last, best hope on earth. This was the moment, this was the time when we came together to remake this great nation so that it may always reflect our very best selves and our highest ideals.

"*This was the moment*" *is a curious construction. By using the past tense in that way—*hypallage, *of a sort—Obama allows the voice of the speech to look back on the present moment as if both in the flow of time and out of it; as if the decision has already been made. For both the religious believers who built America and the religious believers to whom Obama is addressing himself, that is no sort of paradox: in God's providential scheme, the decision has already been made, and every moment in history has been leading up to this one.*

That sort of language, for historical reasons, works better in America than it does in the UK. Tony Blair, for instance, was mocked mercilessly for his pull toward the Messianic register. You may remember him, during the Northern Ireland peace talks, announcing gauchely: "A day like today is not a day for sound bites, really. But I feel the hand of history upon our shoulders."

But for Obama, these things can be said with a straight face. Consequently, his incantatory repetitions activate another linguistic folk-memory too. The language of the King James version of the

Bible echoes behind the strophic structure and parallelisms of Obama's speeches.

The Bible enters Obama's oratory, back near the source, through the language of the Founding Fathers—but it also enters his oratory through a more immediate tributary: the rhetoric of the civil rights movement. When Obama sounds like the Bible, he doesn't just sound like the Bible. He sounds like the Bible channeled through Martin Luther King.

Dr. King's own importance in the millenarian scheme isn't just winked at. On two key occasions during his presidential campaign—at the declaration of his candidacy in Springfield, Illinois, and on the night of the New Hampshire primary—Obama invoked the memory of Dr. King in expressly Biblical language.

In the first instance, he said, "We heard a King's call to let justice roll down like water, and righteousness like a mighty stream." In the second, he referred to him as "A King who took us to the mountaintop and pointed the way to the Promised Land." The former quotes Dr. King's injunction to "let justice roll down like waters, and righteousness like a mighty stream," which itself echoes the Book of Amos. The latter is a reference to the "I've Been to the Mountaintop" speech, delivered on the eve of Dr. King's assassination: "I've been to the mountaintop. . . . I've seen the Promised Land."

When Obama said, "Something is happening in America," he was also echoing Dr. King, from that speech: "Something is happening in Memphis. Something is happening in our world." These speeches do more than just allude to Dr. King's own Biblical language—they co-opt it. And with a near-blasphemous pun on Dr. King's name—"a King"—Obama expressly aligns King as martyr/savior/prophet with Jesus Christ.

Made explicit, this may sound crazily overblown. But in the speeches it functions as a sort of bass note—a heart-lifting suggestion rather than a real system of thinking.

But a twining of the religious and the political is a natural one: Obama's politics and his eschatology are arm in arm. In Dreams from My Father, *he described looking at television footage of the civil rights movement as "a form of prayer." The title of his political memoir,* The Audacity of Hope, *is lifted from the first sermon he heard by his pastor Jeremiah Wright—whom he met through his work as a community organizer in Chicago. Wright's church was distinguished by a sign on the lawn reading "Free South Africa," and Obama claims to have experienced a sort of epiphany, hearing that sermon, in which he saw contemporary political history merged with the providential scheme:*

> *In that single note—hope!—I heard something else; at the foot of that cross, inside the thousands of churches across the city, I imagined the stories of ordinary black people merging with the stories of David and Goliath, Moses and Pharaoh, the Christians in the lion's den, Ezekiel's field of dry bones.*

For Obama, as lawyer and politician alike, the American Constitution and the body of law built on it are presented as attaining a sort of sanctity. The language of the Founding Fathers is so deeply rooted in the American unconscious, he wrote in The Audacity of Hope, *that when he was teaching law at Harvard, "Sometimes I imagined my work to be not so different from the work of the theology professors who taught across campus—for, as I suspect was true for those teaching scripture, I found that my students often felt they know the Constitution without having really read it."*

The apotheosis of Obama's providential oratory was his elec-
tion night speech in Chicago. On a drizzly night, standing in
Chicago's Grant Park sandwiched between two vertical sheets of
bulletproof glass, he gave his audience the full fireworks display:

> *If there is anyone out there who still doubts that America is a*
> *place where all things are possible, who still wonders if the*
> *dream of our founders is alive in our time, who still questions*
> *the power of our democracy, tonight is your answer.*
>
> *It's the answer told by lines that stretched around schools and*
> *churches in numbers this nation has never seen, by people who*
> *waited three hours and four hours, many for the first time in*
> *their lives, because they believed that this time must be different,*
> *that their voices could be that difference.*
>
> *It's the answer spoken by young and old, rich and poor, Demo-*
> *crat and Republican, black, white, Hispanic, Asian, Native Amer-*
> *ican, gay, straight, disabled and not disabled. Americans who sent*
> *a message to the world that we have never been just a collection of*
> *individuals or a collection of red states and blue states.*
>
> *We are, and always will be, the United States of America.*
>
> *It's the answer that led those who've been told for so long by*
> *so many to be cynical and fearful and doubtful about what we*
> *can achieve to put their hands on the arc of history and bend it*
> *once more toward the hope of a better day.*
>
> *It's been a long time coming, but tonight, because of what we*
> *did on this date, in this election, at this defining moment, change*
> *has come to America.*

The familiar elements of an Obama speech are already in
place: the syntheton and tricolon; the anaphora; the encompass-
ing ethos appeal . . .

The speech's great double movement of expansion in space and time is also already established: the spiral out from the moment to the grand arc of history; from the individual voter, patiently waiting for hours in the street, to a great national movement. Here is that same movement reprised and expanded later in the speech: from me (humble individual) to you (immortal collective), and from the backyards of Des Moines to the earth—the message that "our stories are singular but our destiny is shared."

Also still vividly present is Obama's deftness in anchoring his high style to something folksier and more intimate. It won't have been, I daresay, in a deliberate echo of Nixon's "Checkers" speech that Obama turned from addressing the watching world to his two children: "Sasha and Malia, I love you both more than you can imagine. And you have earned the new puppy that's coming with us to the White House." Actually, the clever bit there is the change of addressee.

Obama preserved that connection to the human scale by anchoring the final section of his speech to the life of 106-year-old Ann Nixon Cooper.

This election had many firsts and many stories that will be told for generations. But one that's on my mind tonight's about a woman who cast her ballot in Atlanta. She's a lot like the millions of others who stood in line to make their voice heard in this election except for one thing: Ann Nixon Cooper is 106 years old.

She was born just a generation past slavery; a time when there were no cars on the road or planes in the sky; when someone like her couldn't vote for two reasons—because she was a woman and because of the color of her skin.

And tonight, I think about all that she's seen throughout her century in America—the heartache and the hope; the struggle

and the progress; the times we were told that we can't, and the people who pressed on with that American creed: Yes we can.

At a time when women's voices were silenced and their hopes dismissed, she lived to see them stand up and speak out and reach for the ballot. Yes we can.

When there was despair in the dust bowl and depression across the land, she saw a nation conquer fear itself with a New Deal, new jobs, a new sense of common purpose. Yes we can.

When the bombs fell on our harbor and tyranny threatened the world, she was there to witness a generation rise to greatness and a democracy was saved. Yes we can.

She was there for the buses in Montgomery, the hoses in Birmingham, a bridge in Selma, and a preacher from Atlanta who told a people that "We Shall Overcome." Yes we can.

A man touched down on the moon, a wall came down in Berlin, a world was connected by our own science and imagination.

And this year, in this election, she touched her finger to a screen, and cast her vote, because after 106 years in America, through the best of times and the darkest of hours, she knows how America can change.

Yes we can.

Using Ann Nixon Cooper's life, he draws an arc through the twentieth century to the present, and from the segregated South to the moon.

Obama is just as careful with his sound effects as he is with his figural structures. The slogan that won him the 2008 election, "Yes we can," draws much of its strength from its being three consecutive stressed syllables. It is a metrical object called a molossus: thump, thump, thump—as in Tennyson's "Break, break, break" or Seamus Heaney's "squat pen rests."

You could, just about, scan "Yes we can" as an anapest (diddy-dum): in response to someone who says "No you can't," you might retort "Yes we can." But you can be sure that Obama does not. The official transcript of his speech at the New Hampshire primary, for instance, punctuates it thus: "Yes. We. Can." The molossus gives an aural solidity to the message of determination.*

So it is all the more powerful that—anaphora being his characteristic figure—in this speech he reached for epistrophe, *and made that slogan the repeated phrase. Where his campaign speeches had stressed the beginnings of his flights of speech, the climax of the Chicago address stressed the ends: "At a time when women's voices were silenced . . . Yes we can. When there was despair . . . Yes we can. When the bombs fell . . . Yes we can." Here, his means really were his ends.*

How do you follow a speech like that? This, for Obama, was not a rhetorical question. His victory speech in Chicago contained an understandable element of triumph: as its figural setup suggests, it affirmed the idea of a historical process culminating.

Many expected the rhetorical style of Obama's inauguration address to match or exceed it. But the speech he gave the following January in Washington was very different in tone indeed. It looked forward rather than back—and though no less crafted than its predecessor, it was altogether more somber in tone. This was not a speech made to surf a mood of ecstasy—it was one, rather, whose task was to avoid triumphalism.

---

*Another winning slogan, "I Like Ike," scanned the same way. It occurs to me that Neil Kinnock, when he started goonishly bellowing, "We're *all right*! We're *all right*!" at the 1992 Sheffield rally, may have been attempting to co-opt the molossus magic, but lost the election because of a weak first syllable.

That we are in the midst of crisis is now well understood. Our nation is at war, against a far-reaching network of violence and hatred. Our economy is badly weakened, a consequence of greed and irresponsibility on the part of some, but also our collective failure to make hard choices and prepare the nation for a new age. Homes have been lost; jobs shed; businesses shuttered. Our health care is too costly; our schools fail too many; and each day brings further evidence that the ways we use energy strengthen our adversaries and threaten our planet.

These are the indicators of crisis, subject to data and statistics. Less measurable but no less profound is a sapping of confidence across our land—a nagging fear that America's decline is inevitable, and the next generation must lower its sights.

Today I say to you that the challenges we face are real. They are serious and they are many. They will not be met easily or in a short span of time. But know this, America—they will be met.

The language of hopes and dreams, moonshots, mountains, and promised lands is gone. Instead here is a sober vocabulary of shuttered shops ("shuttered," rather than "closed"—Obama's street-level enargia *here turned to darker purpose) and lowered sights, quantified in the dull round of "data and statistics."*

In part, this can be attributed to expectation management. You spend the election selling people hope with a capital H— then once it's in the bag you draw their attention to the small print. But it is also a matter, at least on the face of it, of making a determined appeal to his defeated opponents. He's no longer speaking as the triumphing leader of the Democratic Party, but as the president and commander in chief. Like it or not, he has to work with the Republicans and, more frightening still, Hillary Clinton.

And like it or not, they have to work with him. This is a speech designed to convey the tone of a jaw being set. There are heavy, fist-thumping stresses in that last sentence on "know," "this," "will," and "met."

> On this day, we come to proclaim an end to the petty grievances and false promises, the recriminations and worn out dogmas, that for far too long have strangled our politics.
>   We remain a young nation, but in the words of Scripture, the time has come to set aside childish things.

"We" is the dominant voice of that speech, and that "we" is placed in a line of struggle that goes through the battlefields of Gettysburg, Normandy, and Khe Sanh, the struggles of the Pilgrim Fathers, slaves, and settlers of the American West. The historical perspective is there, but the glorious workings of Providence are taking a backseat to the hard toil of post-Lapsarian man: "Starting today, we must pick ourselves up, dust ourselves off, and begin again the work of remaking America." We are in Genesis, rather than Revelation.

And it was with a wintrily particular image—more "Must We Really?" than "Yes We Can"—that he ended the speech.

> In the year of America's birth, in the coldest of months, a small band of patriots huddled by dying campfires on the shores of an icy river. The capital was abandoned. The enemy was advancing. The snow was stained with blood. At a moment when the outcome of our revolution was most in doubt, the father of our nation ordered these words be read to the people:
>   "Let it be told to the future world . . . that in the depth of winter, when nothing but hope and virtue could survive . . . that the

*city and the country, alarmed at one common danger, came
forth to meet it."*

*America, in the face of our common dangers, in this winter of
our hardship, let us remember these timeless words. With hope and
virtue, let us brave once more the icy currents, and endure what
storms may come.*

*Let it be said by our children's children that when we were
tested, we refused to let this journey end, that we did not turn back
nor did we falter; and with eyes fixed on the horizon and God's
grace upon us, we carried forth that great gift of freedom and delivered it safely to future generations.*

*In the contrast between his victory speech and his first inaugu-
ral address, Obama demonstrated his mastery of an overarching
rhetorical virtue:* kairos. *Before it is anything else, a speech needs
to be suited to the moment of its speaking.*

EPIDEICTIC RHETORIC

EPIDEICTIC, OR DISPLAY RHETORIC, has often tended to look rather like the neglected stepchild of the rhetorical triumvirate. Forensic and deliberative rhetoric are both at the center of the great functions of the state. Giant buildings in the middle of the world's biggest cities—pillared law courts and Gothic debating chambers—are devoted to them.

But the rhetoric of praise and blame? Not so much. There aren't praise palaces in the average town—unless you count churches and mosques, which aren't quite the same thing. And though I for one would love there to be government-funded buildings erected in perpetuity for the purpose of calling your enemies rude names in public, I don't see it happening.

As well as being tricky to pronounce, epideictic rhetoric is neither quite one thing nor the other. It overlaps substantially with forensic rhetoric, inasmuch as the grounds on which you praise or blame someone will be substantially influenced by what they have done in the past.

Dave is to be deplored *because* he cheats at Monopoly: and my audience is only likely to be convinced he's a bad guy if I bring his actions into evidence. And if Mark Antony's funeral oration doesn't have a bit of a deliberative kick to it—that is, an implied exhortation to his audience to hoist the traitors—I don't know what does.

Likewise, there's an admixture of epideictic rhetoric in most of the other two branches of oratory: deciding what to do, and establishing what happened, invariably leads you into questions of what it means to take a virtuous course of action, who it is proper to emulate, and what we can infer from the characters of those involved in an incident under dispute.

So by just the same token as you can argue that display rhetoric is marginal to the other two kinds, you can also argue that it underpins them. And more to the point, for very many of us today, the only full-dress formal oratory we're likely to engage in is epideictic.

Epideictic rhetoric covers the speeches you hear at weddings from the best man, the maid of honor, and the father of the bride. It covers the speeches you hear at funerals and the language of obituaries. Epideictic rhetoric first emerged some years later than the other two branches, and its flowering is credited to a second-generation sophist called Isocrates, who lived between 436 and 338 BC.

Isocrates wanted to rescue the reputation of sophistry from the Platonic charge that it was the linguistic equivalent of selling snake oil. Against Plato's hostility to anything that distracted from discovering the eternal verities of philosophy, Isocrates insisted that the worldly and practical objectives of politics were deserving objects of study. In the fallen world, these are what we have to work with.

There is no science of human affairs, but sound judgment, as opposed to knowledge, is both possible and necessary to strive for. And one of the things Isocrates emphasized, as Aristotle was to do also, was the importance of *kairos*, or timing: a speech had to be fitted to its moment. What carried the day at one instant would work not at all at another. Here was a rhetoric of pragmatism, a rhetoric involved in the world.

He founded his own school of rhetoric, where he sought to emphasize that persuasive skill should be at the service of knowledge and wisdom: that they worked in concert, and that the ideal orator would also be a virtuous man: *kalos kai agathos*.

In *Against the Sophists*, Isocrates inveighed against the shysters who were giving rhetoric teachers a bad name: "They pretend to search for truth, but straightway at the beginning of their professions attempt to deceive us with lies."

No doubt with an eye to his own exorbitant tuition fees, he sarcastically mocked teachers who professed to impart all the skills necessary to a good citizen for "an insignificant price," and who were guilty of mechanistically "applying the analogy of an art with hard and fast rules to a creative process."

Proper teaching of rhetoric, according to Isocrates, was no more nor less than the imparting of principles that would show us how to act in the world, and as his peroration put it:

> Let no one suppose that I claim that just living can be taught;
> for, in a word, I hold that there does not exist an art of the kind
> which can implant sobriety and justice in depraved natures.
> Nevertheless, I do think that the study of political discourse
> can help more than any other thing to stimulate and form such
> qualities of character.

In taking this view he anticipated the tradition that was to put rhetoric at the center of civic education. Cato defined an orator as "a good man with experience of speaking,"* and Cicero—in marked contrast to the cynical picture painted in Gorgias of the ignorant leading the ignorant—warned: "No one can speak well, unless he thoroughly understands his subject."**

Isocrates, in other words, recognized that rhetoric need not be, or should not be, independent of value judgments. Concentrating not on immediate advantage but on perfection of style—work that was not only useful but beautiful, that "while best displaying the ability of those who speak, brings most profit to those who hear"—Isocrates gave epideictic rhetoric its own space in the world.

But I want to start by taking a closer look at something that predates Isocrates: namely, Gorgias's encomium to Helen, one of the first examples of epideictic rhetoric to survive.

Gorgias set out to praise Helen, and—here we see a definite tincture of the judicial in his speech—to argue that she was not to blame for the destruction of Troy. He starts with a *dialysis*: suggesting a number of possible reasons for her move to Troy: "For either by will of Fate and decision of the gods and vote of Necessity did she do what she did, or by force reduced or by words seduced or by love possessed."

These are addressed point by point. Let us suppose it was the first, he says. The will of the gods is beyond human power to resist—and it is in the nature of things not for the strong to be

---

Vir bonus dicenti peritus.
**Dicere enim bene nemo potest, nisi qui prudenter intelligit.*

compelled by the weak but for the weak to be compelled by the strong.* Therefore she was blameless in the matter.

If, on the other hand, she was dragged away by mortal force and raped, he continues—stating, to modern ears, the obvious—nor then is she to blame: "Surely it is proper for a woman raped and robbed of her country and deprived of her loved ones to be pitied rather than pilloried."

But the next point is one that Gorgias pays particular attention to. What if she was "by words seduced"? This gives him the opportunity to launch into a direct explanation of the power of rhetoric itself: "Speech is a powerful lord, which by means of the finest and most invisible body affects the divinest works: it can stop fear and banish grief and create joy and nurture pity." He joys in the paradox of condemning the very practice he seeks to extol. "All who have and do persuade people of things do so by molding a false argument," he says.

If everyone had a wide and perfect knowledge of the past, apprehension of the present, and foreknowledge of the future, speech would not hold the power it does. But since we find it hard to recall the past, are fuzzy on the present, and know nothing of the future, "On most subjects most men take opinion as counselor to their soul, but since opinion is slippery and insecure it casts those employing it into slippery and insecure successes."

This, incidentally, is more or less the exact argument that, a couple of millennia later, is implied by the work of the economist

---

*Here, he appeals to one of the "topics" Aristotle was to set out—templates governing the relationships between ideas. Here, the inference is made that if in general the gods are stronger than mortals, the rule holds in this instance too.

Joseph Stiglitz. Free markets, he says, work perfectly fairly as long as everyone involved has access to the same information. Asymmetries of information are what distort markets—and are, we might add, the main reason advertising works.

Gorgias advances Helen's case by analogy with his dismissal of the previous possibility: "What cause then prevents the conclusion that Helen similarly, against her will, might have come under the influence of speech, just as if ravished by the force of the mighty?" That's *erotema*, by the way. See how making the whole proposition a yes/no question (and one that implies its own answer) craftily shifts attention away from the possibility that persuasion and main force might not be equivalent? "The persuader, like a constrainer, does the wrong," concludes Gorgias deadpan—in the course of a speech whose whole purpose is persuasion.

> The effect of speech upon the condition of the soul is comparable to the power of drugs over the nature of bodies. For just as different drugs dispel different secretions from the body, and some bring an end to disease and others to life, so also in the case of speeches, some distress, others delight, some cause fear, others make the hearers bold, and some drug and bewitch the soul with a kind of evil persuasion.

Finally, he says, if it was love that brought her to Troy, then she is no more to blame for that. Once again, he builds by analogy on his previous proofs: "If, being a god, Love has the divine power of the gods, how could a lesser being reject and refuse it? But if it is a disease of human origin and a fault of the soul, it should not be blamed as a sin, but regarded as an affliction."

All of this may well seem fair enough. To a modern audience, Gorgias's attempt to exonerate Helen looks less perverse than it would to his Attic contemporaries. But to Gorgias's audience it would have been rather like putting a poster of George W. Bush up in a common room at Sarah Lawrence College. Her culpability in the destruction of Troy was a given: Gorgias identifies her at the outset as "a woman about whom the testimony of inspired poets has become univocal and unanimous as has the ill omen of her name, which has become a reminder of misfortunes."

That perversity is a clue as to what's going on here. The encomium is a performance: at once a shop window for Gorgias's own practice as a teacher of rhetoric, and a straight description of the power of rhetoric itself. It is not purely instrumental: Helen's reputation is the occasion for the speech, not its motive. It is suggestive as to which sort of arena we find ourselves in that the people Gorgias imagines himself refuting are poets.

Gorgias's conclusion is one of self-congratulation: "I have by means of speech removed disgrace from a woman; I have observed the procedure which I set up at the beginning of the speech; I have tried to end the injustice of blame and the ignorance of opinion; I wished to write a speech which would be a praise of Helen and *a diversion to myself*" [my emphasis].

When he writes "a diversion to myself," Gorgias is pointing out the ludic nature of epideictic rhetoric. It draws much of its power from delight. Good rhetoric is an entertainment to speaker and audience alike. Delight is the sugar that makes the medicine go down.

We've spoken about the pleasures to be had from rhetoric of praise and exoneration. But epideictic rhetoric also covers speeches of open attack, and one of the gutsiest instances of it

that I've come across is the speech given by Alfred E. Smith at a citizens' meeting in New York in June 1919.

Alfred "Al" E. Smith was a phenomenally gifted politician, who having left school at fourteen to help support his fatherless family, rose to the governorship of New York in 1919. There, he found himself under attack from one of the most powerful men in the nation, the newspaper baron William Randolph Hearst.

Hearst was notoriously unscrupulous in using his newspapers—he owned a coast-to-coast chain of them—to settle personal scores and broker political influence. Hearst had wanted Al Smith to lower the price of milk—and when Smith refused, Hearst had used his newspapers to accuse him of starving children.

Smith challenged Hearst to debate him in public at a meeting called by the citizens' committee in Carnegie Hall. The tycoon refused to show*—and so Smith had the floor to himself. Rather than conciliate Hearst, Smith went on the attack.

In his exordium, Smith asked for absolute hush, and sought to corral the audience into understanding what followed as being of the utmost gravity: "I feel that I am here tonight upon a mission as important not only to myself but to this city, this state and this country as I could possibly perform."

That elegant and resonant sentence does a lot of work. It first of all keys into an appeal to ethos. Rather than the self-defense of a politician at bay, it casts the beleaguered Smith as part of a continuum, the representative of something larger that is under attack. It seeks to ally his interests with those of his audience, and their interests with something wider still.

---

*"I know the color of his liver," Smith told his audience, "and it is whiter, if that could be, than the driven snow."

Note the classic three-point *auxesis*—the tricolon "this city, this state and this country," of which countless near-variants can be found in political speeches through the ages. As an enthymeme, the hidden premise of this is that the interests of city, state, and country are identical—which, of course, they very seldom if ever are.

Note, too, the way in which—rather than announcing a simple defense of his policy position, effectively taking a passive role, Smith announces that he's on an active "mission" and one of, using hyperbole, the greatest importance possible. Already he has turned defense into attack, passive into active—and with this idea of a mission he folds an implied sense of future action into the framing of his speech. Here, an energizing coloring of deliberative rhetoric enters his discourse.

Then, it's both barrels for Citizen Kane, who has perpetrated what Smith calls "the gravest abuse of the power of the press that was ever wielded by a newspaper or by an individual in the history of this country."

"I cannot think of a more contemptible man," he says, and then starts again as if momentarily dumbfounded by the enormity of Hearst's wrongdoing, a figure known as *interruptio* or *aposiopesis*:

> My power of imagination fails me to bring into my mind's eye a more despicable man than the man that exploits the poor. Any man that leads you to believe that your lot in life is not all right, any man that conjures up for you a fancied grievance against your government or against the man at the head of it, to help himself, is breeding the seeds of anarchy and dissatisfaction more disastrous to the welfare of the community that it is used in than any other teaching that I can think of, because,

at least, the wildest anarchist, the most extreme Socialist, the wildest radical that you can think of may at least be sincere in his own heart.

That great rolling sentence has as the engine of its forward movement the figure of anaphora: "any man that . . . any man that . . . ," which itself echoes and expands the *anadiplosis* of "man . . . man" used in the previous sentence. And the effect of the sentence is, of course, to torpedo any ethos appeal Hearst might seek to make.

The bogeymen of anarchism and socialism (as it is implied, also false friends to the poor) are raised, nearly irrelevantly, simply in order to contrast them with Hearst himself—who as well as being a baddie is an insincere baddie. This is, it's worth noting, a classic anti-rhetorical stance. Hearst's rabble-rousing through his newspapers is dismissed as self-serving and slippery: just the sort of rhetoric, in other words, of which Plato would have disapproved.

Smith continues:

> He [the wildest radical] may think that it is right when he preaches it. But the man that preaches to the poor of this or of any other community discontent and dissatisfaction to help himself and to make good his side of the argument and to destroy, as he said himself he would, the Governor of the State, is a man as low and as mean as I can picture.

Here the figures of amplification are in full effect: that nicely alliterative *synonymia*—"discontent and dissatisfaction"—sits alongside the larger parallelism of "to help himself and to make good his side of the argument," and the sentence is further stuffed

with little parentheses ("as he said himself he would") and *poly-syndeton* ("of this or of any other community").

Bear in mind that most of the sentence no more than reiterates in different words what has already been said. All of this works, through its rhythm and the anticipation, to lend the maximum possible force to that stinging final clause.

You'll notice, too, how sparing Smith is with Hearst's actual name, instead casting him repeatedly as "the man that . . . "—a powerful trope known as *antonomasia*, where an epithet or description is substituted for a proper name, or vice versa. This has the effect, essentially, of casting the unnamed subject for the duration of the speech as something less or something more than human: a personification, in effect, of the qualities the orator attributes to him.

William Randolph Hearst, of course, is long gone. A more modern example still is worth bringing in. And there are few more accomplished contemporary proponents of the rhetoric of blame and insult than Eric Cartman, the foul-mouthed nine-year-old fattie from *South Park*.

In 1999's *South Park: Bigger, Longer and Uncut*, Cartman produces his negative-energy equivalent of Isocrates's panegyricus or Gorgias's encomium to Helen: the foot-stomping sing-along "Kyle's Mom's a Bitch."

The song's dominant figural strategy—the bass note, if you like—is *epistrophe*: that is, the repetition of a word or phrase at the end of a sentence or line.* Thus, the opening stanza (sung allegro):

---

*It's of course worth acknowledging that, since it's in the form of a song, figures of repetition like that are far more likely to crop up. All this is no more than to point to what should be apparent throughout these pages, which is that there's often a very close coincidence between rhetoric and poetics. Verse or song form can steer you toward certain effects, like a bottom settling gratefully into a comfy chair.

> *Kyle's mom's a bitch!*
> *She's a big fat bitch!*
> *She's the biggest bitch in the whole wide world!*
> *She's a stupid bitch!*
> *If there ever was a bitch!*
> *She's a bitch to all the boys and girls!*

Note, though, the virtuosic way in which other figures are interwoven. The first three lines use auxesis—the arrangement of clauses in a sequence of increasing extravagance. She's not just a bitch, but a big fat bitch. In fact, she's the biggest bitch in the whole wide world. Line three is also an instance of hyperbole.

The next triplet of lines offers a neat little anadiplosis, the figure in which the phrase that ends one line begins the next. "Bitch" is suddenly the departure point of line six rather than its destination—and Cartman opens the line out into an ethos appeal. His audience (or so, at the time, he thinks) is made up entirely of nine-year-old children: exactly the "boys and girls" with whom he seeks to ally himself against the supposed enemy.

That's enough for Kyle, who interjects: "Shut your fucking mouth Cartman!"*

Cartman does not shut his mouth, continuing with a touch of isocolon:

> *On Monday she's a bitch,*
> *On Tuesday she's a bitch,*
> *On Wednesday though Saturday she's a bitch!*
> *Then on Sunday just to be different,*
> *She's a super King Kamehameha bitch!*

---

*Though it stands in isolation, here, Kyle's futile yelp may be a little poignantly categorized as *ekphonesis*.

Then it's the turn of apostrophe, as he interrupts himself to reach out, again, to his audience:

> *Come on! You all know the words!*

And next it's *erotema*, or the rhetorical question. See how he draws his listeners in?

> *Have you ever met my friend Kyle's mom?*
> *She's the biggest bitch in the whole wide world!*

Digressio is next, as Cartman leaves his central theme to cast aspersions on her hairdresser . . .

> *She's a mean old bitch,*
> *And she has stupid hair!*

. . . before launching into a bravura demonstration of *epizeuxis*, repeating the word "bitch" no fewer than fifteen times in a row.

> *She's a bitch, bitch, bitch, bitch, bitch, bitch, bitch,*
> *bitch, bitch, bitch, bitch, bitch, bitch, bitch, bitch!*

And so, magnificently, it goes on—including an interlude that appears to be sung by other children in Mandarin, French, Dutch, and what might be Swahili*—only to come to an inglorious end.

---

*It would be stretching a point to describe this as Asianism.

It becomes clear that Kyle's mom is standing right behind Cartman as—stomping and howling and waggling his jazz-hands—he brings his sung peroration to its climax. The smiles fall off the children's faces to be replaced with expressions of horror as Eric sings, oblivious, on. As well as being an instance of dramatic irony, this is also, as Isocrates would have been the first to remind him, a terrible failure of *kairos*.

CHAMPIONS OF RHETORIC VII

The Unknown Speechwriter

HAVE YOU EVER HEARD *the phrase "the Founding Fathers"? Do you know anything about Judson Welliver? If the answers to these questions, in order, are "yes" and "no"—as for most readers they will be—I rest my case. Judson Welliver (1870–1943) is the man who minted that phrase, and as "literary executive secretary" to President Warren Harding is widely regarded as having been the first presidential speechwriter.**

As I wrote very near the beginning of this book, it is to the power of the word rather than the power of the sword that we

---

*In America, current and former presidential speechwriters meet at the Judson Welliver Society.

owe most of the history of Western civilization. But where are the memorials?

There exist, here and there, statues to great orators—though in the modern age it is as warriors that they are normally pictured, a horse and a sword being that much more butch on a sculpture than a toga and a mouth set to catch flies. But where we are invited to shed a manly tear at any number of eternal flames dedicated to the memory of this Unknown Soldier or that one, where is the flame dedicated to the Unknown Speechwriter?

To fight anonymously is regarded as an office of honor. To write anonymously—and here, we go all the way back to that atavistic mistrust of the sophists in ancient Athens—is seen as the opposite. To "put words in someone else's mouth" is the act of the conniver and the trickster, and to speak another's words is seen as somehow shameful—a de facto undermining of your ethos appeal.

That seems unfair, and in this chapter I'd like briefly to offer these men and women a cheery salute, whoever and wherever they are. If not an eternal flame, let this chapter serve as a brief candle.

We all remember Margaret Thatcher announcing, "You turn, if you want to. The lady's not for turning" in response to people questioning her direction of the economy. But few of us will remember the 1948 stage play—Christopher Fry's The Lady's Not for Burning—*on which her phrase punned.* And fewer still will have heard the name of Ronald Millar (1919–1998), who actually wrote the line for her. The literary allusion aside, is that not a fine instance of a speechwriter capturing exactly the temper of the politician for whom he is writing?*

---

*It's said Mrs. Thatcher herself didn't.

A good speechwriter doesn't put words into a politician's mouth, and an effective politician won't let one do so: for the former, the task of writing against character is too difficult; for the latter, the risks of putting someone else in charge of your mouth are too high.

To adapt Pope, admiring the poet who could write "what oft was thought, but ne'er so well exprest," the speechwriter aims to write what the speaker thinks, in the most eloquent terms in which the speaker might plausibly express it.

Ronnie Millar also wrote Mrs. Thatcher's first—apparently extempore—speech from the doorstep of Number 10 Downing Street in 1979 after her election as prime minister:

> *I know full well the responsibilities that await me as I enter the door of Number 10 and I'll strive unceasingly to try to fulfill the trust and confidence that the British people have placed in me and the things in which I believe. And I would just like to remember some words of St. Francis of Assisi* which I think are really just particularly apt at the moment. "Where there is discord, may we bring harmony. Where there is error, may we bring truth. Where there is doubt, may we bring faith. And where there is despair, may we bring hope." And to all the British people—howsoever*

---

*As an appeal to authority, incidentally, the St. Francis of Assisi reference is hard to beat. Or is it? The scholarly journalist Christopher Howse, writing in the *Daily Telegraph*, has the real story: "The words were put into Lady Thatcher's mouth by Ronald Millar, her chief speechwriter. He probably thought the words had indeed first been uttered by St. Francis of Assisi. In reality, they date back no earlier than 1912. They appeared in a pious French magazine called *La Clochette*, published by a group founded in 1901 by Father Esther Bouquerel, who perhaps wrote them. They were fastened on St. Francis after being printed on the back of a picture of him in 1920."

they voted—may I say this. Now that the election is over, may we get together and strive to serve and strengthen the country of which we're so proud to be a part. And finally, one last thing: in the words of Airey Neave, whom we had hoped to bring here with us, "There is now work to be done."

Mrs. Thatcher had asked Millar "almost shyly," a few days before the election, if he had thought of anything she might say in the event of becoming prime minister. He had had the supposed St. Francis quote on the back burner, but didn't tempt fate by handing it over until the results were in.

When she read it on election night, his memoirs[1] recorded, "Her eyes swam. She blew her nose." It was dispatched at four in the morning to be typed up by a Central Office secretary—who, if the version of the Thatcher Foundation is correct, also burst into tears.

The Thatcher Foundation's website (www.margaretthatcher .org) has a discussion of the speech's history that gives a good window into the closeness of the interaction between speechwriter and politician.

It preserves, for instance, a facsimile of the typed draft in note form, with Mrs. Thatcher's manuscript alterations. She has underlined "discord," "harmony," "error," and "truth," and seems to have tried above all to qualify any notes of triumphalism that might be used against her (this address does quite similar work, in miniature, to Barack Obama's inauguration address).

Where it says "know the great responsibilities that await as I enter this door," she has inserted "but humbling" after "great." Where the typescript says: "will strive to fulfill the trust that has been placed in me and the things in which we believe," she has inserted "unceasingly" after "strive," "and confidence" after

"trust" (for rhythmic reasons, presumably, and to balance "strive unceasingly"—"trust and confidence" does no semantic work that "trust" doesn't do on its own). She has also struck out "me and," and fretted over "the things in which we believe," replacing "we" first with "my party," and then with "I."

"Humbling" didn't survive to the delivered version—nor did "great," come to that. "Me and" made it in, whether deliberately or not. But the most significant alteration (not in this draft) was apparently made at Millar's suggestion. To avoid the Messianic tone, the original prayer—which said "where there is discord may I *bring harmony . . . where there is error may* I *bring truth" [my emphasis]—was amended to "may* we *bring harmony . . . may* we *bring truth."*

The final speech was delivered with the help of an aide-mémoire scribbled in blue felt-tip—she concealed it in her hand, and consulted it only once.

It reads (in as good a transcription as I can manage):

HM—accepted
Know great responsibilities
—enter door.
Strive unceasingly: fulfil
trust
Discord—harmony
Error—truth
Doubt—faith
Dispair*—hope

---

*As well as being a leader who didn't know the meaning of surrender, it turns out she was also one who didn't know the spelling of *despair*. The handwriting's sketchy, but I'm pretty damn sure that's an "i."

> *British people—however*
> *they voted*
> *come together*
> *serve—strengthen*
> *A.N. "there's work to be done"*

Here, surely, is a fine example—whatever your politics—of how a speechwriter and a politician can work together, hand in glove, to produce something that lives.

For every Margaret Thatcher there is a Ronnie Millar; for every Barack Obama, a Jon Favreau; for every John F. Kennedy, a Ted Sorensen ("Ask not what your country can do for you, but what you can do for your country," was Sorensen's).

The importance of these men and women is attested to by the long-running political drama The West Wing*—widely praised for its verisimilitude. In a nice scene displaying a speechwriter put on his mettle, it shows with just what ease and pragmatism the ancient figures are still used.*

Toby Ziegler, White House communications honcho, finds himself talking to a policewoman, Rhonda Sachs, near a mob of anarchists demonstrating against the World Trade Organization.

TOBY: *You want the benefits of free trade? Food is cheaper.*

SACHS: *Yes.*

TOBY: *Food is cheaper, clothes are cheaper, steel is cheaper, cars are cheaper, phone service is cheaper. . . . [*You feel me building a rhythm here? That's 'cause I'm a speechwriter and I know how to make a point . . . *] It lowers prices, it raises income. [*You see what I did with "lowers" and "raises" there?*]*

SACHS: *Yes.*

TOBY: *[It's called the science of listener attention. We did repetition, we did floating opposites, and now you end with
the one that's not like the others. Ready?] Free trade stops
wars. [And that's it.] Free trade stops wars! [And we figure out a way to fix the rest!] One world, one peace. [I'm
sure I've seen that on a sign somewhere.]*

SACHS: *God, Toby . . . Wouldn't it be great if there was someone around here with communication skills who could go
in there and tell them that?*

*To return to real politics, a consideration of the Unknown
Speechwriter also offers one of the rare opportunities this subject
affords to turn our attentions to a woman. Among the best-
respected speechwriters of the twentieth century is Peggy Noonan,
who wrote for Ronald Reagan—Jon Favreau is on record as holding her in the highest regard, whatever their ideological differences,
and reportedly consulted her before writing Obama's inauguration
speech.*

*If Ronnie Millar's negotiations with Mrs. Thatcher about her
Downing Street address give a sense of speechwriter and principal
working together on the hoof, Noonan's memoirs[2] give a sense of
how the relationship goes when the full apparatus of an established administration is in swing.*

*"I began my career writing for the ear," says Noonan, who got
her start as a news writer for a Boston radio station. Even then she
couldn't resist an oratorical flourish, and she couldn't resist edito-
rializing; her script for Dan Rather after the acquittal of President
Reagan's would-be assassin John Hinckley began, "Something is
wrong here. Wrong about this age of millionaire assassins . . ." She*

confesses that during her time in the White House, "I experi-
mented with writing speeches in free verse, which may give you an
idea of what you're occasionally in for."

Her memoirs are, it should be said, tough, folksy, and win-
ningly bonkers. When all of her contemporaries were protesting
the Vietnam War, Noonan was a teen Republican of some cussed-
ness. So her relationship with Reagan, as she represents it, was one
part political crush and one part real crush.

Here's how she describes her first encounter with the Gipper:

> *I first saw him as a foot, a highly polished brown cordovan wag-*
> *ging merrily on a hassock. I spied it through the door. It was a*
> *beautiful foot, sleek. Such casual elegance and clean lines. But*
> *not a big foot, not formidable, maybe even a little . . . frail. I*
> *imagined cradling it in my arms, protecting it from unsmooth*
> *roads.*

The first time that one of Noonan's draft speeches came back
marked "Very good—RR," she says, she "cut it out and taped it to
my blouse, like a second-grader with a star."

She adored Reagan, but when she went to the White House as
his speechwriter, she bitterly resented being asked to write for
Nancy. On feminist grounds, it seems. On one occasion that she
was forced to, she says, "I wrote a nice bad speech, so sugary she'd
have to lick her fingers afterward. 'My life didn't begin until I met
Ronnie . . . '" Afterward, she reports with satisfaction, "Jim Rose-
bush [a senior presidential aide] called. 'Congratulations,' he
said. 'She loved it!'"

So, as I say, slightly bonkers. But Noonan did write some sen-
sationally good speeches for her hero, and in a chapter called, nat-

urally, "Speech! Speech!" she sets out how she saw her job in char-
acteristically rococo language.

> A speech is part theater and part political declaration; it is a per-
> sonal communication between a leader and his people; it is art;
> and all art is a paradox, being at once a thing of great power and
> great delicacy. . . . A speech reminds us that words, like children,
> have the power to make dance the dullest beanbag of a heart.

When she writes that a speaker "will tell us who he is and what
he wants and how he will get it and what it means that he wants it
and what it will mean when he does or does not get it," she is in entire agreement with Aristotle. When she says that speeches are not
only "the way we measure public men, they have been how we tell
each other who we are," she is in entire agreement with Aristotle.

Noonan is a true believer in the force of oratory as a way of
shaping tribal identity, and of the importance of literary techniques in conveying political ideas. (Most of Washington's political professionals, she says, are not: they call speeches "the rah
rah" and are more interested in advertisements.)

"Sound bites," she argues with unanswerable rightness, have
always existed—but they are not, as some younger speechwriters
seem to think, raisins to be plonked onto a bowl of porridge. They
should arise inevitably from the natural expression of the text:
"They are part of the tapestry—they aren't a little flower somebody sewed on."

Likewise, she describes how policy wonks undervalue speechwriters, casting themselves as "substantive types," writers as "word-
smiths," and forcing the "wonderful, clean, shining, perfectly
shaped and delicious vegetables" of Noonan's words and ideas

through the bureaucratic meat grinder and rendering them "a smooth, dull, textureless puree."

Working in an environment like the White House, Noonan says, reaching for another culinary image, "The speech is a fondue pot, and everyone has a fork." (She also says, still not straying from the kitchen, that "a good speech is really a sausage skin, the stronger it is the more you shove in.") The president's aides accept this or that invitation, and mark it down as the opportunity to make this or that point. The speechwriters lobby to be assigned the speech. They are supported by researchers, and will be given anything between a few days and a fortnight to write it.

Noonan would start by assembling relevant books, previous speeches, and background information on the issues, audience, and event. As she researched, she'd jot notes, fragments of phrases, and thoughts, "take them home and stare at them." Then in the writing phase, she'd read poetry and biographies—Walter Jackson Bate's biography of Dr. Johnson, and Ezra Pound's Cantos *("I don't think I ever understood a one. It didn't matter, the anarchy of the language and the sweeping away of the syntax had force."*)*

---

*Interesting and apposite, this point about the force of sweeping away syntax, and not just because Noonan herself has the ugly habit of running two sentences together with a comma splice. As should by now be apparent, ungrammatical language (one-word sentences, hypallage, absent main verbs, etc.) works fine in spoken rhetoric. In his book *Winning Arguments*, Jay Heinrichs argues persuasively that though George W. Bush is mocked for his verbal clumsiness, he is actually a highly effective orator. He uses emotive, ethos-laden code words "without the distraction of logic. He speaks in short sentences, repeating code phrases in effective, if irrational order." So when Bush says, "Families is where our nation finds hope, where wings take dream," Heinrichs argues, the fact that it's nonsense is much less important than the fact that the audience hears "families . . . nation . . . wings . . . dream."

She'd draft and redraft, handing a final draft in to her boss on deadline feeling it was hopeless. When she got it back with his marks, she'd reread and "realize for the first time that it was actually pretty brilliant, so delicate and yet so vital, so vital and yet so tender."

Then it would go out to the "staffing process": anything between twenty and fifty members of the White House staff and relevant federal agencies would read and suggest edits . . . and Noonan would have to fight tooth and nail to keep her beloved vegetables intact.

A prime instance came with one of the first big speeches she wrote for Reagan, an address to students in Shanghai for his 1984 trip to China. Playing off the proximity of the Yangtze River to the venue for the speech, Noonan had proudly included in her peroration the metaphor:

> *My young friends, history is a river that takes us as it will. But we have the power to navigate, to choose direction, and make our passage together. The wind is up, the tide is high, and opportunity for a long and fruitful journey awaits us. Generations hence will honor us for having begun the voyage . . .*

Senior advisers in the State Department—unimpressed by Noonan's claim that it was "literature"—regarded the river metaphor as "politically unhelpful" on the grounds that it seemed to echo Marxist ideas of historical determinism, and a long and hilariously literal-minded memo followed, adding that "with the exception of where rivers meet the sea, there is rarely if ever an appreciable tide that affects navigation, and unless the wind is blowing in the proper direction, it is more a nuisance than an inducement to sail."

Noonan in the end triumphed. The delivered version of the speech has the watery qualification that the river "may take us as it will" [my emphasis] but is otherwise substantially as written. Those of us sympathizing somewhat with the State Department over the question of whether rivers have tides, incidentally, will be pleased to know that "the current is swift" replaced "the tide is high."

Noonan's finest hour was Reagan's so-called Pointe Du Hoc speech, delivered on the fortieth anniversary of D-Day from the formidable fortification in Normandy, overlooking both Omaha and Utah Beaches, that the US Army Rangers stormed during Operation Overlord. The speech is, truly, a corker.

Reagan channels the emotional voltage of addressing a crowd of veterans at the scene of their most desperate fight, and turns it into an admonitory message about his vision of the Cold War. The historical moment of a fight against tyranny in 1944 is mapped onto the moment in which the speech is being delivered: it seeks to wire the emotional charge of D-Day into the batteries off which Reagan was running the Cold War.

If this sounds cynical, it isn't. I don't think Reagan was cynical about the Cold War: he believed it was no less of an existential fight than the Second World War. And if you read the Pointe du Hoc speech as an apolitical commemoration of the dead, you haven't read it right. Noonan herself complains that in the editing process, "The speech was losing part of its literature to save time and they kept shoving in last-minute policy and I kept cutting lines to make room."

It opens with that now-familiar trick of funneling huge forces of history into a singular place and time. The clichés don't really matter—indeed, in the crescent rhythm of the opening passage, they help. "Millions cried out for liberation" is, probably intentionally, an echo of Liberty's "huddled masses yearning to be free."

We're here to mark that day in history when the Allied armies joined in battle to reclaim this continent to liberty. For four long years, much of Europe had been under a terrible shadow. Free nations had fallen, Jews cried out in the camps, millions cried out for liberation. Europe was enslaved, and the world prayed for its rescue. Here in Normandy the rescue began. Here the Allies stood and fought against tyranny in a giant undertaking unparalleled in human history.

Then comes the enargia. The soft air of the here-and-now dissolves to the rent air of "this moment" forty years ago.

We stand on a lonely, windswept point on the northern shore of France. The air is soft, but forty years ago at this moment, the air was dense with smoke and the cries of men, and the air was filled with the crack of rifle fire and the roar of cannon.

As Reagan describes the Rangers climbing up the cliffs to assail the fortifications, according to Noonan, the rhythm of the sentences is as it is because "I wanted this to have the rhythm of a rough advance." It does.

The Rangers looked up and saw the enemy soldiers—the edge of the cliffs shooting down at them with machineguns and throwing grenades. And the American Rangers began to climb. They shot rope ladders over the face of these cliffs and began to pull themselves up. When one Ranger fell, another would take his place. When one rope was cut, a Ranger would grab another and begin his climb again. They climbed, shot back, and held their footing. Soon, one by one, the Rangers pulled themselves over the top, and in seizing the firm land at the top of these cliffs, they

began to seize back the continent of Europe. Two hundred and twenty-five came here. After two days of fighting, only ninety could still bear arms.

Then comes the great lump-in-throat moment of the speech: a four-part anaphoric *auxesis,* followed by an apostrophe *to the veterans themselves.*

Behind me is a memorial that symbolizes the Ranger daggers that were thrust into the top of these cliffs. And before me are the men who put them there.

These are the boys of Pointe du Hoc. These are the men who took the cliffs. These are the champions who helped free a continent. These are the heroes who helped end a war.

Gentlemen, I look at you and I think of the words of Stephen Spender's poem. You are men who in your "lives fought for life . . . and left the vivid air signed with your honor."

"The boys of Pointe du Hoc . . . " That's affecting because it is so familiar an idiom, not presidential but fraternal. And it is more affecting because they were *boys. The effect is, somehow, to collapse time—to bring the boys, living and dead, from forty years ago and make them vivid in the here and now. Noonan says the phrase was a "happy steal" from a baseball memoir called* The Boys of Summer.

It signals a break into the plain style—the style of which Reagan was an absolute master. From the airy grandeur of his opening remarks—with its "terrible shadow," its "undertaking unparalleled in human history," and its mellifluously dactylic invocation of "liberty"—he has descended to the affectionately conversational.

His next line is "I think I know what you may be thinking right now," and shortly thereafter he is telling another war story as you might recount a visit to the shops: "Suddenly, they heard the sound of bagpipes, and some thought they were dreaming. Well, they weren't . . ."

The speech—essentially epideictic in theory—ends with a strong deliberative thrust: "Here, in this place where the West held together, let us make a vow to our dead. Let us show them by our actions that we understand what they died for." By the time you get there, what audience—with the boys of Pointe du Hoc sitting right there, and the dead looking on in silent reproach—is going to find it easy to decline? Noonan nailed that one, no question.

It seems fitting that this salute to the Unknown Speechwriter should end with a reminder of why such a salute is needed. In What I Saw at the Revolution, the relentlessly upbeat Noonan recalls a poignant moment. After all those years of protecting the presidential feet from unsmooth roads, she says, "Years later Ronald Reagan turned to me and said, with wistfulness: 'I used to write my own speeches, you know.'"

THUS IT CAN BE SHOWN . . .

THAT'S HOW WE USED to do perorations in our essays at school, isn't it? You wrote an "Introduction," saying what you were going to show. Then an essay showing it. Then a "Conclusion" that always seemed to begin with the unearthly phrase "Thus it can be shown that . . ." and that more or less restated your introduction.

Well. I hope that this book has done more than that. As I send it out into the world—"go, litel boke!"—I do so with the wish that, rather than just mechanically demonstrating a set of propositions, it has given you a sense of the way argument can live.

If they have done anything, I fervently hope that these pages have shown that rhetoric is not a dry, narrow, out-of-date academic subject: rather, that it gathers in the folds of its robe everything that makes us human. Rhetoric is everywhere language is, and language is everywhere people are. To be fascinated by rhetoric is to be fascinated by people, and to understand rhetoric is in large part to understand your fellow human beings. I want to pass on not knowledge, in this book, but love.

That was where Aristotle, to me, hit on something far more valuable than Plato. He saw the world was compromised and imperfect, and that we don't live in a world of abstract forms: we live in a world of people. He saw that human beings are not actuated by abstract knowledge but by fear and desire, and that as long as there are people, they will spend their whole lives trying to talk each other round. Rather than turn away in dismay, he worked to understand that. And what he found was wonderful.

In the West, traditions ascribe the parenthood of the persuasive arts to gods (Hermes, who is both the trickster and the messenger god) and to heroes (wily old Odysseus), but gods and heroes are no more than mirrors in which we see ourselves. They are metonyms. They are figures.

People have been talking each other in and out of fights and in and out of bed since the first syllable formed on the first ape-like prehistoric lip. The total corpus of everything they've ever said is the object of study: the patterns that obtain across centuries are testament to our commonality; the ceaseless variation testament to the power and elasticity of invention. Rhetoric is inexhaustible.

If language is the air, rhetoric is the weather—from the gentlest and most uplifting spring day to thunder that rattles the windows in their frames. It's out there. It obtains. It's everywhere. Sail before the wind.

Glossary

Alliteration is a concept most of us are familiar with from being taught poetry. It's a rhetorical figure too. The repetition of consonant sounds is a way of wiring words and concepts together. It's particularly handy in the age of the sound bite, where politicians and advertisers alike need slogans to stick in the mind. Think of all the "Affirmative Action" and "Bank Bailouts" we hear of. See also *assonance*.

Amplificatio is a generalized term for anything that tends to expansion in expression or effect: heightened or circumlocutory language, elaborate comparisons, and so forth. Anything that pushes "the cat sat on the mat" in the direction of "Princess Tiddleyboo, feline paragon, Queen of the Jellicle armies and scourge of the vole, curled her Persian person onto the Persian rug of distant Araby" would come under *amplificatio*. See also *auxesis*.

Anacoluthon is breaking off a sentence so the first half you write, the second part is grammatically different.

Anadiplosis is a particularly elegant and effective figure—typically combining a figure of repetition with one of amplification. Like the Itsy-Bitsy Spider going end over end up the waterspout, *anadiplosis* uses the end of one phrase as the beginning of the

next. "She swallowed the cat to catch the bird; she swallowed the bird to catch the spider; she swallowed the spider to catch the fly . . ."

Anamnesis describes the process of calling the past to mind.

Anaphora is the repetition of words or a phrase at the beginning of a clause or sentence. A fine example comes to us from the Book of Ecclesiastes, via the Byrds: "A time to be born, a time to die / A time to plant, a time to reap / A time to kill, a time to heal / A time to laugh, a time to weep."

Antanaclasis is a special case of *ploce* (q.v.) and *paronomasia* (q.v.), where a word is repeated but changes its meaning. You'll sometimes hear a recovering alcoholic explain that he turned himself in to Alcoholics Anonymous because "I was sick and tired of feeling sick and tired."

Antimetabole: See *chiasmus*.

Antithesis is balancing one term or clause with another of contrasting force. When in his song "Bright Eyes," Art Garfunkel confronts the heartbreaking reality that rabbits don't live forever, he asks: "How can the light that burned so brightly suddenly burn so pale?"

Antonomasia is the use of an epithet or nickname in place of a name. You're using it if, in response to someone saying something nerdy, you say, "Hark at clever-clogs!" Or, "All right, Poindexter. No more Mountain Dew for you. . . . " Arguably a special case of *metonymy* (q.v.).

Apodioxis is the indignant rejection of an opponent's argument as so absurd that it was an impertinence to introduce it. Very popular among members of the current political class when asked a question they don't want to answer. "I won't dignify that with a response" is the set form in political debate. "Next question," delivered icily, is the version you see most often in celebrity interviews. When, in the film *Wayne's World*, the protagonist rejects a proposition with the exclamation "And monkeys might fly outta my butt!" he's using a form of *apodioxis*.

Apoplanesis is the use of *digressio* (q.v.), or a quick change of subject, to avoid an issue. "Your breath smells of smoke. Have you been smoking?" "Oh look! A bee!"

Aporia is where you appear to break off to debate a tricky point with yourself—feigned indecision being a good way of appearing conscientiously to take your opponent's points on board. It's a good way of faking sincerity, in other words. "Should I kill Bond? Or should I tell him my master plan and then kill him? Decisions, decisions . . . "

Aposiopesis is where you pretend you don't know where you're going next. Note: "pretend." The speaker breaks off as if words have failed him. If they really have failed him, woe betide him. Or perhaps not. Pope remarks drily that this is a splendid figure for ignoramuses to use, because you can ask, "'What shall I say?' when one has nothing to say; or 'I can no more,' when one really can no more."

Apostrophe in Greek means "turning away." This figure describes the rather theatrical moment when a speaker suddenly changes the implied addressee of the speech—breaking off to address an abstract idea, an inanimate object or someone who's not there. Earl Spencer's funeral address for Diana, Princess of Wales, effectively shifts to address the dead princess early on. When you exclaim, "Ye gods!" you are apostrophizing. Likewise, the author of a wonderfully cockeyed Scottish translation of Catullus's poem on Lesbia's dead sparrow—"Weep, weep ye Loves and Cupids all* / And ilka man o' decent feelin': / My lassie's lost her wee, wee bird / And that's a loss, ye'll ken, past healin.'"

Argumentum ad Populum is an appeal to the authority of the crowd. "Western Australia is a great place: six billion flies can't be wrong."

Asianism: The names of the figures also include terms for defects and failures of rhetoric—whether logical or stylistic. *Asianism*— named for the bombastic style of Greek oratory said to have proliferated among the different populations of Asia—is the word for

---

*"Loves and Cupids" are also an instance of personification.

a ridiculously periphrastic high style. Associated with *bomphilogia* (q.v.) or *macrologia* (q.v.). *Atticism* (q.v.) is its opposite.

Atticism is a crisp, unornamented, aphoristic style. The opposite of *Asianism* (q.v.).

Assonance is the repetition of vowel sounds. As with *alliteration* (q.v.) it works to associate words together and make them memorable. "Naming and Shaming" relies on assonance.

Asyndeton is the omission of conjunctions. Cf. Churchill: "Silent, mournful, abandoned, broken, Czechoslovakia recedes into the darkness." The opposite of *polysyndeton* (q.v.).

Auxesis is a generalized term for cranking things up. *Climax* (q.v.) is a form of *auxesis*, for instance, as is *hyperbole* (q.v.)—but at trope level *auxesis* can be as simple as the use of inflated language. When a politician calls a soldier a "warrior" and the dead "the fallen," or when a shampoo ad talks about "cleansing" rather than cleaning, that's auxesis. Erasmus in *De Copia* explains: "We use a more violent word in place of the normal one in order to heighten what we were saying; for example to say 'slain' for killed or 'highway robber' for 'dishonest.'" See also *amplificatio*.

Bomphiologia is extreme *circumlocutio* (q.v.). Windbaggery. See Polonius for details, or Glendower's threat to "summon spirits from the vasty deep." See also *macrologia*.

Chiasmus or *antimetabole* puts four terms in a crisscrossed relation to each other—in the form ABBA. "Ask not what your country can do for you, but what you can do for your country," said John F. Kennedy. "Your manuscript is both good and original; but the parts that are good are not original, and the parts that are original are not good," Dr. Johnson told an aspiring author. And Theodore Roosevelt characterized as the central condition of human progress "conflict between the men who possess more than they have earned and the men who have earned more than they possess."

Circumlocutio or *circumlocution*, to give it its not-very-different English name (see also *periphrasis*), is to talk around a point. Some-

times it describes simple euphemism—"I understand you have a problem with your unmentionables, Mr. Smith?"—but it can cover the use of a descriptive phrase to substitute for a name. Rumpole's referring to his wife as She Who Must Be Obeyed would be an instance of *circumlocution*, as is the substitution of the Homeric epithet "the spud-faced nipper" for Wayne Rooney's given name. Too much *circumlocutio* tips over into *bomphiologia* (q.v.) or *macrologia* (q.v.).

Climax is where a series of successive clauses and sentences build up in force and importance. The scientist George Wald, for instance, speaking against the atomic bomb in 1969, said: "I think we've reached a point of great decision, not just for our nation, not only for all humanity, but for life upon the earth."

Comprobatio is complimenting the audience in the hopes that they will look more kindly on your case. The opposite of what Ricky Gervais was doing when he hosted the Golden Globes.

Concessio or *paromologia* is the conceding of a minor point in order to gain a more important one. It is the "yes, but . . . " figure. "Sir: you're *drunk*." "I am drunk. And you're ugly. But in the morning, I shall be sober . . . "

Correctio: See *metanoia*.

Decorum is a term of wide and vital application: it means fitting your speech in terms of style and address to the audience it is intended to persuade. A full discussion is to be found in the section on style.

Dialysis is a figure of argument in which you set out disjunctive alternatives. "Either you were stealing from the company, or you transferred $100,000 into your bank account by accident. If the former, you're a crook. If the latter, you're an idiot. Either way, you're fired."

Diazeugma is *zeugma* (q.v.) the other way around: a single subject governs several verb clauses. "The man standing in that dock, your honor, killed my wife, abused my children, twisted the head off my cat, painted the walls with the blood of my pet tortoise, and afterward wiped his hands on my budgerigar."

Digressio is a generalized term for exactly what it sounds like (a fairly good guide to a lot of rhetorical terms): a digressive sidetrack or anecdote, sometimes used to add force to an argument by analogy, sometimes to distract from a tricky point, and sometimes to jolly the audience along.

Division is the third part of a speech, setting out the areas of disagreement. See p. 91.

Enargia ("Picture the scene . . .") is a generalized term for the orator's effort to paint a mental picture of a scene or person (this special case of *enargia* is sometimes called *prosopographia*) so vivid that the audience feels as if it's actually there. Lanham's discussion of the subject quotes an ancient description of the orator Lysias, who allows a hearer to feel he can "see the actions which are being described going on and that he is meeting face to face the characters in the orator's story." David Lloyd George used *enargia* brilliantly in the speech to Parliament where he announced the so-called People's Budget of 1909:

> Have you been down a coal mine? I was telling you I went down one the other day. We sank down into a pit half a mile deep. We then walked underneath the mountain, and we did about three-quarters of a mile with rock and shale above us. The earth seemed to be straining—around us and above us—to crush us in. You could see the pit props bent and twisted and sundered until you saw their fibers split. Sometimes they give way, and then there is mutilation and death. Often a spark ignites, the whole pit is deluged in fire, and the breath of life is scorched out of hundreds of breasts by the consuming fire.

Enumeratio is another that sounds like what it is. In argument, it's the brisk numbering off of points. "One for the money, two for the show . . ."

Epiplexis is when you ask a pointed series of rhetorical questions in order to express indignation or grief. Job's complaints to God—roughly: What have I done to deserve this?—are dominated by this

figure: "Is it good unto thee that thou shouldest oppress, that thou shouldest despise the work of thine hands, and shine upon the counsel of the wicked? Hast thou eyes of flesh? Or seest thou as man seeth? Are thy days as the days of man? Are thy years as man's days, that thou enquirest after mine iniquity, and searchest after my sin?"

Epistrophe is *anaphora* (q.v.) backward: it's where you repeat the word or phrase at the end rather than the beginning of the clause. Hat-tip to Joe Stalin for this appropriately backward-themed instance from a 1931 speech urging Russians to get with the Five Year Plan: "All beat her [the old Russia]—because of her backwardness, because of her military backwardness, cultural backwardness, political backwardness, industrial backwardness, agricultural backwardness."

Epizeuxis is extreme repetition: the same word over and over again with nothing in between. Suitable for moments of high drama, cf. King Lear: "Howl, howl, howl, howl! O ye are men of stones." Or flat banality, cf. Tony Blair: "Education, education, education."

Erotema, also called *erotesis,* or *interrogatio,* is a question that implies but doesn't expect an answer: "Why would a girl like you be interested in a schlub like me?" It's commonly known as the rhetorical question. There are several variations on the theme, such as *hypophora* (q.v.) and *epiplexis* (q.v.).

Erotesis: See *erotema.*

Ethos is the attempt to establish a speaker's authority with the audience.

Exordium is the first part of a speech (see p. 84).

Figure is anything that makes language interesting. That is, in the extended sense, everything that happens in language. See *trope.*

Hendiadys is a form of circumlocution: a stylized expression where an adjectival phrase is broken up into a pair of nouns. It's sometimes used as a reflex of pomposity rather than with stylistic design—because it inflates one thing into two, it has an amplificatory effect. But nobody seems very good at thinking of clear-cut and/or important examples in English. "Grace and favor" for "gracious favor" (or "favorable grace")? "Out of the goodness of his heart" for "out of his good heart"? "Nice and generous" for "nicely generous"? The

strong hunch I have is that in English the two-noun version, very often, isn't so much figurative as the natural form of the expression. Just as quantitative meter doesn't really work in English verse, *hendiadys*—though, as I understand it, it is all over the shop in Latin—doesn't really have an important place in English rhetoric.

Horismus is a pithy, sometimes almost aphoristic definition: "Man is an ape that tells jokes." It is specially used when the definition involves a contrastive element. On the other side of the coin is *systrophe* (q.v.).

Hypallage is a muddling of the agreements or uses of words. Sometimes it's a vice of pretension (Bottom in *A Midsummer Night's Dream* is often cited as a paragon of the form), sometimes a sly grab at humorous effect, and sometimes the result of a winningly inept translation. The opening lines of the 1991 Japanese computer game, *Zero Wing*, spawned a long-running Internet catchphrase thanks to the unrivaled *hypallage* of their English translation: "Somebody set up us the bomb. Main screen turn on. All your base are belong to us. You have no chance to survive make your time."

Hyperbaton is the general term for a disruption in the expected word order. "This is the sort of nonsense up with which I will not put"— versions of which sentence are attributed to Winston Churchill— is a humorous instance.

Hypophora is where you ask a whole series of questions and answer them: "Why do birds suddenly appear / Every time you are near? / Just like me, they long to be / Close to you. // Why do stars fall down from the sky / Every time you walk by? / Just like me, they long to be / Close to you."

Hysteron Proteron is a form of *hyperbaton* (q.v.): a jiggling of the word order to put things back to front. (*Hysteron proteron* means "the last for the first"—as described in Bob Dylan's "The Times They Are A-Changin.'") When Take That, in their comeback single "The Flood," sing, "The defenders of the faith, we are," they are using the figure. In song lyrics, *hysteron proteron* and other disturbances of natural word order are sometimes indications of simple

ineptitude rather than a striving for figural effect—but I can't imagine that's the case here.

Interrogatio: See *erotema*.

Isocolon is the use of a series of clauses of roughly the same length and similar grammatical structure. The model and rhetorician Jerry Hall shows how: "My mother said it was simple to keep a man: you must be a maid in the living room, a cook in the kitchen, and a whore in the bedroom."

Kairos is timing—the ability to make an argument at the right moment. Arguments can fail or prosper according to the circumstances in which they're delivered.

Logos is the attempt to present a plausible argument in logical or apparently logical terms.

Macrologia: See *bomphiologia*.

Metanoia or *correctio* is the stagy business of saying something, then retracting it and qualifying it. A favorite figure of ex-girlfriends: "I hate you. No, I don't hate you. I *pity* you."

Metaphor, like *simile* (q.v.), is something you will have learned about in primary-school English. *Simile* says one thing is *like* another thing; *metaphor* behaves as if one thing *is* another. When, in "Creep," Radiohead's Thom Yorke sings, "You're just like an angel," he is using a *simile*. When someone greets his wife, "Hello, angel," he is using *metaphor*. *Simile* is the uniformed beat cop, with his badge on his chest; *metaphor* is the plainclothes officer.*

Metonymy is a figure closely associated with *synecdoche* (q.v.). These are regarded by some theorists as drawing their power from the most fundamental ways in which language works. Both involve referring

---

*I remind you of the figure of *metaphor* here only because it flocks, slightly, with *metonymy* (q.v.)—and because, like *metonymy*, it is understood by some historians of rhetoric to be a fundamental figure. The sexist mentioned in my paragraph on *metonymy* might call a woman "doll"—which is a metaphorical usage. If *metonymy* works on contiguity ("skirt" is associated with woman), *metaphor* works on similarity or identity: "Doll" is a substitute for "woman"— as well it might end up being if you go round talking like that.

to something obliquely. *Metonymy* works by substituting an associated attribute for what is referred to. *Synecdoche* works by substituting a part for the whole, or vice versa. You can spend many happy hours arguing about what they mean, and whether the latter is a subset of the former. If you're the sort of person who calls a grown woman a "piece of skirt," you're being *metonymic*. If you're the sort of person who calls your car your "set of wheels," you're being *synecdochic*. In both cases, though this isn't a technical term from rhetoric, you're being an *asshole*.

Mycterismus, considered among the flowers of rhetoric, belongs to the extensive and delightful knot-garden of belittlement and sneering. I include it because Puttenham gave it an especially pleasing English name: "fleering frumpe." It is a figure both of style and delivery: an insult to one's opponent delivered with an appropriately slighting gesture. Mycterismus is the ostentatious yawn as you interrupt his peroration with "Give us a break!" Puttenham wrote of it: "In some smiling sort looking aside or by drawing the lip awry or shrinking up the nose, as he had said to one whose words he believed not, 'No doubt, sir, of that.'"

Narration is the second part of a speech, setting out the facts as generally understood (see p. 87).

Occultatio, occasionally mistakenly called *occupatio*—the result of a long-ago transcription error—is a figure that allows you to bring in all sorts of material while pretending you're not going to talk about it. "Because I'm a nice guy," you might tell your girlfriend in the middle of a row at a dinner party, "I'm not going to embarrass you by telling everyone about that time you got drunk and slept with Russell Brand." A formalized version has become common in courtroom dramas: a lawyer launches a whole line of outrageous questioning that, when it is objected to by the other side, he meekly but smugly withdraws. Chaucer *adores* this figure: in *The Knight's Tale*, he spends fifty lines of verse enumerating in agonizing detail all the things he's *not* going to tell you about a funeral. The Greek term is *paralipsis*.

Occupatio: See *occultatio*.

Panegyric is a praise-speech. The opposite of a *philippic* (q.v.).

Paralipsis: See *occultatio*.

Paromologia: See *concessio*.

Paronomasia is the general term for wordplay. Although the former American Defense Secretary Donald Rumsfeld was castigated for it by the dunderheads at the Plain English Campaign (he was given their "Foot in Mouth" award), his "known unknowns" speech was his finest hour: philosophically robust, wittily paronomasic, and of exemplary clarity. "Reports that say that something hasn't happened are always interesting to me, because as we know, there are known knowns; there are things we know we know. We also know there are known unknowns; that is to say we know there are some things we do not know. But there are also unknown unknowns—the ones we don't know we don't know."

Pathos is the attempt to move the audience's emotions.

Periphrasis: See *circumlocutio*.

Peroration is the final part of an argument: summing-up. See p. 103.

Philippic is an aggressive *ad hominem* attacking speech—named after Demosthenes's famous orations against Philip of Macedon.

Pleonasm is the inclusion of words that are grammatically or semantically superfluous. At this moment in time I myself am visibly exemplifying pleonasm, as you can see with your own eyes.

Ploce is a general word for the repetition of a word. See also *polyptoton* and *antanaclasis*. "I've got soul but I'm not a soldier," in the Killers song, is a sort of banjaxed combination of *polyptoton* and *antanaclasis*. It was memorably sent up by the comedian Bill Bailey, who proclaimed, "I've got ham but I'm not a hamster."

Polyptoton is a special case of *ploce* (q.v.), where a word changes form as it is repeated. "Who watches the watchmen?" for example.

Polysyndeton is, in a nutshell, the overuse of conjunctions. It can give an emphatic sense of grandeur to a bare list of things, however. During the Easter Rising of 1916, the rebels proclaimed, "We hereby proclaim the Irish Republic as a Sovereign Independent State, and

we pledge our lives and the lives of our comrades-in-arms to the cause of its freedom, of its welfare, and of its exaltation among the nations." "Of its," repeated three times, is grammatically redundant but rhetorically effective. The opposite of *asyndeton* (q.v.).

Proof refers to both the arguments available to support your case and the fourth part of a speech, in which those arguments are advanced. See p. 93.

Prosopographia is an especially vivid description of a person. A subset of *enargia* (q.v.).

Refutation is the fifth part of a speech, in which you attack your opponent's arguments. See p. 99.

Simile: See *metaphor*.

Symploce is where *anaphora* (q.v.) and *epistrophe* (q.v.) come together, like a stack of sandwiches. Here's Malcolm X: "Much of what I say might sound bitter, but it's the truth. Much of what I say might sound like it's stirring up trouble, but it's the truth. Much of what I say might sound like it's hate, but it's the truth."

Synathroesmus (also *congeries*, or *accumulatio*) is the heaping-on of words, either of similar meaning—"Itsy-bitsy teeny-weeny yellow polka-dot bikini"—or in summation of the broader argument of the speech: "He schemed, he plotted, he lied, he stole, he raped, he killed, and he parked in the mother-and-child slot outside the supermarket despite having come on his own . . ."

Synecdoche: See *metonymy*.

Syntheton is where two terms are joined by a conjunction. Truth and justice. Liberty and livelihood. Color and creed. Fish and chips.

Systrophe, a great pile of qualities that nevertheless don't add up to an explicit definition, is the complementary term to *horismus* (q.v.). Hamlet's "What a piece of work is a man" speech is usually the example given, but I prefer the *Danger Mouse* theme song: "He's the greatest / He's fantastic / Wherever there's danger he'll be there / He's the ace / He's amazing / He's the strongest, he's the quickest, he's the best / Danger Mouse / Danger Mouse / *Danger Mouse!*" etc., etc.

Tmesis: I've included this not because it's something you see all that often, but because I like the name. It means sticking a word or phrase into the middle of another word. Do people really do that? Abso-frickin'-lutely!

Tricolon: The best-known *tricolon* in the history of the world, probably, is a remark attributed to Caesar: *Veni, vidi, vici*—"I came, I saw, I conquered."* The *tricolon* is a set of three units of speech put in a row, and it has remained an absolute staple of oratory from that day to this. A television ad now urges us to recreate Caesar's feat in the consumer sphere: "Find it. Get it. Argos it." So pervasive is the *tricolon*—and so naturally and effectively does it fall on the ear—that even phrases that aren't *tricola* are sometimes misremembered as if they were. Winston Churchill actually said: "I have nothing to offer but blood, toil, tears, and sweat." But collective memory has adapted this to the more euphonious *tricolon* "blood, sweat, and tears"—which is also more metaphorically coherent, since it excludes the one term that's not a bodily fluid. A *tricolon crescens*, or rising tricolon, is one where the terms get longer; a *tricolon diminuens* where they get shorter.

Trope is a *figure* (q.v.) that changes the meaning of a word.

Zeugma is a tricksy figure in which several clauses are governed by a single word, usually a verb. Puttenham called it "Single Supply." Flanders and Swann, in their song "Have Some Madeira, M'Dear," really go to town on this figure: "He had slyly inveigled her up to his flat / To view his collection of stamps / And he said as he hastened to put out the cat / The wine, his cigar and the lamps . . . " Specialists divide *zeugma* into *prozeugma*, *hypozeugma*, and *mesozeugma* depending, respectively, on whether the verb comes before the clauses it governs, after them, or in the middle of them. See also *diazeugma*.

---

*The smart alecks among you will note that this is also a fine instance of *asyndeton*. And *isocolon*. And *climax*.

Figures by Theme

It may be helpful, too, to suggest some thematic groupings for the figures. These are necessarily loose and personal, but they give, I hope, a sense of the sort of work figures do.

THE THREE RS: REPETITION, REPETITION, REPETITION

Alliteration, Anaphora, Anadiplosis, Assonance, Epistrophe, Epizeuxis, Ploce, Polysyndeton, Symploce

FIGURES OF CONTRAST AND PARALLELISM

Antithesis, Antonomasia, Diazeugma, Isocolon, Metaphor, Metonymy, Synecdoche, Simile, Paronomasia, Tricolon, Zeugma

FIGURES OF AMPLIFICATION

Auxesis, Amplificatio, Asianism, Circumlocutio, Climax, Digressio, Hendiadys, Pleonasm

FIGURES OF REDUCTION OR ABBREVIATION

Atticism, Asyndeton

FIGURES OF DISRUPTION

Aporia, Apoplanesis, Aposiopesis, Chiasmus/Antimetabole,
Hypallage, Hyperbaton, Hysteron Proteron, Tmesis

FIGURES OF ARGUMENT

Apodioxis, Concessio, Dialysis, Enargia,
Enumeratio, Horismus, Metanoia/Correctio, Systrophe

FIGURES OF ADDRESS: ARE YOU TALKIN' TO ME?

Anamnesis, Apostrophe, Argumentum ad Populum,
Comprobatio, Epiplexis, Erotema/Erotesis/Interrogatio,
Hypophora, Mycterismus, Occultatio/Paralipsis

For anyone interested in exploring the figures further, two resources have been invaluable to me, and I can't recommend them too
highly.

Online, there's the brilliantly organized Silva Rhetoricae:
    http://rhetoric.byu.edu/.

Offline, there's Richard A. Lanham's *A Handlist of Rhetorical Terms*,
2nd ed. (Berkeley: University of California Press, 1991).

KEY CONCEPTS

THE THREE APPEALS

Ethos, Pathos, and Logos

THE THREE BRANCHES OF RHETORIC

Forensic (Judicial)—Associated with the past
Deliberative (Political)—Associated with the future
Epideictic or Display Oratory—Associated with the present

THE FIVE CANONS OF RHETORIC

Invention—Discovery of proofs
Arrangement—Shaping of argument
Style—Giving argument a form in language
Memory—Absorbing the argument
Delivery—Putting the argument across

THE SIX PARTS OF A SPEECH

Exordium (also *prooimion*)
Narration (also *diegesis, prothesis,* or *narratio*)
Division (also *divisio, propositio,* or *partitio*)
Proof (also *pistis, confirmatio,* or *probatio*)
Refutation (also *confutatio* or *reprehensio*)
Peroration (also *epilogos* or *conclusio*)

Notes

INTRODUCTION

1. John Bender and David E. Wellbery, *The Ends of Rhetoric: History, Theory, Practice* (Stanford: Stanford University Press, 1990), 25.

RHETORIC THEN AND NOW

1. Translation from the Greek, as in Vincent Farenga, "Periphrasis on the Origin of Rhetoric," *Modern Language Notes* 94 (1979): 1033–1055.

2. Thomas A. Cole, "Who Was Corax?" *Illinois Classical Studies* 16 (1991): 65–84.

3. This is from Benjamin Jowett's 1871 translation, available at http://classics.mit.edu/Plato/gorgias.html.

4. Aristotle, *The Art of Rhetoric*, trans. Hugh Lawson-Tancred (London: Penguin, 1991).

5. Steven W. May, "George Puttenham's Lewd and Illicit Career," *Texas Studies in Literature and Language* 50 (Summer 2008): 143–176.

FIVE PARTS OF RHETORIC

1. Quintilian, *Institutes of Oratory*, 3:3.

THE FIRST PART OF RHETORIC: INVENTION

1. Aristotle, *Rhetoric*, VII, 2, 12–13.

THE SECOND PART OF RHETORIC: ARRANGEMENT

1. Richard A. Lanham, *A Handlist of Rhetorical Terms* (Berkeley: University of California Press, 1991), 171.
2. *Ad Herennium*, I, 4, 8, trans. Harry Caplan (Cambridge, MA: Harvard, 1954).
3. *Rhetoric*, V, 1.
4. *Institutes of Oratory*, V, 7, 4–5.

CHAMPIONS OF RHETORIC II:
MARCUS TULLIUS CICERO

1. Desiderius Erasmus, *Ciceronianus—Or, A Dialogue on the Best Style of Speaking*, trans. Izora Scott (New York: Teachers College, Columbia University, 1908).

THE THIRD PART OF RHETORIC: STYLE

1. In *A Companion to Roman Rhetoric*, ed. William Dominick and Jon Hall (Oxford: Blackwell, 2007).
2. *Rhetoric*, IX, 3, 8
3. Richard A. Lanham, *A Handlist of Rhetorical Terms*, 2nd ed. (Berkeley: University of California Press, 1991), 78.

CHAMPIONS OF RHETORIC III: ABRAHAM LINCOLN

1. Carl J. Richard, *The Founders and the Classics: Greece, Rome and the American Enlightenment* (Cambridge, MA: Harvard, 1994), 24.
2. Garry Wills, *Lincoln at Gettysburg: The Words that Remade America* (New York: Simon and Schuster, 1992).

THE FOURTH PART OF RHETORIC:
MEMORY

1. John O'Keefe and Lynn Nadel, *The Hippocampus as a Cognitive Map* (Oxford: Clarendon Press, 1978).

2. Cicero, *De Oratore*, II, 360.

3. Quintilian, *Institutes of Oratory*, XI, 2, 7.

4. *Ad Herennium*, III, xvi, 28.

5. Ibid., III, xix, 32.

6. *Ad Herennium*, III, xx, 33.

7. Ibid.

CHAMPIONS OF RHETORIC IV:
HITLER AND CHURCHILL

1. *Blood, Toil, Tears and Sweat: Winston Churchill's Famous Speeches* ed. David Cannadine (London: Cassell, 1989).

2. Andrew Roberts, *Hitler and Churchill: Secrets of Leadership* (London: Weidenfeld & Nicolson, 2003).

3. Richard Overy, *The Dictators: Hitler's Germany and Stalin's Russia* (London: Allen Lane, 2004).

THE FIFTH PART OF RHETORIC:
DELIVERY

1. "They Don't Make Speeches Like They Used To," *The Times*, January 20, 2011.

2. Gyles Brandreth, *The Complete Public Speaker* (London: Sheldon Press, 1983).

3. John Bulwer, *Chirologia: or the naturall language of the hand. Composed of the speaking motions, and discoursing gestures thereof. Whereunto is added Chironomia: or, the art of manuall rhetoricke. Consisting of the naturall expressions, digested by art in the hand, as the chiefest instrument of eloquence* (London: Thomas Harper, 1644).

DELIBERATIVE RHETORIC

1. *Ad Herennium*, III, v, 9.

2. Still available online: http://www.guardian.co.uk/commentisfree
/2010/feb/25/falklands-britains-expensive-nuisance.

CHAMPIONS OF RHETORIC V:
MARTIN LUTHER KING

1. See especially John H. Patton, "'I Have a Dream': The Performance of Theology Fused with the Power of Orality," in *Martin Luther King Jr. and the Sermonic Power of Public Discourse*, ed. Carolyn Calloway-Thomas and John Louis Lucaites (Tuscaloosa: Alabama University Press, 1993).

2. Alexandra Alvarez, "Martin Luther King's 'I Have a Dream': The Speech Event as Metaphor," *Journal of Black Studies* 18 (March 1988).

3. For more on this, see David A Bobbitt, *The Rhetoric of Redemption: Kenneth Burke's Redemption Drama and Martin Luther King Jr's 'I Have A Dream' Speech* (Oxford: Rowman and Littlefield, 2004).

4. Drew Hansen, *The Dream: Martin Luther King, Jr., and the Speech That Inspired a Nation* (New York: Ecco Press, 2003).

JUDICIAL RHETORIC

1. Edward P. J. Corbett and Robert J. Connors, *Classical Rhetoric for the Modern Student*, 4th ed. (Oxford: Oxford University Press, 1999).

CHAMPIONS OF RHETORIC VII:
THE UNKNOWN SPEECHWRITER

1. Ronald Millar, *A View from the Wings* (London: Weidenfeld, 1993).

2. Peggy Noonan, *What I Saw at the Revolution* (New York: Random House, 1990).

Index

Page references for glossary entries are in **bold**; those for footnotes are followed by n